Sports Illustrated

The Hockey Book

1959 | Jacques Plante's goalie mask, the first worn regularly in the NHL.

MATTHEW MANOR/HOCKEY HALL OF FAME

DOMINIK HASEK
The Dominator, Buffalo Sabres.
1998
Photograph by NICK CARDILLICCHIO

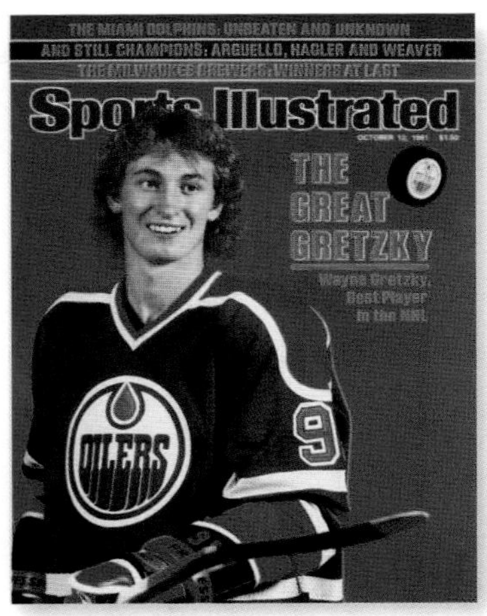

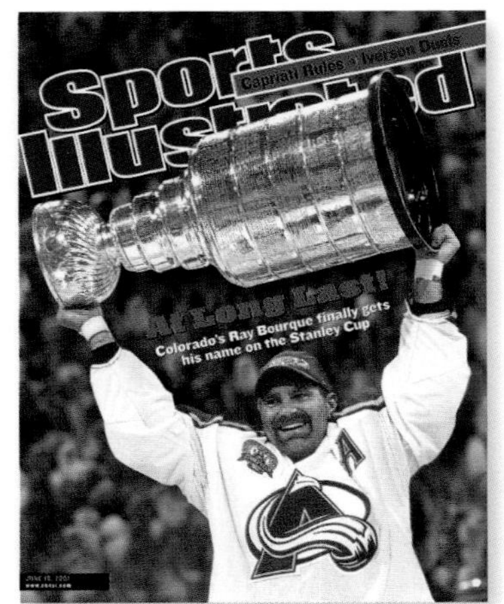

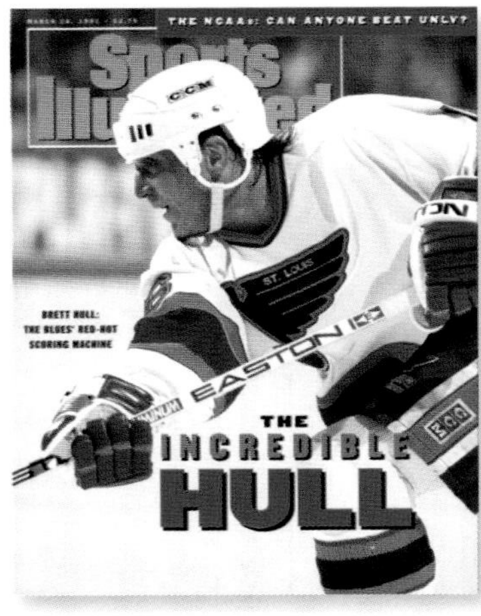

The Hockey Book

KOSTYA KENNEDY *Editor*

STEVEN HOFFMAN *Designer*

RICHARD O'BRIEN *Senior Editor* DAVID SABINO *Associate Editor*

CRISTINA SCALET *Photo Editor* DON DELLIQUANTI *Assistant Photo Editor*

KEVIN KERR *Copy Editor* JOSH DENKIN *Associate Designer*

SARAH KWAK *Reporter* STEFANIE KAUFMAN *Project Manager*

HOCKEY HALL OF FAME *Archives and Historical Reference*

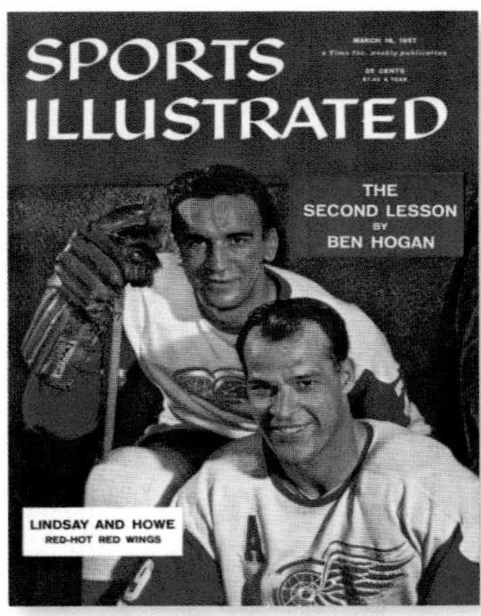

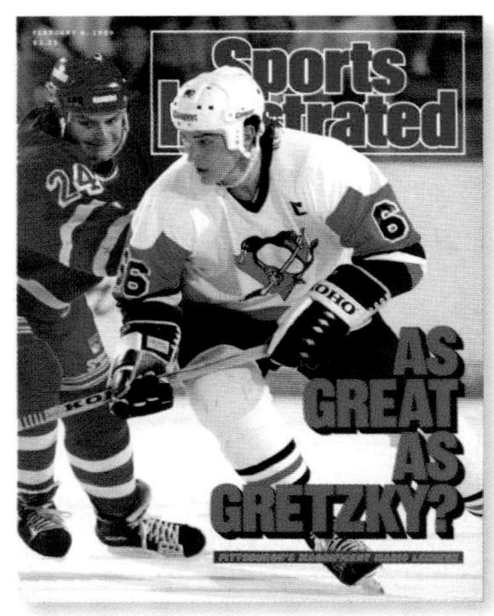

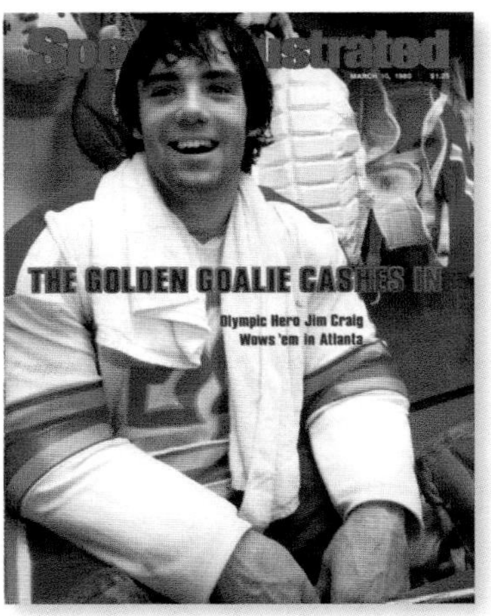

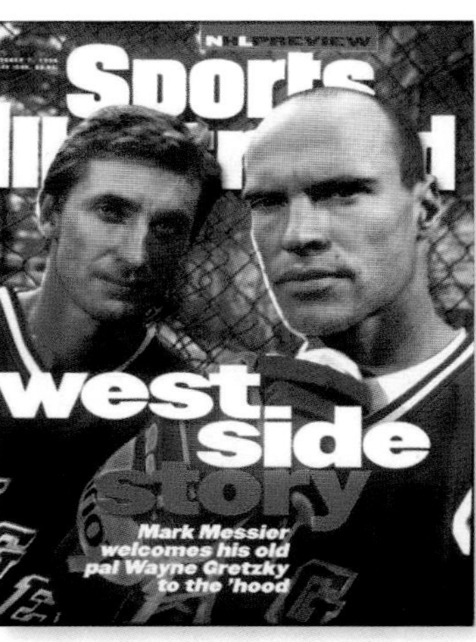

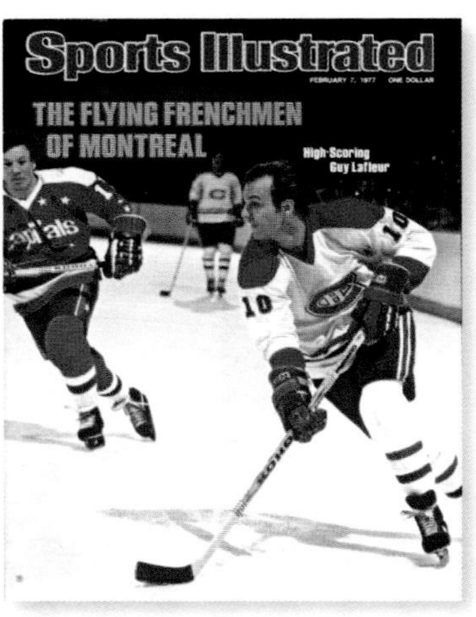

Sports Illustrated

Contents

12 INTRODUCTION *by Michael Farber*
26 ERA: BEGINNINGS, 1875 *through* 1925–26
34 AN INNOCENT AT RINKSIDE *by William Faulkner*
40 FLYER FROM FLIN FLON *by Mark Mulvoy*
46 THE PANTHEON: FORWARDS
48 MEET THE BOY WONDER *by E.M. Swift*
56 TWIN PILLARS *by Michael Farber*
64 ERA: ESTABLISHMENT, 1926–27 *through* 1945–46
72 THE ART OF THE FACE-OFF *by Michael Farber*
80 SPORTSMEN OF THE YEAR: THE U.S. OLYMPIC TEAM *by E.M. Swift*
90 SMOOTH OPERATOR *by Steve Rushin*
96 ERA: ORIGINAL SIX, 1946–47 *through* 1966–67
104 SINGLE-MINDED *by Gary Smith*
112 LEAGUE OF HIS OWN *by Michael Farber*
116 THE PANTHEON: DEFENSEMEN
118 SPORTSMAN OF THE YEAR: BOBBY ORR *by Jack Olsen*
126 ON AND ON AND ON . . . *by E.M. Swift*
132 ERA: EXPANSION, 1967–68 *through* 1978–79
138 WHEN HELL FROZE OVER *by Allen Abel*
144 BOZO THE BRUIN *by George Plimpton*
150 THE HANDSOME HERO OF THE HAWKS *by Kenneth Rudeen*
156 ELEVEN SECONDS *by E.M. Swift*
162 ERA: GRETZKY, 1979–80 *through* 1990–91
168 THE PANTHEON: GOALTENDERS
170 THE PIONEER *by Michael Farber*
172 THE RECORD-BREAKER *by Michael Farber*
178 OVER THE EDGE *by Kostya Kennedy*
184 SUTTER CLUTTER *by Leigh Montville*
190 FIRE ON ICE *by Herbert Warren Wind*
194 ERA: SUNBELT, 1991–92 *through* 2003–04
202 BORIS AND HIS BOYS PLAY A FEW FRIENDLIES *by Mark Mulvoy*
208 DESTINY'S CHILD *by S.L. Price*
216 THE PANTHEON: COACHES
218 WORRYING IS THE WAY TO WIN *by Mark Kram*
226 CHERRY BOMBS *by Leigh Montville*
232 ERA: NEW GAME, 2005–06 *to* PRESENT
242 THE OLD GOALIES' DANCE *by Pete Axthelm*
250 GOODBYE, GREAT ONE *by E.M. Swift*
256 ACKNOWLEDGMENTS

 • ISBN 10: 1-60320-151-3; ISBN 13: 978-1-60320-151-3; LIBRARY OF CONGRESS CONTROL NUMBER: 2010925781 • PRINTED IN CHINA

KURRI
17
TAYLOR
18
FUHR
31

WAYNE GRETZKY

The Great One, as an L.A. King, versus the Oilers.

1988

Photograph by DAVID E. KLUTHO

MARK MESSIER
Captain, New York Rangers.
1996
Photograph by GREGORY HEISLER

GORDIE HOWE
Mr. Hockey, Detroit Red Wings.
1951
Photograph by BETTMANN/CORBIS

CLUB ATHLÉTIQUE CANADIEN
Before being renamed the Montreal Canadiens.
1912
Photograph by IHA

C
CAC
CAC

INTRODUCTION

BY MICHAEL FARBER

SEE. BOBBY ORR IS FLYING.

LOOK CLOSELY AT THE PHOTOGRAPH THAT MIGHT BE AS FAMILIAR TO SOME OF YOU AS THE SNAPSHOTS OF YOUR KIDS' FIRST BIRTHDAYS. ORR IS SUSPENDED IN MID-AIR: HORIZONTAL, STICK RAISED TRIUMPHANTLY IN HIS RIGHT HAND, A LOOK OF RAPTURE MINGLED WITH AMAZEMENT THAT CREASES A YOUNG FACE, A VISCERAL JOY THAT RADIATES EITHER BECAUSE HE HAS JUST SCORED THE STANLEY CUP-WINNING GOAL OR

RAY LUSSIER/BOSTON HERALD/BREARLEY COLLECTION

ORR'S CAREER was already in full flight when he scored The Goal, and completed the Bruins four-game sweep of the Blues.

because he has just sprouted wings. (Forty years later, I still can't decide.) He was 22 then. He is 22 now, Peter Pan hovering above the Never Never Land of the Boston Garden ice. Unlike Bobby Clarke, who had his own fabulous jack-o'-lantern smile, Orr never gravitated to a desk job with an NHL team and never dropped the diminutive. Bob? Not him. Robert Gordon Orr remained Bobby, unbounded. He would not grow up. He clung to the trappings of his youth, making kids of any of us who ever dreamed of soaring.

Orr happened to be airborne that long ago Mother's Day because a disgusted St. Louis Blues defenseman named Noël Picard had tripped him after the goal. (I'm guessing this is the origin of the phrase "hoisted with your own Picard." Or not.) Blessedly Ray Lussier, a photographer for the *Boston Record-American*, captured that gravity-defying voyage, a solo flight around the circumference of our imagination. Lussier shot most of that Game 4 of the finals hunkered on a stool in the corner of the east end of the Garden, poking his camera through a hole in the plexiglass. At the end of regulation he ambled to the west end where the Bruins would be attacking in overtime. There he spied a vacant stool. Now May 10, 1970, was unseasonably warm. The temperature outside on Causeway St. was 93°. And the photographer who had previously occupied that west end stool had wandered off to do the most natural thing in hockey: grab a beer. This could be a challenge in the old Garden. The passageways in the lower bowl were narrow, and the concession stands always seemed crammed with rough men and big-haired women with fingernails painted an alternating black and gold. Thus this exercise in thirst-slaking apparently took a little longer than scheduled, so that the luckless photographer returned to his former stool at what would have been about one minute into overtime if Orr had not ended the NHL season at the 40-second mark. When the rival shooter started to harangue Lussier for pilfering the photo spot, Lussier packed up his gear and said, "I got what I needed." He had what we all needed: irrefutable proof that man could fly.

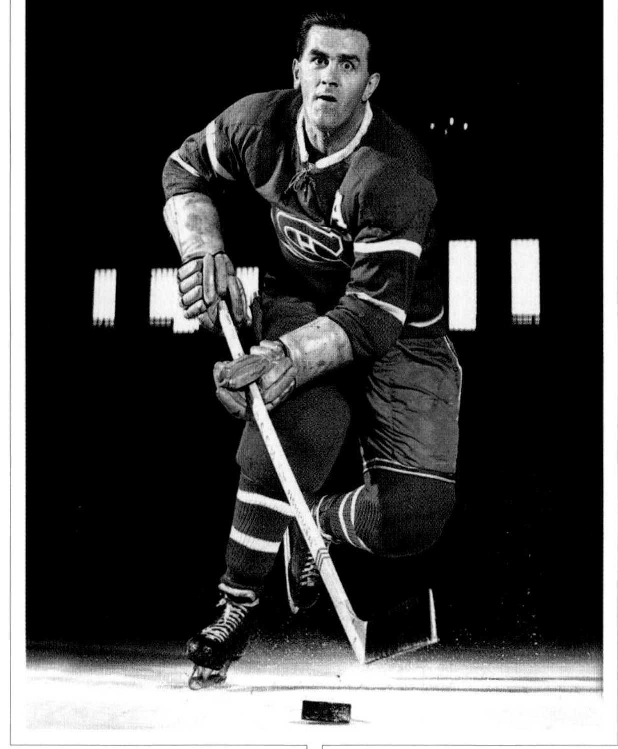

THE INTENSITY of the Rocket's glare could frighten goalies who knew what was coming next: He scored 544 career goals.

DAVID BIER STUDIOS

SOMETHING HAS BEEN LOST IN translation. Seventeen thousand square feet of ice does not fit onto a 37-inch screen, not when the puck is one-inch thick and three inches in diameter. This is a sport that begs to be seen live, where speed and noise and artistry and violence and happenstance and intricate geometry converge into the most delightful of spectacles. Like the people say, you shoulda been there. Maybe you can hear the national anthem at the United Center from home (assuming the feed you're watching is not in commercial), but you can't feel it through your soles unless you go to Chicago's new madhouse on Madison. You can follow the play at the Bell Centre in Montreal on a living-room screen, but you can't share a sense of community with 21,000 of the hockey-obsessed unless you make a pilgrimage. In person, the game reveals itself in all its delicious nuances. And until some network invents a better glowing puck, it will not be video images but rather insightful words and, yes, remarkable photographs that serve as the noblest handmaids of the game.

An example: The eyes of Maurice (Rocket) Richard. Those eyes, Orr's knees, Gretzky's hands, Gordie Howe's elbows, Mark Messier's shaved skull, Jaromir Jagr's mullet, Patrick Roy's blue-eyed laser stare, Alex Ovechkin's gap-toothed smile, Sidney Crosby's hockey haunches . . . if you were starting a Hockey Hall of Fame of anatomy, physiognomy and tonsorial arts, these would all be part of your inaugural class. Almost everyone knows about the burning coals that were Richard's eyes, even though the Rocket retired in 1960 when sports television, especially in Canada, was in its embryonic stage. Unless you had an end-arena seat at the Montreal Forum in the 1940s and '50s, you never saw those eyes in person. You know what they look like because of this photograph *(above)*, as staged as the running-back-as-Heisman-Trophy pose. Richard—in full stride, puck just ahead of his dead-flat blade, hair pomaded, mouth agape, eyes aglow—advances towards the camera. Then you have the words uttered by brilliant goaltender

Glenn Hall, who, with Chicago and Detroit, did peer into what is now reflexively called the Rocket's red glare. (As far as I can recall, seeing him around Montreal in his later years, Richard's eyes were brown.) "When he came flying towards you with the puck on his stick, his eyes were all lit up, flashing and gleaming like a pinball machine," Hall once said. "It was terrifying."

Now look at the photograph on this page. There is Rocket, shaking hands with Boston goalie "Sugar" Jim Henry. The focus here is not on Richard's enlarged pupils but on a substantial bandage above his left eye where blood oozes from six fresh stitches. Richard had collided with the Bruins' Leo Labine in the second period of Game 7 of the 1952 semifinals, sustaining the gash and a probable concussion. With four minutes left in the third, he returned and would soon score the series-winning goal, carrying the puck from deep in his zone, swooping past defenseman Bill Quackenbush and beating the goalie—Sugar Jim Henry. Richard was a peerless offensive force, but in the photograph he shares a frame with a peer. Henry's right eye is blackened—a puck had struck the maskless goalie there in Game 6—and the angle of Henry's torso leaves an indelible impression. He leans forward from the waist as he shakes Richard's hand. He is practically bowing, yet there is no trace of servility; Henry is displaying profound respect—for the player, and for the game.

To recap: one bloodied eye, one blackened eye and two players imbuing the traditional handshake line with a transcendent reverence for the competition just completed. If there is a better picture of hockey's best self, I haven't seen it.

Richard died of cancer in May 2000, just before the start of the Stanley Cup finals. An astonishing 115,000 mourners filed past his open casket in what is now called the Bell Centre. Some 2,700—including Canadian Prime Minister Jean Chrétien and NHL Commissioner Gary Bettman—filled Notre-Dame Basilica while another 1,500 waited outside to honor the Rocket. He lives on in these pages forever, in vibrant black and white.

THE ORIGINS OF HOCKEY ARE hazy. There are elements of the game that suggest the Irish sport of hurling, the Scottish game of shinty and a game played by the Mi'kmaq First Nations of eastern Canada. The first game of "hockey" might have been played in Windsor, Nova Scotia, Kingston, Ontario or the Northwest Territories. On some days you'd think the veteran NHL coach Ron Wilson invented it. (Just kidding. I love Ron.) The first historian-vetted indoor game occurred March 3, 1875, at the Victoria Skating Rink, between Drummond and Stanley streets, in Montreal. A wooden puck. Nine skaters per side. The dimensions of the Victoria rink, 204 by 80 feet, were remarkably similar to the current NHL size of 200 by 85. Lord Stanley, who in 1892 would donate the most instantly identifiable trophy in North American sports, would watch his first game there.

But while the roots of hockey are Canadian, this is unquestionably a world game. The hockey ethos—Northern, robust, selfless—is transferable, a movable feast as satisfying as watching Scott Niedermayer, say, bring the puck out of his defensive zone. Globally, there are no better fans than the burgundy-clad Latvians, who descend on the world championships most springs fueled by deep passion (and a drop or two of alcohol). There is no more organic North American hockey experience than seeing a game at Michigan's Yost Arena, where rabid Wolverines fans have filled their beloved barn since it was built in 1923. And the best hockey arena in the world doesn't even have four walls; the Swiss team HC Ambri-Piotta plays in Valascia, an arena in southern Switzerland that seats 2,000 and stands 5,000 and is open at both ends. Canadians might treat hockey as their own national chew toy—when Canada beat Team USA for the Olympic gold medal on a Sunday afternoon in Vancouver 2010, 80% of all Canadians tuned in; a Super Bowl would *kill* for such a share of the U.S. public—but there is ample space under the tent for everyone blessed with the hockey gene. Indeed the most significant sporting event in United States history is the 1980 Olympic hockey

SUGAR JIM HENRY lost more games than he won, but he played with a fortitude and respect immortalized in this postgame handshake with Richard.

ROGER JEAN/LA PRESSE

victory over the Soviet Union. All Americans had hockey DNA that day.

Still the raw intensity of Canada's relationship with the sport startled this American, a defrocked New York Rangers fan, who moved to Montreal in 1979, 10 months before the Miracle On Ice. Studying Canada's love for the sport eventually led to what I now call the One Degree of Kevin Bieksa theory, a nod to the Vancouver Canucks defenseman born in Grimsby, Ont. (Other than giving an ineffectual Canadiens goalie the nickname Red Light Racicot and coining the phrase Dead Puck Era to brand the trap-heavy, neutral-zone constipated NHL from the mid-1990s until the 2004 lockout, the Bieksa theory is my lone contribution to the sport.) The point: Canadians take hockey personally because it seems almost everyone is separated by no more than one degree from someone in hockey.

Take my experience. When I moved onto my current street in 1987, Scotty Bowman's parents lived kitty-corner. Raymond Bourque's brother-in-law carried the couch into my living room. The widow of Hall of Famer Buddy O'Connor moved off the block about six months before we came. I used to bump into ex-Canadiens defenseman Dollard St. Laurent at the neighborhood grocery store. My financial planner's brother-in-law played 915 NHL games and is now an assistant coach for the Los Angeles Kings.

Sometimes it seems you can't toss an apple core in this city without hitting a third-line winger.

SO BOBBY FLIES, THE ROCKET BLEEDS, The Great One dangles, St. Patrick stares, Ovie exults. Those are the greats, some of the men who personify the sport and fill this anthology. But before you dig deeper into this book, we leave you with the perhaps more pedestrian but equally illuminative tale of Brendan Witt. Unfortunately in this case there is no visual proof. There is merely the testimony of eyewitnesses who, one morning in December 2009, watched in horror as the New York Islanders defenseman, crossing Arch Street in Philadelphia to fetch his morning coffee at Starbucks, was struck and knocked to the ground by a gold-colored SUV making an illegal left turn.

When bystanders suggested they phone for an ambulance, Witt reportedly said: "I'm O.K. I've got to go play some hockey. I'm a hockey player. No big deal."

This is the hockey heart that beats worldwide, from Minsk to Madison, Wis., from Stockholm to San Jose. The only thing that could have made this a more perfect hockey story was if it had been evening and if Witt, like the anonymous photographer who once abandoned his stool at the Boston Garden, had been crossing the street in search of a postgame beer.

LOU CAPOZZOLA

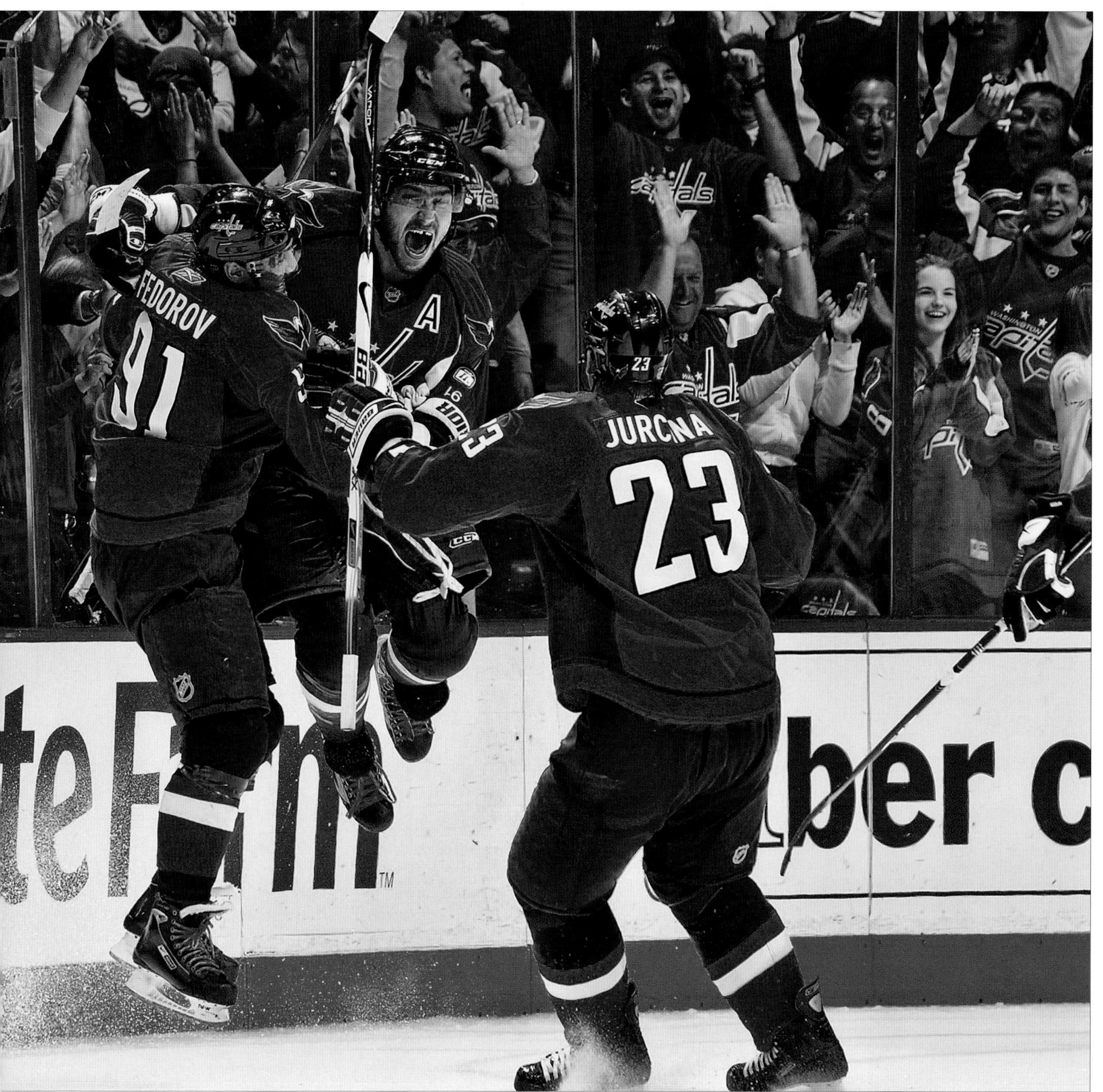

THERE'S NO PLACE LIKE RINKSIDE: At any moment Ovechkin can touch off the crowd with his wondrous offensive ability, as well as his jubilant goal celebrations.

Sports Illustrated

The Hockey

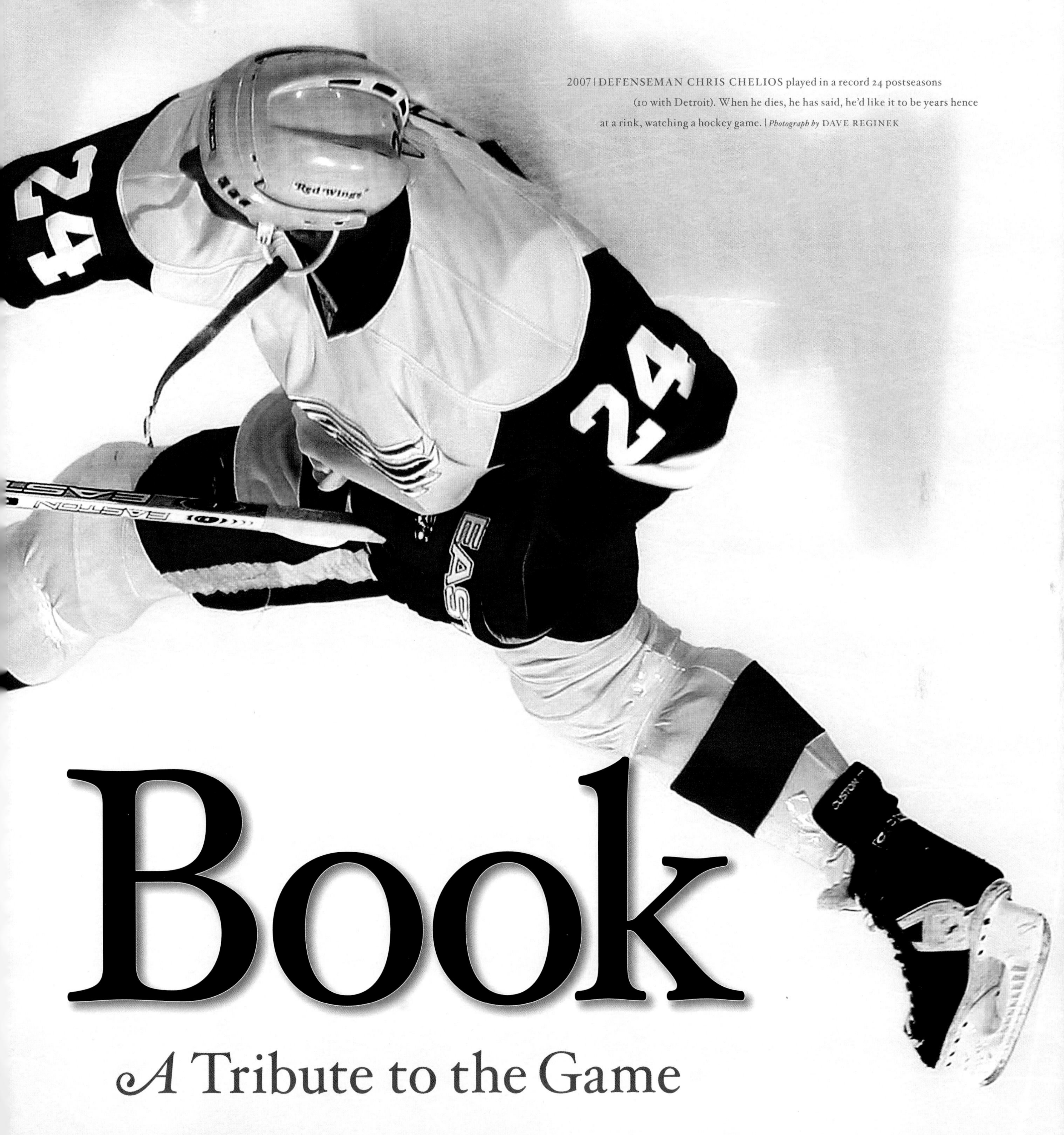

2007 | DEFENSEMAN CHRIS CHELIOS played in a record 24 postseasons (10 with Detroit). When he dies, he has said, he'd like it to be years hence at a rink, watching a hockey game. | *Photograph by* DAVE REGINEK

Book

A Tribute to the Game

COURTESY HOCKEY HALL OF FAME

1914 | THIS PUCK was engraved (with a misspelling) after the Toronto Blue Shirts used it to beat the Victoria Aristocrats and win the Stanley Cup. | *Photograph by* DAVID N. BERKWITZ

1930 | GOALIE CLINT BENEDICT wore this leather mask for a few games after a shot by Howie Morenz shattered his cheekbone. | *Photograph by* HOCKEY HALL OF FAME

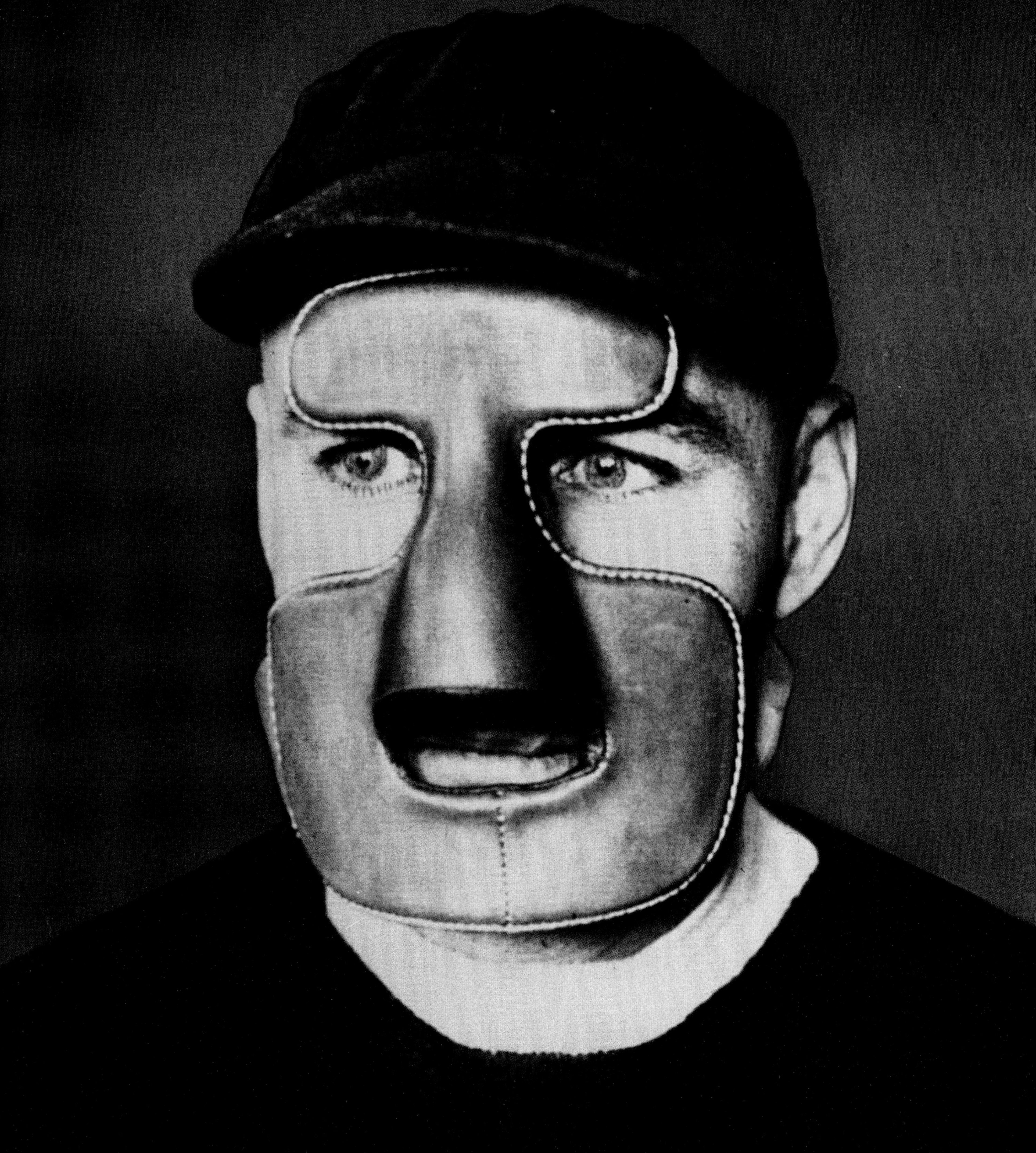

2009 | ALEXEI YASHIN (19) had the puck here, but in the end his Russian squad lost 7–6 to the World team captained by Jaromir Jagr in the first KHL All-Star Game, held in Moscow's Red Square. | *Photograph by* VITALY BELOUSOV

TISSOT
СОГАЗ
СМПБАНК

1963 | THE RED WINGS' Larry Jeffrey found himself stuck stick-up behind seven-time Norris Trophy winner Doug Harvey of the Rangers. | *Photograph by* JOHN G. ZIMMERMAN

1955 | AT THE Montreal Forum a visit by the Bruins was often a treat: The Habs were 14–0 against Boston in playoff series between '53 and '87. | *Photograph by* HY PESKIN

Beginnings

1875 *through* 1925–26

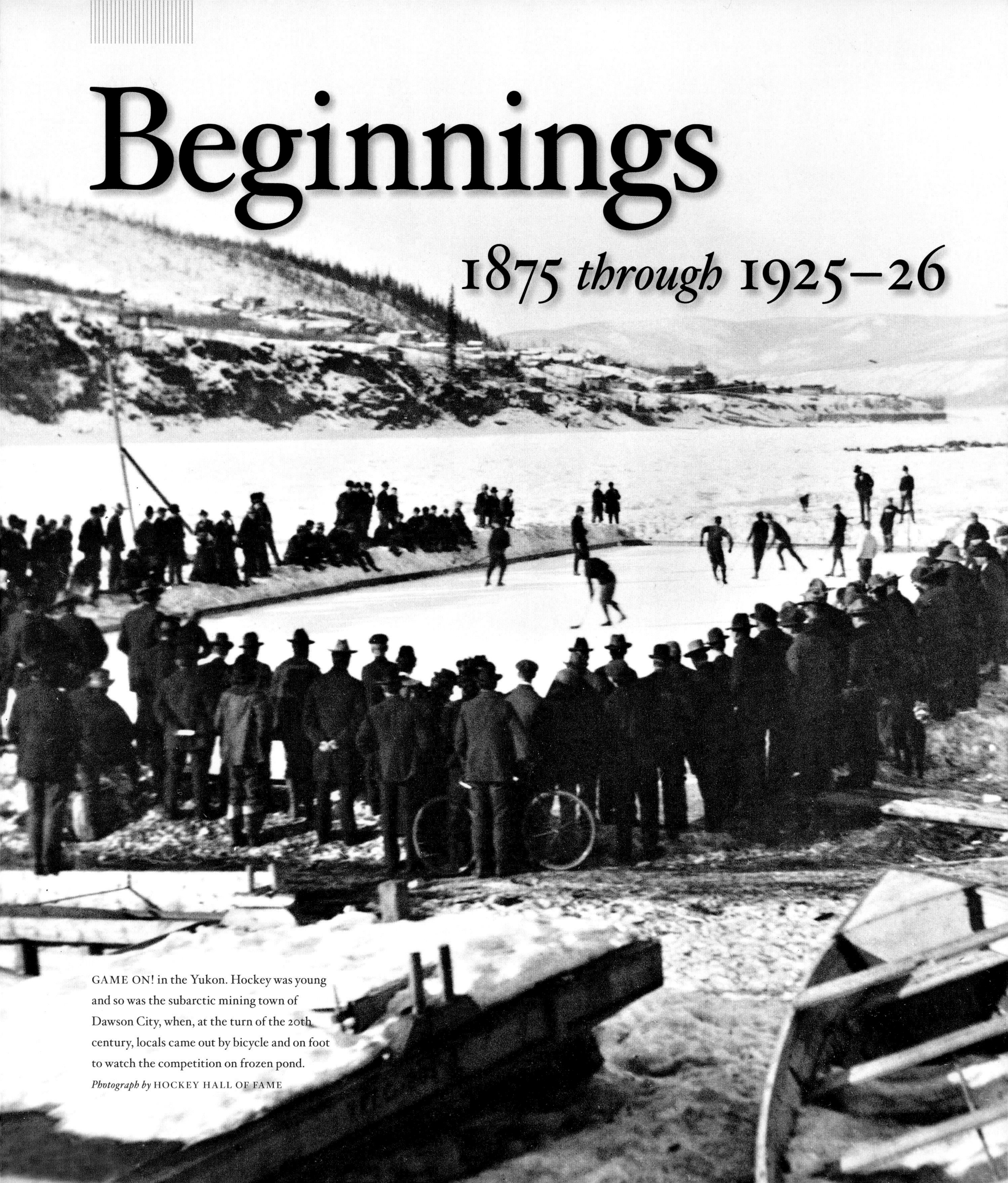

GAME ON! in the Yukon. Hockey was young and so was the subarctic mining town of Dawson City, when, at the turn of the 20th century, locals came out by bicycle and on foot to watch the competition on frozen pond.
Photograph by HOCKEY HALL OF FAME

> ALL-STARS OF THE ERA <

FIRST TEAM

FORWARD
CY DENNENY
SENATORS, BRUINS

FORWARD
JOE MALONE
CANADIENS, TIGERS, BULLDOGS

FORWARD
FRANK MCGEE
SILVER SEVEN, ABERDEENS, SECONDS

DEFENSEMAN
ART ROSS
ANDERERS, SENATORS, ELKS

DEFENSEMAN
LESTER PATRICK
ARISTOCRATS, WANDERERS, METROPOLITANS

GOALIE
GEORGES VÉZINA
CANADIENS

SECOND TEAM

FORWARD
CYCLONE TAYLOR
MILLIONAIRES, KINGS

FORWARD
NEWSY LALONDE
CANADIENS, CRESCENTS

FORWARD
HOBEY BAKER
PRINCETON TIGERS

DEFENSEMAN
SPRAGUE CLEGHORN
SENATORS, ST. PATRICKS, CANADIENS, BRUINS

DEFENSEMAN
EDDIE GERARD
SENATORS

GOALIE
CLINT BENEDICT
SENATORS, MAROONS

COACH
PETE GREEN
SENATORS

> NICKNAMES <

Aurel [Little Giant] Joliat ^
George [Buck] Boucher
Harry [Punch] Broadbent
Francis [King] Clancy
Carson [Shovel Shot] Cooper
Bert [Pig Iron] Corbeau
Samuel [Rusty] Crawford
Wilfred [Shorty] Green
Albert [Toots] Holway
Albert [Battleship] Leduc
Edouard [Newsy] Lalonde
Fred [Steamer] Maxwell
Howie [the Stratford Streak] Morenz
John [Crutchy] Morrison
Didier [Cannonball] Pitre
George [Goldie] Prodgers
[Bullet] Joe Simpson
Eddie [the Edmonton Express] Shore
Reginald [Hooley] Smith
Frederick [Cyclone] Taylor
Georges [the Chicoutimi Cucumber] Vézina

STATISTICAL LEADERS

GOALS

CY DENNENY	225
BABE DYE	176
JOE MALONE	143
REG NOBLE	141
NEWSY LALONDE	124

ASSISTS

CY DENNENY	77
FRANK NIGHBOR	77
REG NOBLE	70
GEORGE BOUCHER	58
HARRY CAMERON	51

POINTS (ALL SKATERS)

CY DENNENY	302
BABE DYE	215
REG NOBLE	211
FRANK NIGHBOR	197
JOE MALONE	175

POINTS (DEFENSEMEN)

GEORGE BOUCHER	154
HARRY CAMERON	140
SPRAGUE CLEGHORN	120
BERT CORBEAU	110
GOLDIE PRODGERS	88

GOALIE WINS

CLINT BENEDICT	126
GEORGES VÉZINA	103
JOHN ROACH	65
JAKE FORBES	61
ALEX CONNELL	41

GOALS AGAINST AVERAGE*

ALEX CONNELL	1.58
CLINT BENEDICT	2.71
JAKE FORBES	2.97
GEORGES VÉZINA	3.28
JOHN ROACH	3.34

*MINIMUM 66 NHL GAMES

>>WISH YOU WERE THERE

The First Indoor Hockey Game

MARCH 3, 1875 • VICTORIA SKATING RINK, MONTREAL Comprised mainly of students from McGill University, 18 players, nine per side, take the ice in what is also believed to be the first game (inside or out) using positions, standardized goals, goaltenders, a referee, goal judges and uniforms. The focus of everyone's attention is a small wooden disc that replaces the usual item, a lacrosse ball.

Montreal AAA 3, Ottawa Generals 1

MARCH 22, 1894 • VICTORIA SKATING RINK, MONTREAL After a four-way-tie atop the Amateur Hockey Association of Canada standings, the first Stanley Cup playoffs are held. Quebec withdraws, giving Ottawa a bye to the finals where it meets defending champ Montreal, which beat its city-rival, the Montreal Victorias in a semifinal match. The AAA's Billy Barlow scores in both games, including the Cup-clinching goal in the 3–1 final.

Ottawa Silver Seven 23, Dawson City Nuggets 2

JANUARY 16, 1905 • DEY'S ARENA, OTTAWA Three days after losing Game 1 of the Stanley Cup challenge to the Silver Seven 9–2, and four days after completing a harrowing, 24-day odyssey through blizzards and sub-zero temperatures via dog sleds, boat and train (the gold mining town of Dawson City in the Yukon is 4,400 miles from Ottawa) the Nuggets are routed in Game 2. Silver Seven superstar Frank McGee scores 14 goals in the most lopsided game ever played in the quest for Lord Stanley's Cup.

Montreal Wanderers 10, ECAHA All Stars 7

JANUARY 2, 1908 • MONTREAL ARENA, MONTREAL To honor the late Hod Stuart, a standout member of the 1907 Stanley Cup champion Montreal Wanderers who was killed in a diving accident in the Bay of Quinte, a memorial game is organized between the Wanderers and a collection of the best players in the Eastern Canada Amateur Hockey Association. Hockey's first All-Star game raises more than $2,000 for Stuart's widow and two young children.

< Seattle Metropolitans 9, Canadiens 1

MARCH 26, 1917 • SEATTLE ICE ARENA, SEATTLE Seattle's Pacific Coast Hockey Association entry rebounds after dropping the opener of a best-of-five series 8–4 to the visiting powerhouse from Montreal by winning the next three games to become the first U.S.–based Stanley Cup champion. In the Metropolitans' clinching 9–1 victory, Bernie Morris scores six times to give him 14 goals over the four-game set.

Quebec Bulldogs 10, Toronto St. Pats 6

JANUARY 31, 1920 • QUEBEC ARENA, QUEBEC CITY The greatest scorer of his time, Quebec's Joe Malone, breaks Newsy Lalonde's NHL single-game record by notching a still-never-matched seven goals in this regular-season contest against lowly Toronto. Malone nearly set the standard even higher, but his apparent score late in the first period was disallowed. Five weeks later he would add to his legend with a six-goal game.

>MAYHEM MOMENT

FEBRUARY 18, 1899

Montreal Arena

Upset at ref J.A. Findlay for a lenient penalty call on Montreal during the Stanley Cup Challenge, the Winnipeg Victorias *(left)* storm off the ice. Findlay also leaves in disgust but is convinced by other officials to return. Winnipeg players, though, are not willing to return to the ice and Findlay awards Montreal, up 3–2 when play halted, the Cup by forfeit.

> "It was discovered later that some of Winnipeg's players had dressed right after the walkout and left hurriedly to sample the delights of Montreal night life."
>
> —*Brian McFarlane, in his 1967 book* 50 Years of Hockey

> TEAMS OF THE ERA

OTTAWA SENATORS

From 1919–20 through '26–27 no team was better than the Senators, who won four Stanley Cups and 67% of their regular-season games and finished in first place six times. The Senators' roster during this period contained an extraordinary 14 players who would be enshrined in the Hall of Fame including three—George Boucher, Cy Denneny and Frank Nighbor—who played for all four of the Cup winners.

OTTAWA SILVER SEVEN

Winners of nine consecutive Stanley Cup challenges over the course of three seasons (1903–06), the Silver Seven took on all comers to establish themselves as hockey's first true dynasty. The Silver Seven benefited from sterling performances by the most feared scorer of the time, "One-Eyed" Frank McGee (he was blind in one eye), who scored five or more goals in a game eight times during his short 45-game career.

^ VANCOUVER MILLIONAIRES

A charter member of the Pacific Coast Hockey Association, the Millionaires were so named because they paid high salaries to lure top talent such as Fred (Cyclone) Taylor and Newsy Lalonde to the West Coast. Representing the PCHA in the Stanley Cup finals four times, the Millionaires won the only Cup in Vancouver history in 1915 by sweeping three games from the powerhouse Ottawa Senators while outscoring them 26–8.

[DEBUT]		[FINALE]
Sprague Cleghorn	1910–11	Bruce Stuart
George Boucher	1917–18	Art Ross
Punch Broadbent	1918–19	Si Griffis
Babe Dye	1919–20	Tommy Smith
Leo Reise	1920–21	Thomas McCarthy
King Clancy	1921–22	Jack McDonald
Aurel Joliat	1922–23	Eddie Gerard
Howie Morenz >	1923–24	< Joe Malone
Hap Day	1924–25	Goldie Prodgers
Lionel Conacher	1925–26	Georges Vézina

> BY THE NUMBERS

10 | Guineas (about $48.67) spent by Sir Frederick Arthur Stanley on the silver punch bowl that he donated in 1892 to be presented to the leading hockey club in Canada.

7 | Teams in the precursor to the NHL, the NHA, which began in 1909–10: the Cobalt Silver Kings, Haileybury Comets, Montreal Canadiens, Montreal Shamrocks, Montreal Wanderers, Ottawa Senators and Renfrew Creamery Kings.

7 | Seasons the NHL existed only in Canada before adding the Boston Bruins in 1924–25.

16 | Consecutive-game goal-scoring streak in 1921–22 by Ottawa's Punch Broadbent, an NHL record that still stands.

110–3 | Canada's margin of victory over five games at the 1924 Olympics.

36 | Goals scored at those '24 Games in Chamonix by Harry Watson, who remains the record-holder for goals in a single Olympics and a career.

5 | Stanley Cup finals games played in 1919 between the Canadiens and Seattle Metropolitans before a flu epidemic canceled the series.

> PATRICK FACTOR

Brothers Frank and Lester Patrick formed the Pacific Coast Hockey Association in 1911, introducing new guidelines to hockey. Twenty-two of the innovations pioneered in the league—such as forward passing, blue lines, assists, penalty shots and uniform numbers—remain in use today.

1961 | EARL INGARFIELD, here hoping to put one behind Montreal's Jacques Plante, was a bright light for the Rangers in '61–62, scoring 26 goals. | *Photograph by* JOHN G. ZIMMERMAN

2007 | THERE WAS no getting around the defense of Blues goalie Manny Legace, though the Kings' Michael Cammalleri gave a flat-out effort. | *Photograph by* DANNY MOLOSHOK

NHL
.CO
34
Brian's
SOP SHER-WOOD
WOOD

AN INNOCENT AT RINKSIDE

BY WILLIAM FAULKNER

Nobel Prize–winning novelist William Faulkner took in his first hockey game, as SI's guest at Madison Square Garden, where the Montreal Canadiens played the New York Rangers. He recorded these vivid impressions. —*from* SI, JANUARY 24, 1955

THE VACANT ICE LOOKED tired, though it shouldn't have. They told him it had been put down only a few minutes ago following a basketball game, and after the hockey match it would be taken up again to make room for something else. But it looked not expectant but resigned, like the mirror simulating ice in the Christmas store window, not before the miniature fir trees and reindeer and cozy lamplit cottage were arranged upon it, but after they had been dismantled and cleared away.

Then it was filled with motion, speed. To the innocent it seemed discorded and inconsequent, bizarre and paradoxical like the frantic darting of the weightless bugs which run on the surface of stagnant pools. Then it would break, coalesce through a kind of kaleidoscopic whirl like a child's toy, into a pattern, a design almost beautiful, as if an inspired choreographer had drilled a willing and patient and hardworking troupe of dancers—a pattern, a design which was trying to tell him something, say something to him urgent and important and true in that second before it began to disintegrate and dissolve.

Then he learned to find the puck and follow it. Then the individual players would emerge. They would not emerge like the sweating barehanded behemoths from the troglodyte mass of football, but instead as fluid and fast and effortless as rapier thrusts or lightning—Richard with something of the passionate glittering fatal alien quality of snakes, Geoffrion like an agile ruthless precocious boy who maybe couldn't do anything else but then he didn't need to; and others—the veteran Laprade, still with the know-how and the grace.

Excitement: men in rapid, hard, close physical conflict, not just with bare hands, but armed with the blades of skates and the hard, fast, deft sticks which could break bones when used right. He had noticed how many women were among the spectators, and for just a moment he thought that perhaps this was why—that here actual male blood could flow, not from the crude impact of a heavier fist but from the rapid and delicate stroke of weapons, which, like the European rapier or the frontier pistol, reduced mere size and brawn to its proper perspective to the passion and the will. But only for a moment because he, the innocent, didn't like that idea either. It was the excitement of speed and grace, with the puck for catalyst, to give it reason, meaning.

He watched it—the figure-darted glare of ice, the concentric tiers rising in sections, vanishing upward into the pall of tobacco smoke trapped by the roof—the roof which stopped and trapped all that intent and tense watching, and concentrated it downward upon the glare of ice frantic and frenetic with motion; until the by-product of the speed and the motion—their violence—had no chance to exhaust itself upward into space. And he thought how perhaps something is happening to sport in America, and that something is the roof we are putting over it and them. Skating, basketball, tennis, track meets and even steeplechasing have moved indoors; football and baseball function beneath covers of arc lights and in time will be rain- and cold-proofed too. There remain the proper working of a fly over trout water or the taking of a rise of birds in front of a dog or the right placing of a bullet in a deer or even a bigger animal which will hurt you if you don't. But not for long: In time that will be indoors too beneath lights and the trapped pall of spectator tobacco.

But (to repeat) not for long, because the innocent did not quite believe that either. We—Americans—like to watch; we like the adrenalic discharge of vicarious excitement or triumph or success. But we like to do also: the discharge of the personal excitement of the triumph and the fear to be had from actually setting the horse at the stone wall or pointing the overcanvased sloop or finding by actual test if you can line up two sights and one buffalo in time. There must have been little boys in that throng too, frantic with the slow excruciating passage of time, panting for the hour when they would be Richard or Geoffrion or Laprade—the same little Negro boys whom the innocent has seen shadow-boxing in front of a photograph of Joe Louis in his own Mississippi town, the same little Norwegian boys he watched staring up the snowless slope of the Holmenkollen jump one July day in the hills above Oslo.

MOMENTS SIMILAR to this occurred at the game Faulkner attended; to him some players appeared as fluid, as fast and as effortless as rapier thrusts.

EVAN PESKIN

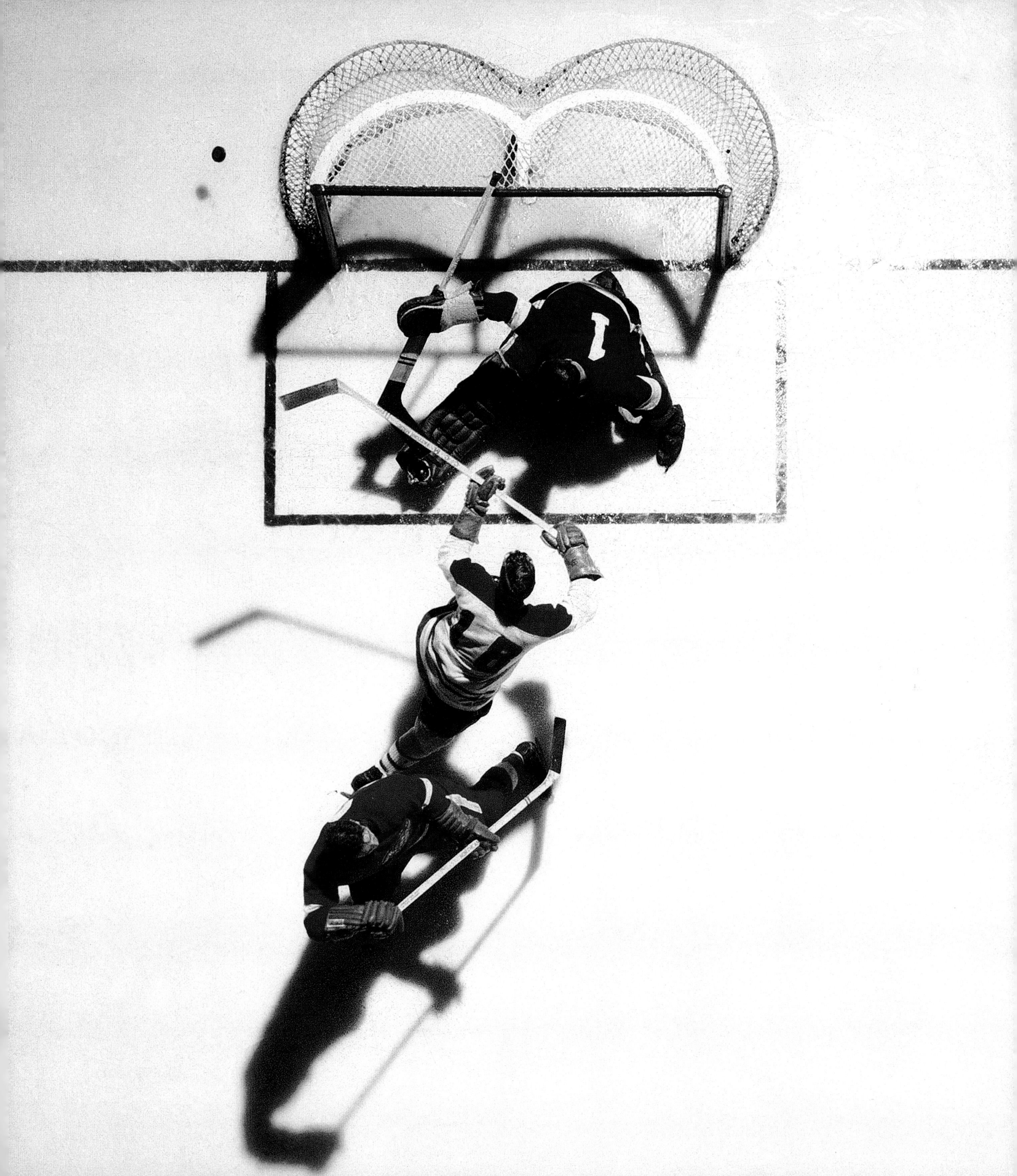

ncou
2010
BULLO
10
22
C
ANADA
BAUER
Supreme ONE95
Reebok

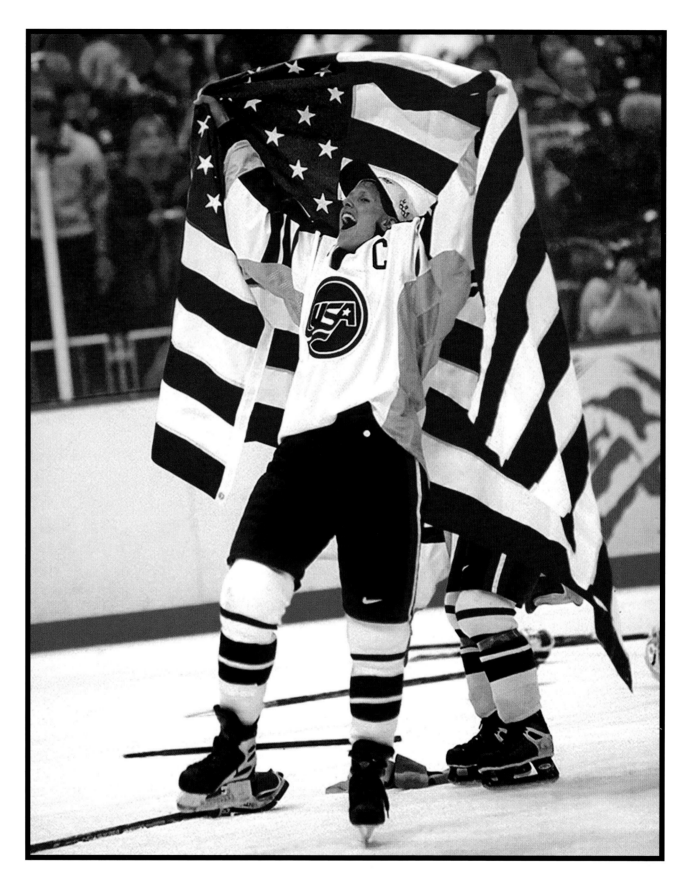

1998 | CAMMI GRANATO captained the U.S. to Olympic gold. She is the first female member of the U.S. Hockey Hall of Fame. | *Photograph by* BRUCE BENNETT STUDIOS

2010 | HAYLEY WICKENHEISER, who was the first woman to score in a pro league, won her third Olympic gold with Team Canada. | *Photograph by* LARRY W. SMITH

> Artifacts

Painted Faces

They're smart and they're good-looking. Goalie masks are not just essential mug protectors but also revealing forms of art and self-expression. The adventurous Gilles Gratton, for example, hoped his custom-made lion mask (below) would scare opponents. His nickname? Gratoony the Loony

GERRY McNEIL
Montreal Royals (EPHL) 1959–60

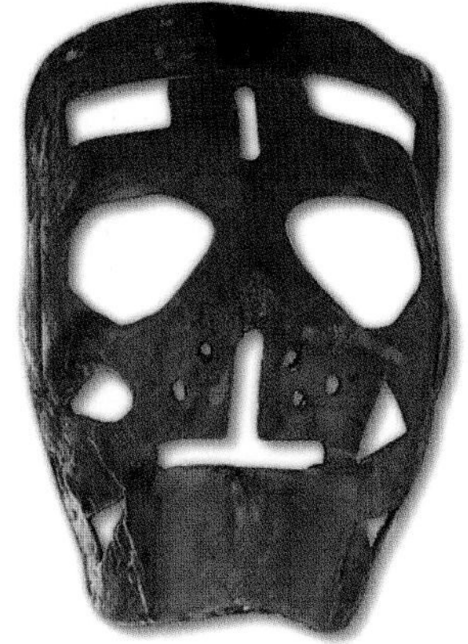

TERRY SAWCHUK
Toronto Maple Leafs 1964–1967

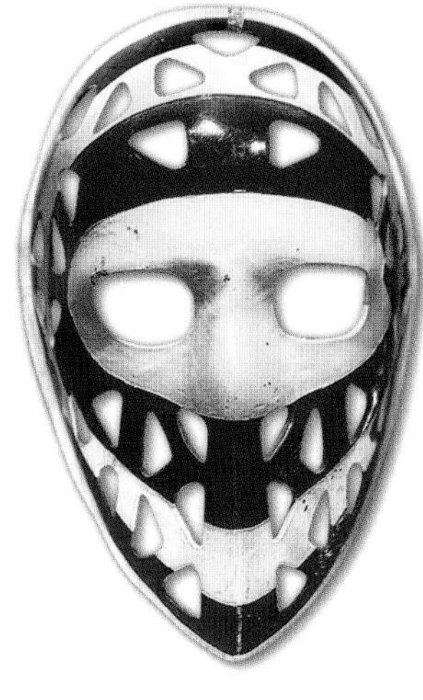

KEN DRYDEN
Montreal Canadiens 1970–1973

EDDIE GIACOMIN
Detroit Red Wings 1976–77

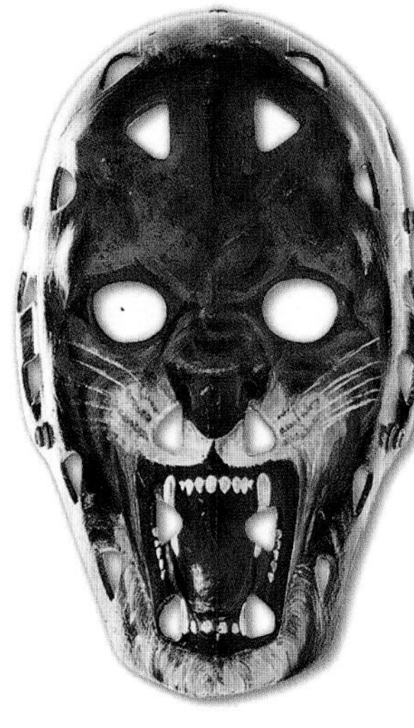

GILLES GRATTON
New York Rangers 1976–77

BILLY SMITH
New York Islanders 1977–78

MIKE PALMATEER
Toronto Maple Leafs 1977–1979

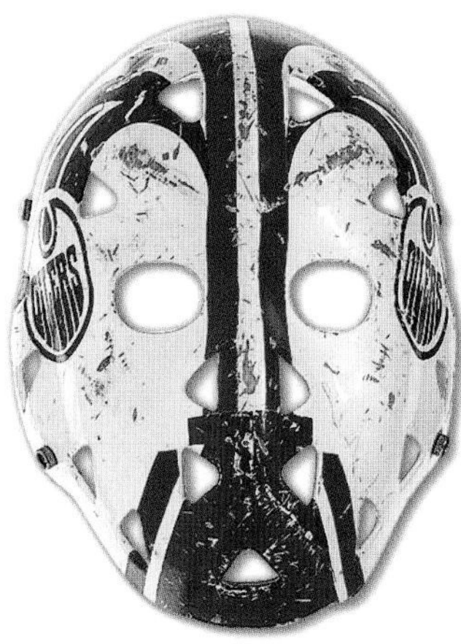

GRANT FUHR
Edmonton Oilers 1983–1985

JON CASEY
Minnesota North Stars 1989–1991

JOHAN HEDBERG
Atlants Thrashers 2009–2010

DAVID N. BERKWITZ (MCNEIL); SCOTT CUNNINGHAM (HEDBERG); DAVE SANFORD/HOCKEY HALL OF FAME (DRYDEN); MATTHEW MANOR/HOCKEY HALL OF FAME (8)

CURTIS JOSEPH
St. Louis Blues 1990–1993

FLYER FROM FLIN FLON

BY MARK MULVOY

The NHL's reigning MVP and the captain of Philadelphia's Broad Street Bullies, Bobby Clarke embodied the hardscrabble spirit of his hometown. —*from* SI, OCTOBER 22, 1973

IGNORE THE INNOCENCE OF HIS angelic face and his all-I-want-for-Christmas smile. To place Bobby Clarke in proper perspective, he must be viewed in several cities. Moscow, for one. There was Team Canada staring at disaster, down two games to the Russians with three to play. As he swept up ice, Clarke happened to be trailing the Soviet star, Valeri Kharlamov. "It suddenly hit me that Kharlamov was killing us while I was only holding my own," Clarke recalls. "I realized that someone had to do something about him." In the heat of that realization Clarke swung his stick and connected with Kharlamov's ankles. The consequence was considerably more damaging than the mere discipline and shaking up Clarke had in mind. The Russian missed the rest of that game and the next one. Clarke got a two-minute slashing penalty. The NHL All-Stars rallied to win the last three games—and the series. "It's not something I was really proud of," Clarke says softly, "but I honestly can't say I was ashamed to do it."

Now move to Philadelphia. Bobby Clarke is not booed in Philadelphia, which is a distinction in itself. As captain of the Broad Street Bullies, also known as the Flyers, Clarke centers the first line, directs the power play, kills penalties and moderates the nightly disputes between the Bullies and their adversaries. Though he tries to keep a low fighting profile in front of his home crowd, Clarke is adept at squirting gasoline on incipient fires. One night Keith Magnuson of Chicago smashed the unsuspecting Clarke into the boards. "Clarke, you're sick," Magnuson snarled.

"I can't help that, dummy," Clarke replied, "but you're stupid, Maggy, and you *can* do something about that. Now buzz off—or I'll send Schultzie after you." Schultzie is winger Dave Schultz. He's large and menacing, the NHL's heavyweight champ. If unfriendly people like Magnuson press their attentions on Clarke, Schultz comes calling. "We've got to protect our leader," he explains

Finally, see Clarke in Flin Flon, Manitoba, his hometown. "I'm pretty reserved when I'm with strangers," Clarke says, "but I swear, drink beer and drive too fast when I'm with my own kind." Clarke is in Flin Flon for a brief August visit so that the people may honor him—the NHL's Most Valuable Player—with a Bobby Clarke Day, complete with an exhibition game to benefit local youth hockey.

This is the summer's happening in Flin Flon, a mining town of 12,000 on the Manitoba-Saskatchewan border. Almost everyone in Flin Flon, including Clarke's father, Cliff, works for the Hudson Bay Mining and Smelting Co. Downtown looks like any community of similar size: an H&R Block tax office, a Kentucky Fried Chicken parlor, a Simpsons-Sears with a sale on color TV sets, a bowling emporium, Schrieder's Clothing Store, a couple of drugstores, a movie theater, three taxi stands and half a dozen cafés, one of which is boarded-up.

It was here that Clarke immersed himself in hockey at the expense of all else, and here that he played junior hockey for coach Pat Ginnell. "I first saw Bobby play in the juvenile finals back in the spring of 1966," Ginnell says. "He had some nice moves, easily the best on the ice, but he sure looked funny with his big glasses, his bucked teeth and the skates his feet were swimming in. Still, there was no way he was going to miss. He became our best player and a tough kid. He'd cut your ears off if he had to. The idea was that if you got Clarke, you'd get Flin Flon."

Now, it is almost game time on Bobby Clarke Day at Flin Flon's Whitney Forum. Clarke sits in a small dressing room with the teenage Bombers who'll be his teammates in the exhibition. Ginnell gives Clarke his old Bomber shirt—number 11. "We retired it when you left," Ginnell says. Clarke tries to pull the jersey over his shoulders. "Sorry, Pat," he says, "it just doesn't fit anymore."

It is doubtful that any of the 2,600 fans who jam the Forum hear the P.A. announcer's introduction of the guest of honor. The noise begins as Clarke steps from the dressing room, and does not subside until he skates to center ice, waves in every direction and pleads for silence. He accepts the gifts—a television set, silverware, jewelry—and he thanks the crowd for coming. "I can never repay Flin Flon for all it has done for me," he says.

The game begins, and in the first minute a youngster named Rob Watt slams into Clarke with his stick raised high. Down goes the Most Valuable Player of the NHL. "Do that again, kid, and I'll take your bleeping head off," Clarke shouts. Later—with just 74 seconds left in the game—Clarke spots Watt skating with his head down in center ice. The ensuing crunch is probably audible in Moscow. Clarke crashed into Watt so hard that the kid is barely able to totter back to his bench.

"Ah, yes," says Jim Bryson, a former Bombers trainer and longtime Flin Flon local, with a smile. "That's our Bobby."

CLARKE, A DIABETIC who slipped to No. 17 in the 1969 draft, became beloved in Philadelphia and led the Flyers to back-to-back Stanley Cups in the mid-'70s.

JOHN OLSON

Cooper
CLARKE R.
16
SHER-WOOD

2003 | THE DEVILS' Joe Nieuwendyk had his game face on in an Eastern Conference finals game in Ottawa; the Senators won, though, 3–2 in OT. | *Photograph by* LOU CAPOZZOLA

2006 | THE PUCK went swifter, higher and farther than Team Canada goalie Martin Brodeur could reach during a game against Switzerland at the Turin Olympics. | *Photograph by* ELSA

torino 2006
torino
30
CANADA
VECTOR
BUSCH
CCM

1952 | IN CASE Canadiens' goaltender Gerry McNeil still couldn't see the puck that had just sped past, the goal judge put the light on for him. | *Photograph by* AP

THE PANTHEON >> *Forwards*

SI's TOP 25

Jean Béliveau
Mike Bossy
Bobby Clarke
Sidney Crosby
Phil Esposito
Sergei Fedorov
Wayne Gretzky
Gordie Howe
Bobby Hull
Brett Hull
Jaromir Jagr
Aurel Joliat
Valeri Kharlamov
Guy Lafleur
Newsy Lalonde
Mario Lemieux >
Ted Lindsay
Frank Mahovlich
Mark Messier
Stan Mikita
Howie Morenz
Alexander Ovechkin
Maurice Richard
Bryan Trottier
Steve Yzerman

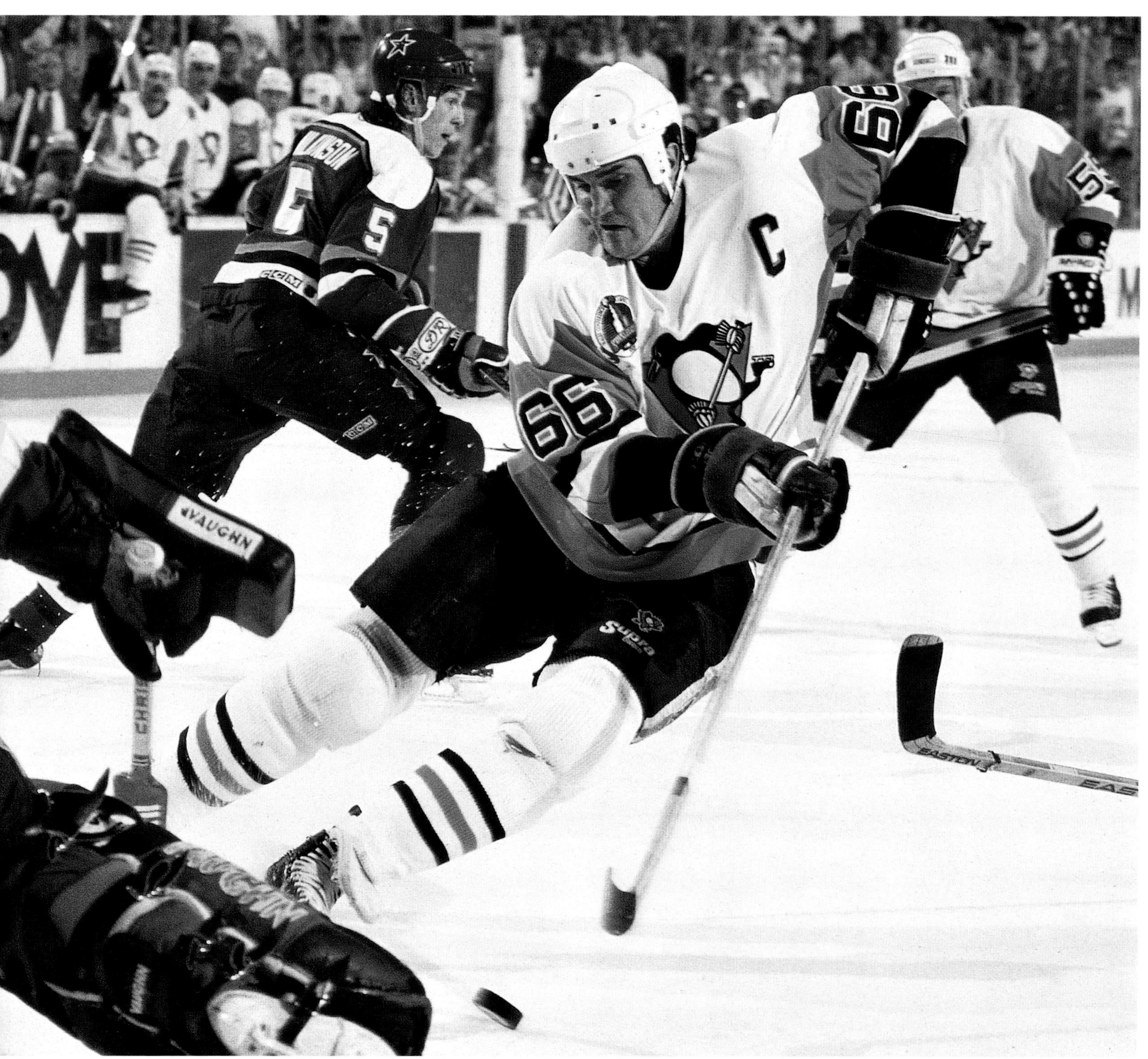

1991 | LEMIEUX LED the NHL in points six times. In '91 he and the Penguins beat the North Stars, and goalie Jon Casey, in the Stanley Cup finals. | *Photograph by* DAVID E. KLUTHO

Cooper
SK 600

MEET THE BOY WONDER

BY E.M. SWIFT

A season before his pro debut in the WHA Wayne Gretzky was drawing large crowds and rewriting the record books as a rookie in rough-and-tumble Junior A. Already, his name had been preceding him for nearly a decade. —*from* SI, FEBRUARY 20, 1978

MORE THAN 7,000 PEOPLE—the largest hockey crowd of the season in Canada's capital—came to the Ottawa Civic Center one night last month to get to the bottom of a 16-year-old wunderkind who plays for the Sault Ste. Marie (Ont.) Greyhounds. His name is Wayne Gretzky. That's with a Zed-K-Y, please. The immigration guy fouled it up when his grandfather came over from Russia. In Peterborough the next night, the same thing happened: largest crowd of the year even though the last-place Greyhounds provided the opposition. The night after that, it was the same story in Hamilton: first sellout of the year for a Junior A game, and in a blizzard to boot, everyone out getting stuck in the snow to see some kid called The Great Gretzky, whom every paper in Ontario has hailed as the next Bobby Orr since he was eight years old, 4' 4" and 70 pounds.

Gretzky is not just another star of the future. He is there, Canada's answer to Steve Cauthen and Nadia Comaneci, one of those rare youths who leapfrogs the stage where they speak of potential, whose talent is already front and center, which, incidentally, is the position he plays for the Greyhounds. Skating in the Ontario Junior A Major Hockey Association (OHA) Gretzky has exploded onto the Junior scene like no one since Guy Lafleur—and before that Orr. If Wayne Gretzky were never to play another hockey game, thousands of Canadian kids would remember him into their dotage. He is the stuff of their dreams; that, lacking size, lacking strength, lacking speed, they, too, can somehow make it.

He is now a wiry (read "skinny") 155 pounds spread over 5' 11", but he should fill out enough to keep the pros happy. Gretzky describes his speed as "brutal"—meaning slower than slow. Gretzky's shot is accurate, but far from overpowering. And if you expect to see him mucking it up in the corners, forget it. Still, without question, he is the most exciting Junior hockey player since Lafleur left Quebec City in 1971.

"They compare me to Orr and Lafleur, and that's very flattering," says Gretzky in his best "shucks, who, lil-ol-me?" tone. "But basically, my style is different from anyone else's."

Gretzky's talent is all in his head. "He's the smartest kid I've ever seen," says Fred Litzen, Sault Ste. Marie's head scout who has evaluated talent for 40 years. Gretzky knows not only where everyone is on the ice, but he also knows where they're *going.* Uncanny anticipation, people call it.

While Gretzky's straight-ahead speed is something less than overwhelming, his mobility makes him nearly impossible to check, and his quickness—"Oh God, he's got terrific reflexes," says Litzen—makes him a superb forechecker in the mold of Bobby Clarke, the player after whom Gretzky models himself the most. Right now, Gretzky has a knack with the puck equal to anyone's, at any level. "From the red line to their net I play a solid game compared to anyone in the NHL," he says. And somehow such a statement from a 16-year-old does not have a cocky ring. It shouldn't, because it's true.

When he was five, nearly three years after his father, Walter, strapped skates onto his tiny feet and shoved him onto the flooded backyard rink, Gretzky made the Brantford, Ont., novice all-star team, a squad usually made up of 10- and 11-year-olds. That led to an interview with the local television station at age six; a Toronto *Globe and Mail* feature at eight; a film clip on national television at nine. His career as a media darling was rolling. At 11 he scored 378 goals in 68 games, including three in 45 seconds in the third period of a game in which Brantford trailed 3–0. The legend grew, far faster than the boy.

After being the third player selected in the midget draft held by the OHA last spring, Gretzky was expected to need time to adjust to the rougher, faster pace of the mother lode of North American hockey. He didn't. He scored a hat trick in his first game with Sault Ste. Marie, and has been at the top of the OHA scoring race ever since. In his first 48 games Gretzky had 54 goals and 87 assists for 141 points. He has already shattered the rookie record of 137 points in a season. You wouldn't know that the Greyhounds were in the cellar by the way the press flocks into the dressing room after the games. Inside, reporters crowd around Gretzky, ignoring the rest.

Orr? LaFleur?

"In 25 years in this business," says Harry Wolfe, the radio voice of the Greyhounds. "I have never seen a kid capture the imagination of the Canadian public like Wayne Gretzky."

LIKE ANY ROOKIE Gretzky was subject to hazing—prank calls, Vaseline in the hair. But his teammates also held him in awe, realizing he was in a class by himself.

LANE STEWART

1956 | THE REF was on top of the action as a pair of Gordies—that's Detroit's Howe checking Toronto's Hannigan—clashed in the Cup semifinals. | *Photograph by* BETTMANN/CORBIS

1958 | RED WINGS center and three-time Lady Byng winner Alex Delvecchio politely eased his way between an official and the Rangers' Jack Evans. | *Photograph by* HY PESKIN

KOHO
2

1997 | RED WINGS defenseman Slava Fetisov, the former CSKA Moscow star, was stopped by Colorado's imposing Patrick Roy here, but Detroit won the game—and the conference finals. | *Photograph by* DAVID E. KLUTHO

1959 | A SHOT by the Rangers' Andy Bathgate bloodied the Canadiens' Jacques Plante and inspired him to be the first goalie to routinely wear a mask. | *Photograph by* BETTMANN/CORBIS

1957 | A STILL UNBLEMISHED Plante put his best face forward against the Rangers en route to winning the third of his seven Vezina Trophies. | *Photograph by* JOHN G. ZIMMERMAN

TWIN PILLARS

BY MICHAEL FARBER

Both of them sophomores, both of them sensations, Sidney Crosby and Alexander Ovechkin were being counted on to raise the NHL's profile. —*from* SI, NOVEMBER 2, 2006

MAYBE IT'S NOT A CATCHY marketing slogan, but the NHL has this going for it: The players are generally nice people. It is the sport's peculiar blessing that it employs some of the roughest athletes, who are also among the most down-to-earth, the kinds of guys who would give you the shirts off their backs. Or in the case of Sidney Crosby, a jersey. After three hours in a photo studio with Alexander Ovechkin not long ago, posing in light that flattered them almost as much as their stats from incandescent rookie seasons in 2005–06, Crosby tugged off his black number 87 Penguins sweater, held it out to Ovechkin, clothed in his Capitals gear, and asked almost shyly, "Want to trade?"

Crosby, 19, and Ovechkin, 21, are not friends in a conventional sense. Indeed, they barely know each other. Their paths crossed in four Pittsburgh-Washington games last season, and they socialized and traded phone numbers after the NHL awards ceremony in June, when Ovechkin was named the league's rookie of the year over Crosby in a landslide (124–4 in first-place votes) that will strike future generations as an anomaly. Their careers are linked not only by age and talent, but also by their status as the foundation for a league trying to rebuild itself. After getting its on-ice product in order following the 2004–05 lockout, the NHL is trying to regain a foothold in the casual sports fan's imagination. The league isn't as concerned that Crosby and Ovechkin get to know each other this season as it is that you get to know them.

Ovechkin, at 6' 2" and 220 pounds, is rangy and raw and unconventionally handsome, his open face dominated by a nose that slaloms to the left. Crosby, 5' 11" and 199 after adding five pounds of muscle in the off-season, is compact, thick through his haunches, preternaturally poised and slick in his appearance. Ovechkin, from Moscow, is playful even in his second language. Crosby, from Nova Scotia, is sober even in his first. Ovechkin, a winger with a righthanded shot, is brimming with speed and manic invention, wallpapers defensemen and scores goals that seem to defy the laws of physics. Crosby, a center with a lefthanded shot, can slow the tempo or quicken it, a puppet master who makes deft passes and flicks precise wrist shots.

"On ice, rivals," Ovechkin says, "but in the league for sure [we are] partners."

Says Crosby, "We're from opposite places, but we can relate to similar things." Each may be the only player in hockey who really understands what it is like to be the other. The way Bill Gates can identify with Warren Buffett. The way Magic Johnson could understand Larry Bird.

The NHL hopes it is in possession of two talents able to cross from athlete to celebrity. The standard measure of hockey's blessed (Ovechkin became the second rookie ever with 50 goals and 100 points; Crosby became the youngest player with a 100-point season) has always been how quickly they lead a team to a Stanley Cup. Ovechkin and Crosby will be judged on that, but also on their ability to move the NHL into the national conversation.

For Crosby, being one of the faces of hockey "is something I've grown into, like tying my skates"—since he was anointed by Wayne Gretzky as a future NHL record-breaker when Crosby was 15 years old. The gregarious Ovechkin is seizing his moment. "I love to do crazy things," Ovechkin says. "Like [at] the draft." There, he sat at Washington's table and delighted fans when he took G.M. George McPhee up on his offer to go to the podium and announce the Capitals' two first-round picks.

More recently, on a public square in Toronto, a mob of 100 businessmen and students greeted Ovechkin as if he were the Muscovite next door. The occasion was the release of *NHL 07*, an EA Sports game that features Ovechkin on the cover; and when his virtual face appeared on a monitor, to take a penalty shot, Ovechkin studied the likeness and asked, "Why am I not smiling?"

Then, he laughed.

"It's a great time for me," Ovechkin says. "When people come up and say, 'Please sign [an autograph]' because they know you and love hockey, and you play in a great city where people watch and scream and have a great time, the energy comes to you. And you play the same way."

Ovechkin didn't adapt quite so easily to *NHL 07*. He was about 0 for 20 taking penalty shots on the console until he selected a new player, with whom he deked and beat the goalie. That virtual player, whom Ovechkin used to go five hole, wore a black number 87 Penguins jersey.

CROSBY AND THE PENGUINS pushed past Ovechkin and the Capitals in a stirring, seven-game playoff series in 2009.

GREGORY SHAMUS/NHLI/GETTY IMAGES

CCM
capitals
A
WASHINGTON
87
C
SUPREME

2000 | AFTER TWO DECADES as a Bruin, Ray Bourque put his defensive skills on display with the Avalanche—and won his first Stanley Cup. | *Photograph by* DARREN CARROLL

STARS
26
BOURQUE
77

20

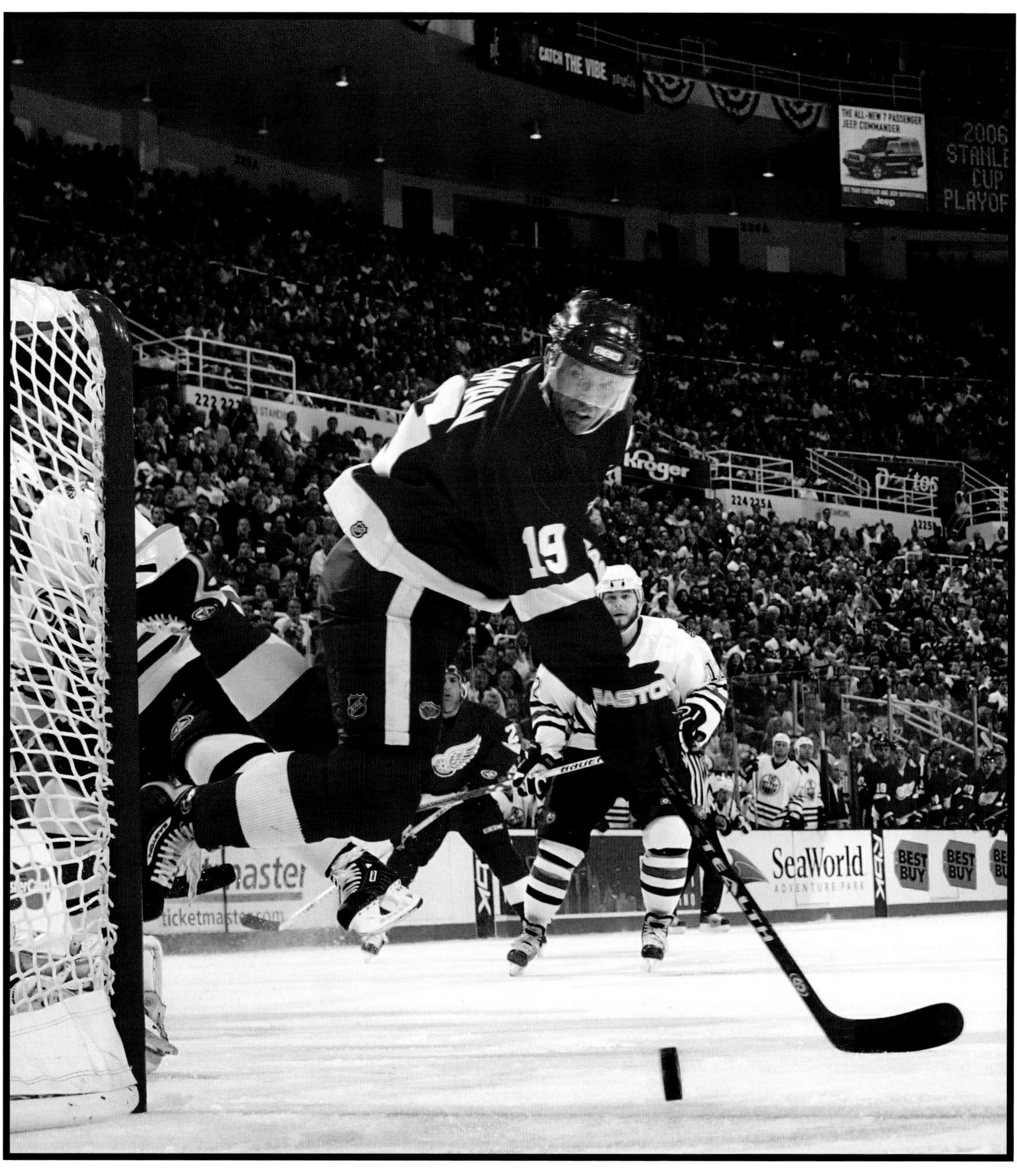

2006 | AFTER 22 soaring seasons with Detroit, Steve Yzerman closed out his career in the playoffs' first round against the Oilers. | *Photograph by* DAVID E. KLUTHO

1958 | FANS FOUND the action diverting as the Red Wings' Marcel Pronovost and the Rangers' Red Sullivan got tangled up near the Garden boards. | *Photograph by* HY PESKIN

SHER-WOOD
LLE
CANADIAN

1977 | GOALTENDER KEN DRYDEN went belly-up against the Bruins, but still led Montreal to the second of four straight Stanley Cups. | *Photograph by* CO RENTMEESTER

Establishment

1926–27 *through* 1945–46

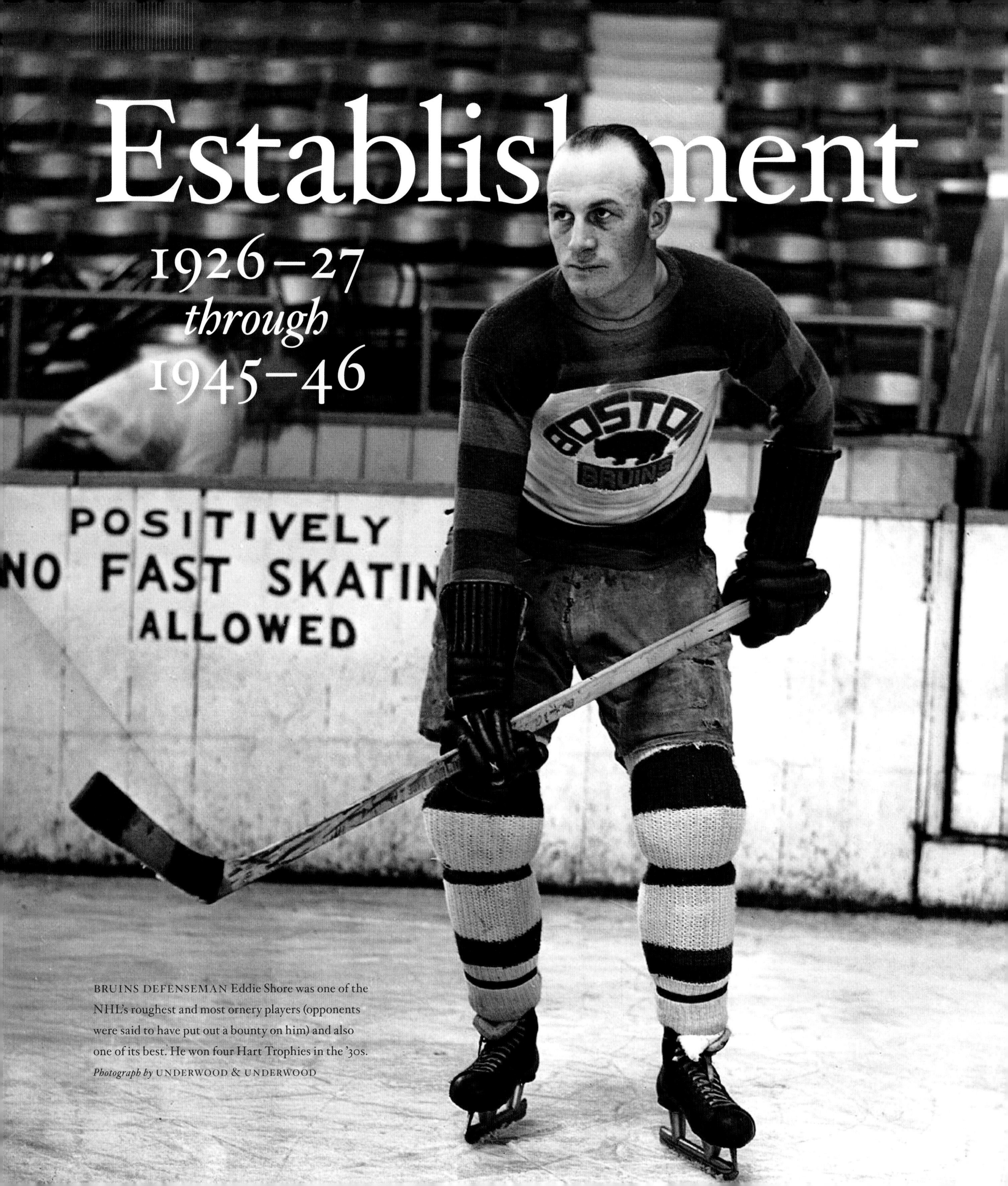

BRUINS DEFENSEMAN Eddie Shore was one of the NHL's roughest and most ornery players (opponents were said to have put out a bounty on him) and also one of its best. He won four Hart Trophies in the '30s.
Photograph by UNDERWOOD & UNDERWOOD

>ALL-STARS OF THE ERA<

FIRST TEAM	SECOND TEAM
LEFT WING BUSHER JACKSON MAPLE LEAFS, AMERICANS, BRUINS	LEFT WING AUREL JOLIAT CANADIENS
CENTER HOWIE MORENZ CANADIENS, BLACK HAWKS, RANGERS	CENTER SYD HOWE RED WINGS, SENATORS, EAGLES
RIGHT WING DIT CLAPPER BRUINS	RIGHT WING CHARLIE CONACHER MAPLE LEAFS, AMERICANS, RED WINGS
DEFENSEMAN EDDIE SHORE BRUINS, AMERICANS	DEFENSEMAN SYLVIO MANTHA CANADIENS, BRUINS
DEFENSEMAN LIONEL CONACHER MAROONS, AMERICANS, BLACK HAWKS	DEFENSEMAN EBBIE GOODFELLOW RED WINGS
GOALIE GEORGE HAINSWORTH CANADIENS, MAPLE LEAFS	GOALIE TINY THOMPSON BRUINS, RED WINGS

COACH
DICK IRVIN
CANADIENS, MAPLE LEAFS, BLACK HAWKS

>NICKNAMES<

Walter [Turk] Broda ^
Clarence [Taffy] Abel
Max [Dipsy-Doodle Dandy] Bentley
Hector [Toe] Blake
Helge [Bulge] Bostrom
Frank [Mr. Zero] Brimsek
Victor [Dit] Clapper
Frederick [Bun] Cook
Rosario [Lolo] Couture
Napoleon [Bunny] Dame
Clarence [Happy] Day
Art [Nosey] Gauthier
Mel [Sudden Death] Hill
Rennison [Dinny] Manners
Charles [Rabbit] McVeigh
Jim [Peggy] O'Neill
Cliff [Fido] Purpur
Eddie [Old Blood and Guts] Shore
Ralph [Bouncer] Taylor
Nels [Old Poison] Stewart
Cecil [Tiny] Thompson

STATISTICAL LEADERS

GOALS	
NELS STEWART	290
HARVEY JACKSON	241
SYD HOWE	237
DIT CLAPPER	228
BILL COOK	228

ASSISTS	
BILL COWLEY	328
SYD HOWE	291
FRANK BOUCHER	261
TOE BLAKE	248
DIT CLAPPER	246

POINTS (ALL SKATERS)	
SYD HOWE	528
BILL COWLEY	510
HARVEY JACKSON	475
DIT CLAPPER	474
NELS STEWART	473

POINTS (DEFENSEMEN)	
FLASH HOLLETT	313
BABE PRATT	284
EDDIE SHORE	284
EARL SEIBERT	276
OTT HELLER	231

GOALIE WINS	
TINY THOMPSON	284
GEORGE HAINSWORTH	246
DAVE KERR	203
LORNE CHABOT	201
TURK BRODA	173

GOALS AGAINST AVERAGE*	
GEORGE HAINSWORTH	1.93
ALEX CONNELL	1.97
CHUCK GARDINER	2.02
LORNE CHABOT	2.04
TINY THOMPSON	2.08

*MINIMUM 300 NHL GAMES

>>WISH YOU WERE THERE

Red Wings 1, Montreal Maroons 0 (6OT)

MARCH 24, 25, 1936 • MONTREAL FORUM The longest game in NHL history (176 minutes, 30 seconds) ends when 21-year old Mud Bruneteau beats goalie Lorne Chabot in Game 1 of a best-of-five Cup semifinals. Detroit goalie Norm Smith makes 90 saves; Chabot 66.

Canadiens 4, Bruins 2

MARCH 18, 1945 • BOSTON GARDEN Having been shut out the previous night against Chicago despite being awarded a penalty shot, Montreal's Maurice (Rocket) Richard beats goaltender Harvey Bennett late in the third period to become the first NHL player to score 50 goals in 50 games.

Maple Leafs 3, Red Wings 1

APRIL 18, 1942 • MAPLE LEAF GARDENS, TORONTO After dropping the first three games the Leafs complete the greatest comeback in Stanley Cup finals history by sweeping the final four. In the third period of Game 7 Toronto's Pete Langelle scores what proves to be the Cup-clincher when he puts a rebound into an empty net that has been vacated by Detroit goalie Johnny Mowers, breaking a 1–1 tie.

Bruins 3, New York Americans 0

DECEMBER 20, 1938 • BOSTON GARDEN Rookie goaltender Frank Brimsek completes his sixth shutout in seven games, a feat never again achieved, earning the nickname "Mr. Zero."

Rangers 3, Maple Leafs 2

APRIL 13, 1940 • MAPLE LEAF GARDENS Bryan Hextall, the NHL's leading goal scorer, caps the Rangers' first Stanley Cup run in seven years by beating goalie Turk Broda 2:07 into overtime of Game 6, giving New York its third OT victory in the best-of-seven series. The Broadway Blueshirts would wait 54 years to hoist the Cup again.

v Maple Leafs 7, NHL All Stars 3

FEBRUARY 14, 1934 • MAPLE LEAF GARDENS A benefit for Toronto forward Ace Bailey, whose career was ended by a vicious, near-fatal hit from Boston's Eddie Shore that fractured Bailey's skull on Dec. 12, 1933, is sponsored by the NHL as a way to avoid a Bailey lawsuit. Before a crowd of more than 14,000, Bailey's uniform No. 6 is retired—the first such honor bestowed on an NHL player—and Bailey and Shore make peace, shaking hands at center ice.

>MAYHEM MOMENT

APRIL 13, 1927

Ottawa Auditorium

After Boston loses a cheap-shot and penalty-marred deciding Game 4 of the 1927 Stanley Cup finals, the Bruins reserve defenseman Billy Coutu *(left)* confronts referees Jerry Laflamme and Billy Bell on their way to the officials' dressing room. In the encounter Coutu punches Laflamme and slams Bell to the ground.

"For striking referees Bell and Dr. Laflamme, player Coutu is expelled from the National Hockey League and is fined $100."

—Official statement issued by NHL president Frank Calder, who was in attendance in Ottawa for the Stanley Cup finals, April 1927

> TEAMS OF THE ERA

^

TORONTO MAPLE LEAFS

After purchasing the franchise for $165,000 in 1927, Conn Smythe, who had built the original New York Rangers, changed the name of the sad-sack St. Patricks to the more patriotic Maple Leafs. Coinciding with the opening of Smythe's state-of-the-art Maple Leaf Gardens in 1931, the team (which had never won a title) improved dramatically, reaching 10 Stanley Cup finals and winning seven championships over the next 20 seasons.

MONTREAL CANADIENS

Only four of Montreal's record 24 championships came during this period but as was the case for much of the franchise's 101-year history the Canadiens sent out the game's greatest talents. In 1927–28 Howie Morenz, perhaps the NHL's first true superstar, became the league's first 50-point scorer; then in the early 1940s, all eyes were on young forward Maurice Richard, who scored 82 goals over his first two full seasons.

BOSTON BRUINS

Under the leadership of Charles Adams and Art Ross, the Bruins were the most successful early U.S. franchise, winning three Cups between 1929 and '41. Goalie Tiny Thompson led the league in wins five times and in goals-against average four times. He was aided by a host of future Hall of Famers: defensemen Dit Clapper and Eddie Shore, as well as forwards Milt Schmidt, Bobby Bauer and Woody Dumart, a.k.a the "Kraut Line."

[D E B U T] [F I N A L E]

[DEBUT]		[FINALE]
Eddie Shore	1926–27	Newsy Lalonde
Dit Clapper	1927–28	Sprague Cleghorn
Tiny Thompson	1928–29	Cy Denneny
Syl Apps	1936–37	Howie Morenz
Sid Abel >	1938–39	< Babe Siebert
Doug Bentley	1939–40	Eddie Shore
Elmer Lach	1940–41	Charlie Conacher
Maurice Richard	1942–43	Ebbie Goodfellow
Harry Lumley	1943–44	Frank Boucher
Ted Lindsay	1944–45	Mush March

> BY THE NUMBERS

509 | Games played by Reg Noble, the final active player from the NHL's first season. He retired in 1933 at age 36 having scored 167 goals in 16 seasons.

14 | Shutouts for Canadiens goalie George Hainsworth in 1926–27 to earn the NHL's first Vezina Trophy. He took over in net for Montreal after Georges Vézina died of tuberculosis a year earlier.

11 | Shutouts in 1928–29 for Pittsburgh Pirates goalie Joe Miller.

9 | Wins for Miller in '28–29 (he also had five 0–0 ties).

16 | Years, 11 months, age of left wing Armand (Bep) Guidolin when he debuted with the Bruins on Nov. 12, 1942. He remains the youngest NHL player ever.

14 | Members of the initial class of the Hockey Hall of Fame—including Lord Stanley of Preston—inducted in 1945.

310 | Goals allowed in 50 games in '43–44 by the Rangers' Tubby McAuley, the only goalie in history to play at least 25 games and have a goals against average above 6.00 (6.24).

> PATRICK FACTOR

Rangers general manager, coach and former defenseman Lester Patrick, 44, replaces an injured Lorne Chabot as goaltender to lead his team to a 2–1 overtime win in Game 2 of the 1928 Stanley Cup finals versus the Montreal Maroons. In so doing he becomes the oldest player to participate in the finals.

c. 1912 | HOBEY BAKER

c. 1913 | JOE MALONE

c. 1910 | SPRAGUE CLEGHORN

c. 1927 | CY DENNENY

c. 1908 | FRED (CYCLONE) TAYLOR

c. 1924 | CLINT BENEDICT

HOCKEY HALL OF FAME (5); JAMES RICE/HOCKEY HALL OF FAME (BENEDICT)

2007 | SHARKS CENTER Joe Thornton won the Hart Trophy in 2005–06, one of three seasons in which he led the NHL in assists. | *Photograph by* PETER READ MILLER

CCM
19
A

1970 | EACH TIME that the Bruins' playful goalie Gerry Cheevers took a puck in the mask he had a line of stitches painted to mark the spot. | *Photograph by* DICK RAPHAEL

THE ART OF THE FACE-OFF

BY MICHAEL FARBER

Though the intricacies of the draw can sometimes be overlooked, success on face-offs often means the difference between winning and losing. —*from* SI, APRIL 27, 1998

THE FACE-OFF CAME IN THE Dallas Stars' defensive zone with 9.9 seconds left in the first period of a game against the Phoenix Coyotes. It was one of those felicitous moments when a fan can either get a running start toward the concession stands or stay to watch hockey reveal itself. For Dallas's Guy Carbonneau it was his 10th face-off of the period and maybe the 30,000th since the start of his NHL career in 1983–84 with the Montreal Canadiens. He has all sorts of information on opposing centers stored in his brain. As he straddled the boards and hopped onto the ice, Carbonneau was calculating the variables in his next matchup. Carbonneau is a righthanded shot who is strong drawing to his backhand, but he was having an off night. His opponent, Bob Corkum, is Phoenix's best face-off man; he is also a righthanded shot and most likely would try to draw the puck back to the point. By the time Carbonneau reached the face-off circle, he knew what he wanted to do. The puck dropped, sticks flashed and Carbonneau drew the puck behind him to defenseman Dan Keczmer, who carried it behind the net and skated out the clock.

Mediocre face-off men may remember their wins; outstanding ones remember their losses. The night before in a hotel lobby Carbonneau, who's among the best in NHL history, had re-created a scene from 1985: Stanley Cup quarterfinals, overtime of Game 7, face-off against Peter Stastny of the Quebec Nordiques, to the right of Canadiens goalie Steve Penney. Carbonneau lost the draw, then lost Stastny, who drew the puck to the point and skated to the net, where he tapped in the rebound of a shot by Pat Price. "That face-off really affected me," says Carbonneau. "It took a long, long time to recover. My worry was that the organization would never let me take a face-off in that situation again. It changed me. It made me think harder about face-offs."

Hockey people think about face-offs all the time. Coaches study video of opponents' draws and chart how each of their face-off guys fare against the other teams'. On many clubs, 10 minutes of face-off drills follow each practice. During games teams will sometimes send a second center onto the ice on a key draw in case their top face-off man gets tossed from the circle for either trying to anticipate the drop of the puck too aggressively or failing to align properly in the circle.

The rule of thumb is, 90% of the face-off men will draw to their backhand 90% of the time. "Everybody's better on their backhand because they're [raking] their entire blade over the entire dot," says Philadelphia's Eric Lindros. "You don't have as much strength on your forehand as on your backhand." There's a biomechanical explanation that involves the oblique muscles—from the face-off stance, the muscles that control trunk rotation have more range of motion and generate greater speed turning to the backhand side—but that's oblique to most players. All they know is, in critical situations they stick with their best move.

The beauty of the face-off, though, is not the similarity of styles but their diversity. Stastny liked drawing to his forehand. Ron Francis wins many of his face-offs with his feet. Mark Messier might slash an opposing center as the puck is dropped to give his opponent something to think about on subsequent draws. Carbonneau is a resolute backhand artist who can also win a face-off on the forehand or by tying up his opponent's stick and kicking the puck to a teammate.

The purity of the one-on-one battle—a skill predicated on hand-eye coordination and reaction time—can be polluted if a linesman drops the puck on the edge of the dot, which is two feet in diameter, instead of in its middle. Former Canadiens center Jacques Lemaire says he lost an overtime draw to the Sabres' Gilbert Perreault in Game 5 of the 1975 semifinals when a linesman dropped the puck practically in Perreault's skates. "After that [Canadiens coach] Scotty Bowman never wanted to use me in those situations," Lemaire says. "For years, when there was a defensive-zone face-off, I'd just skate to the bench, pissed off, because he wasn't going to use me. Every time I talk to my centers about face-offs, I flash back to that puck dropping."

As a child, Derek Sanderson, the former Bruins face-off magician, learned face-off math from his father, Harold, while watching the peerless Teeder Kennedy take draws for the Maple Leafs on *Hockey Night in Canada*. "The way my father figured, if you won a draw, it guaranteed your team at least five seconds of clear puck possession," says Sanderson. "Don't you want to control the puck several more minutes a game than the other team? This isn't basketball, where you inbound the ball to get a play started. Or football, where you snap it. This is a fight over a loose puck, and the team that wins those face-offs will win the game."

CARBONNEAU, who's in white, and teammate Joe Nieuwendyk worked on draws in practice, seeing each drill as a chance to hone the nuances of their technique.

DAVID E. KLUTHO

CCM

1976 | PEOPLE CALLED the Bruins' Terry O'Reilly the Tasmanian Devil; the California Seals' Mike Christie (3) found out why. | *Photograph by* BRUCE BENNETT STUDIOS

2007 | DUCKS ENFORCER George Parros, an economics major at Princeton, took Blackhawks heavyweight David Koci to school. | *Photograph by* JONATHAN DANIEL

48
WWW

BAUER
BAUER

2009 | AN ANNUAL super series among Canadian and Russian all-star juniors yields high-energy highlights; here Russian goalie Alexander Zalivin turns aside the Quebec league's Luke Adam (19). | *Photograph by* RICHARD WOLOWICZ

> Film Study

Reel Heroes

Hockey movies have long showcased some of Hollywood's biggest stars: John Wayne, Paul Newman, Rita Hayworth and a five-year-old Donald Duck

1977

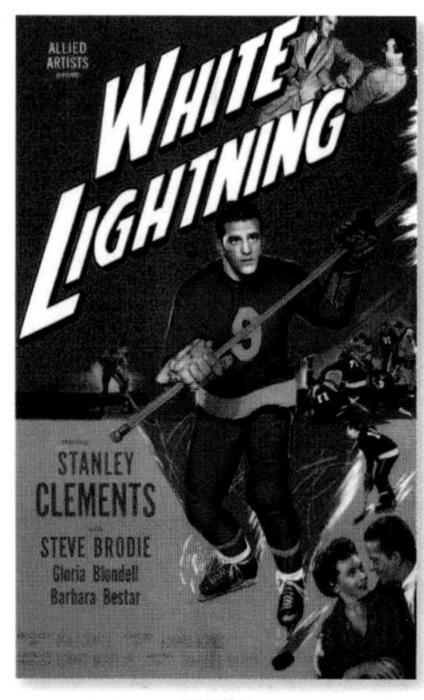

1953

1992

1992

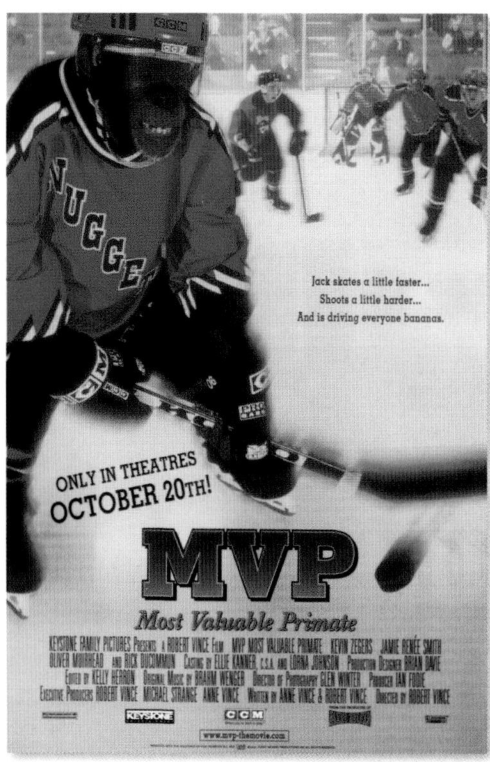

2000

1937

1939

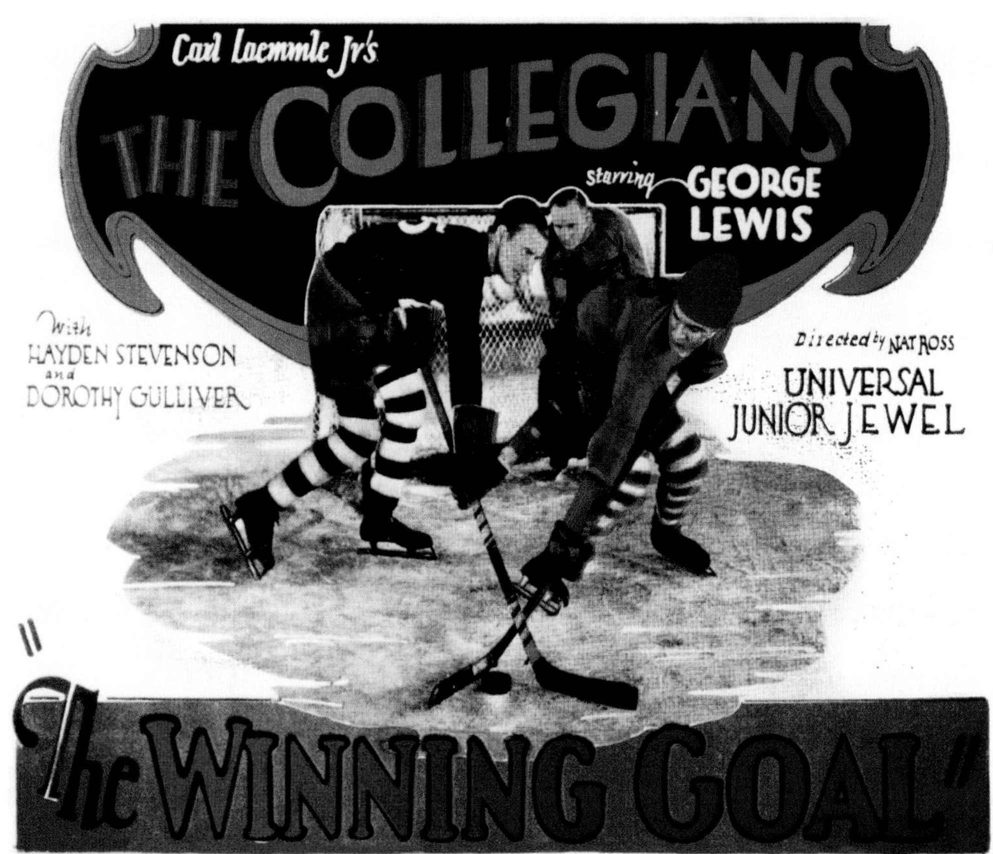

1920

1999

1937

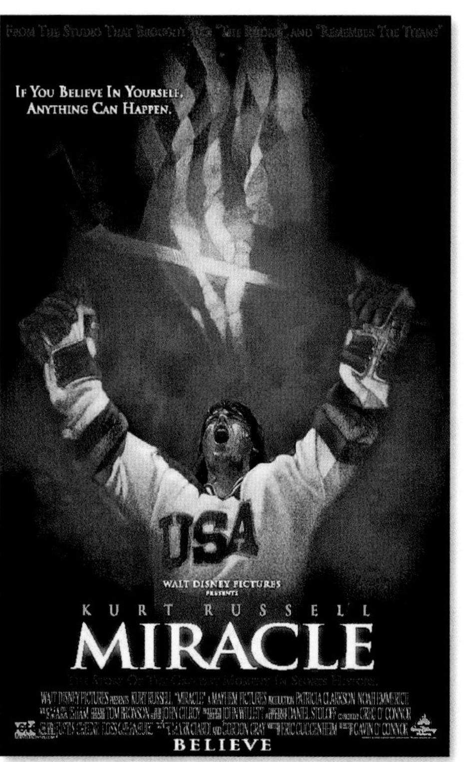

2004

SPORTSMEN OF THE YEAR: THE U.S. OLYMPIC TEAM

BY E.M. SWIFT

With a miraculous victory over the Soviet Union, the unheralded U.S. hockey team and its taskmaster coach inspired the country. After that they won the gold medal. —*from* SI, DECEMBER 22, 1980

THE IMPACT WAS THE THING. One morning they were fuzzy-cheeked college kids and the next . . . WE BEAT THE RUSSIANS! In Babbitt, Minn., hometown of forward Buzz Schneider, guys went into their backyards and began firing shotguns toward the heavens. Kaboom! Kaboom! WE BEAT THE RUSSIANS! In Santa Monica, Calif., a photographer heard the outcome of the game and went into his local grocery store, run by an elderly immigrant couple. "Guess what," he said. "Our boys beat the Russians." The old grocer looked at him. "No kidding?" Then he started to cry. "No *kidding*?"

In Winthrop, Mass., 70 people gathered outside the home of Mike Eruzione, who had scored the winning goal, and croaked out the national anthem.

One man was listening to the game in his car, driving through a thunderstorm, with the U.S. clinging to a 4–3 lead. He kept pounding his hands on the steering wheel in excitement. Finally he pulled off the highway and listened as the countdown started . . . 5 . . . 4 . . . 3 . . . 2 . . . 1 . . . . WE BEAT THE RUSSIANS! He started to honk his horn. He yelled inside his car. It felt absolutely wonderful. He got out and screamed in the rain. There were 10 other drivers yelling their fool heads off in the rain. They made a huddle, and then they hollered together—WE BEAT THE RUSSIANS! Strangers dancing beside the highway as 18-wheelers zoomed by.

We. The U.S. Olympic hockey team . . . these were our boys. Small-town kids, well-groomed and good-looking, who loved their folks and liked to drink a little beer. Our boys. Young men molded by a coach who wasn't afraid to preach the good old Protestant work ethic, while ever prepared to stuff a hockey stick down an opponent's throat. And don't think that didn't matter, given the political climate—the hostages in Iran; Afghanistan; the pending Olympic boycott of the Moscow Games.

Individually, the players were fine, dedicated sportsmen. But collectively they were a transcendent lot. For seven months they pushed and pulled each other along, until for two weeks in February they—a bunch of unheralded amateurs—became the best hockey team in the world. And they were not just a team, they were a perfect reflection of how Americans wanted to see themselves. By gum, it's still in us! It was certainly still in ***them***.

So for reminding us of some things, and for briefly brightening the days of 220 million people, we doff our caps to them, ***in*** *toto*, Sportsmen of the Year.

Leadership was the key. These guys didn't descend on skates from a mountaintop preaching teamwork and brotherhood. They were all stars, *la crème de la crème*. Many with big egos, big heads. Fifteen of the 20 had been drafted by NHL clubs and considered the Games a stepping-stone to the big time. They could showcase their talents, prove they could handle a grueling schedule, and, thank-you-bub, where do I sign? Herb Brooks, the coach, made it the most painful stepping-stone of their lives.

"He treated us all the same," says every last member of the team. "Rotten."

What kind of competitor did Brooks want? He wanted young, educated kids who were willing to break down stereotypes and throw old wives' tales about conditioning and tactics out the window. He wanted open-minded people who could skate. The players had to learn a new style of play in seven months. In simplest terms, they had to learn what any touch-football player knows—that crisscross patterns and laterals are more effective than the plunge.

That style was easy to sell because weaving, passing, holding on to the puck is a more enjoyable way to play the game. Smashing that stereotype was a cinch. But conditioning? There is no mind in the world open enough to enjoy the tortures of Herbies.

Herbies are a form of wind sprint that many hockey players do, but only the Olympians call them by that name. End line to blue line and back, to red line and back, to far blue line and back, all the way down and back. Rest. Two or three sets of Herbies at the end of practice is about as much punishment as most North American coaches dish out.

Peter Stastny, the Czechoslovakian Olympic star, says the thing that most shocked the international hockey community about the young Americans (average age: 22) was their conditioning. The Soviets had always been at one level, with everybody

THE COMEBACK, semifinal win over the Soviets—who had beaten the U.S. 10–3 in an exhibition before the Games—led to pandemonium in Lake Placid.

HEINZ KLUETMEIER

BROTEN
9

else at a level below. Suddenly there were a bunch of *Americans*, for heaven's sake, whom the Russians had to huff and puff to keep up with in the third period. In the seven games played in the Olympics, the U.S. team outscored its opponents 16–3 in the third period. What got into them? Steroids? Herbies.

Early on, Brooks went to coaches of track and swimming and found out about anaerobics, underloading, overloading, pulse rates, the works. Then he transferred this information to his players, who, because they were educated, because they were open-minded, were willing to listen. Sure, we'll run up and down that hill after practice. Sure, we'll do another Herbie. Twenty-five minutes of sprints without pucks? Sure. And for six months they hated Brooks's guts.

The moment of truth came back in September 1979, after a 4–4 tie in Norway. Brooks, to say the least, was dissatisfied. "We're going to skate some time today," he told the players. Then he sent them back onto the ice.

Forward Dave Silk recalls it this way: "There were 30 or 40 people still in the stands. First they thought we were putting on a skating exhibition, and they cheered. After a while they realized the coach was mad at us for not playing hard, and they booed. Then they got bored and left. Then the workers got bored, and they turned off the lights."

Doing Herbies in the dark . . . it's terrifying. But they did them. Again and again and again. When it ended at last, Brooks had the players coast slowly around the rink so that the lactic acid could work itself out of their muscles. That was when forward Mark Johnson broke his stick over the boards. Mark Johnson, who made the team go. Mark Johnson, who was its hardest worker, its smartest player. Mark Johnson, whom Brooks never, ever had to yell at. And you know what Brooks said—*screamed*—after skating those kids within an inch of their lives? "If I ever see a kid hit a stick on the boards again, I'll skate you till you *die*!" They believed him. And they *would have died*, just to spite him. Says Silk, "I can remember times when I was so mad at him I tried to skate so hard I'd collapse, so I could say to him, '*See what you did?*' " But they weren't an all-star team anymore. They were together in this, all for one. And Brooks was the enemy. Don't think he didn't know it.

THE FANFARE DIDN'T REALLY START to build until after the U.S. beat Czechoslovakia 7–3 in the team's second Olympic match. With little time left in that game Johnson was injured by a dirty check (no pun) and on TV the nation heard the wrath of Brooks firsthand. His proposal to wed a Koho hockey stick with a certain Czechoslovakian gullet provoked 500 irate letters, but it also piqued the curiosity of the nonhockey-minded public. Hey, this guy's *all right*! And those players. They're so *young*. Let's keep an eye on these guys—but what's icing?

Norway . . . Romania . . . West Germany, down they went, each game a struggle in the early going, pulled out in the third period when those nameless kids blew the opposition away. Afterward the players would line up at center ice and smile those big wonderful smiles and *salute the fans*. They'd hoist their sticks to the fans on one side of the rink; then turn and hoist them to the other side. It was a terrific routine.

One reason they still were nameless was that Brooks had forbidden them to attend postgame press conferences, enraging the U.S. Olympic Committee brass and the players' agents. The players understood the reasoning. This team wasn't built around stars, and the press conferences were set up to handle only three players. And so, with no pressure of the spotlight, the players stayed loosey-goosey. Hey, this was *fun*! But the Russians were coming.

The day before the Soviet game, Brooks told his players that the Russians were ripe; lethargic changing lines, their passes lacking crispness. "The Russians were ready to cut their own throats," says Brooks. "But we had to be ready to pick up the knife and hand it to them. The morning of the game I called the team together and said, 'It's *meant to be*. This is your moment, and it's going to happen.' It's kind of corny, and I could see them thinking, Here goes Herb again. . . . But I *believed* it."

U.S. goalie Jim Craig made some big saves early in the game, but the Russians scored first. Five minutes later Buzz Schneider tied it on a 50-foot shot from the left boards. The Soviets took the lead again, but with one second left in the first period Johnson scored to make it 2–2. When the Russians came out for the second period, Vladislav Tretiak no longer was in goal; he'd been

CRAIG, A loner on the team, stopped 21 shots in the gold-medal game, then struck a chord with the nation as he searched the crowd for his father after the victory.

ERIC SCHWEIKARDT

yanked in favor of Vladimir Myshkin who'd shut out the NHL All-Stars in the '79 Challenge Cup. The Soviets got the only goal of the second period and outshot the Americans 12–2.

Brooks told his players to divide the third period into four five-minute segments. They didn't have to tie the game in the first segment, or even the second. There was time. Stay with them. Make them skate. At 8:39 Johnson tied the game 3–3 on a power play. Bedlam. Go, clock, go! "I remember thinking we might actually have a chance to tie," says forward Mark Pavelich. But the U.S. team had barely had a chance to think of that improbability when Eruzione scored what forward John Harrington calls "one of the great slop goals of all time." The puck was behind the Soviet net and Harrington and a defenseman were battling for it. The puck squirted along the boards to Pavelich, who hammered at it and was promptly smashed face-first into the glass. The puck caromed off the boards and slid into the slot, directly to Eruzione, who snapped a wrist shot past Myshkin. Ten minutes to go. U.S.A. 4, U.S.S.R. 3.

And that's how it ended. No one remembers much about those final 10 minutes except that they took forever. No one breathed. The shifts were insanely short because, by the players' admission, no one wanted to be on the ice when the Great Red Bear awoke and there was hell to pay. Craig, who had been tying up the puck at every opportunity during the tournament, slowing down the play, now wouldn't touch it. He was afraid, and rightly so, that if his teammates lined up for a face-off in their own zone and had time to think about the absurdity of leading the Russians, had time to peer up at the clock and brood about the time remaining, their knees would turn to goo.

But they never panicked. Shoot, this was a ball compared with Herbies in the dark. Indeed, if anyone panicked it was the Russians, who misfired shots, who started to throw in the puck and chase it and who, at the end, never pulled their goalie.

And then it was over. The horn sounded, and there was that unforgettable scene of triumph, the rolling and hugging and flinging of sticks. The flags. My god, what a sight. There was the shaking of hands, the staggered, reluctant exit from the ice. But it wasn't until the U.S. players were in the locker room that the enormousness of what they had done hit them. "It was absolutely quiet," recalls backup goalie Steve Janaszak. "Some guys were crying a little. You got the idea that the game wasn't over yet, because no one is ever up a goal on the Russians when a game is over. No one really believed it."

It was then that somebody started a chorus of *God Bless America*, 20 sweaty guys in hockey uniforms chanting, ". . . from the mountains, to the valleys, no-na-na-na-na, na-na-na . . .!" Nobody knew the words. And where was Brooks? Holed up in the men's room, afraid to come out and ruin their celebration. "I almost started to cry," he says. "It was the most emotional moment I'd ever seen. Finally I snuck out into the hall, and the state troopers were all standing there crying. Now where do you go?"

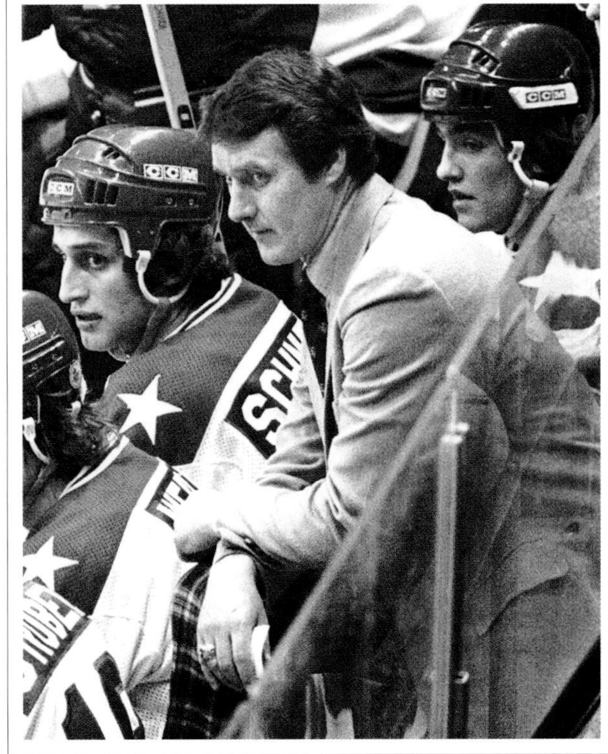

Of course, the tournament wasn't over. If the U.S. had lost to Finland on Sunday, it would have finished in *fourth* place. No medal. Brooks came into the locker room on Saturday, saw guys signing sticks and pictures, and began throwing things around and telling them, "*You aren't good enough for all this attention! You're too damn young! You don't have the talent!*" The eyes rolled and the lips buttoned—but they listened because what he was saying was obvious to all of them. They had come too far to blow it. And on Sunday they won the gold medal 4–2, needing three goals in the third period to do it. Really, they weren't even worried. They *knew* they would do it, because if you can outscore the Russians in the third period, two goals to none, you can sure as heck outscore the Finns.

They counted down the seconds, slapping their sticks on the boards, screaming to each other, to the refs, to the crowd. Again pandemonium, slightly less frenzied than two days before, the handshakes and the gradual retreat from the scene of their triumph.

The final, uplifting moment came at the gold medal ceremony, when Eruzione called his teammates up on the platform with him. After that they marched around the rink singing and carrying on as if they owned the place. They *did* own the place. They owned the whole country for a while. It just made you want to pick up your television set and take it to bed with you. It really made you feel good.

A PERFECTIONIST, a disiplinarian and a brilliant tactician, Brooks felt that by working his players to exhaustion he could unify them. He was right.

1966 | DETROIT DEFENDER Bill Gadsby downsized Chicago's Stan Mikita. It was the last season of a great Gadsby career that included eight All-Star Games. | *Photograph by* JAMES DRAKE

1982 | STOPPING TWO-TIME Norris Trophy winner (and future Hall of Famer) Larry Robinson was a reach for Kings goalie Mario Lessard. | *Photograph by* CRAIG MOLENHOUSE

Cooper
19

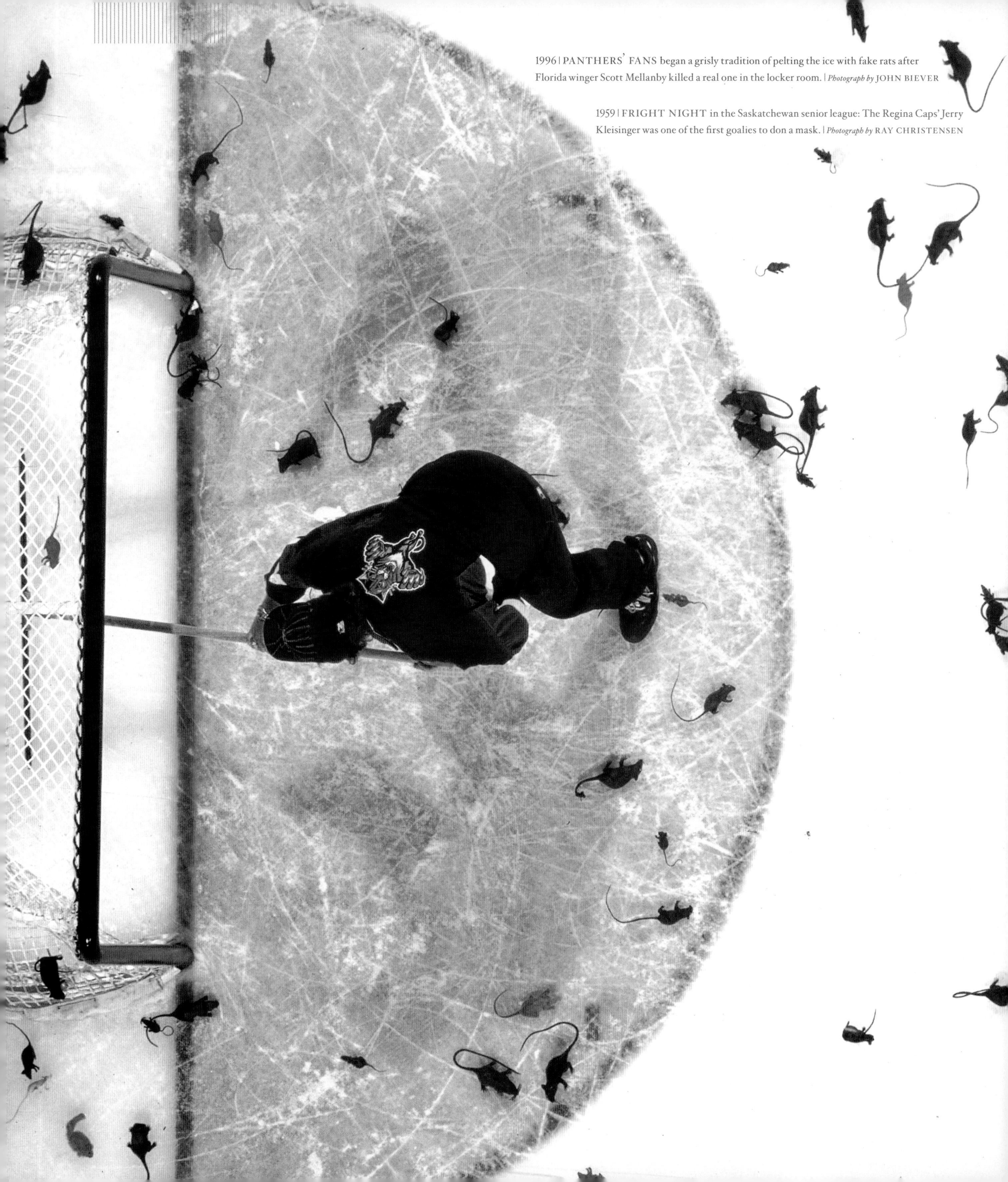

1996 | PANTHERS' FANS began a grisly tradition of pelting the ice with fake rats after Florida winger Scott Mellanby killed a real one in the locker room. | *Photograph by* JOHN BIEVER

1959 | FRIGHT NIGHT in the Saskatchewan senior league: The Regina Caps' Jerry Kleisinger was one of the first goalies to don a mask. | *Photograph by* RAY CHRISTENSEN

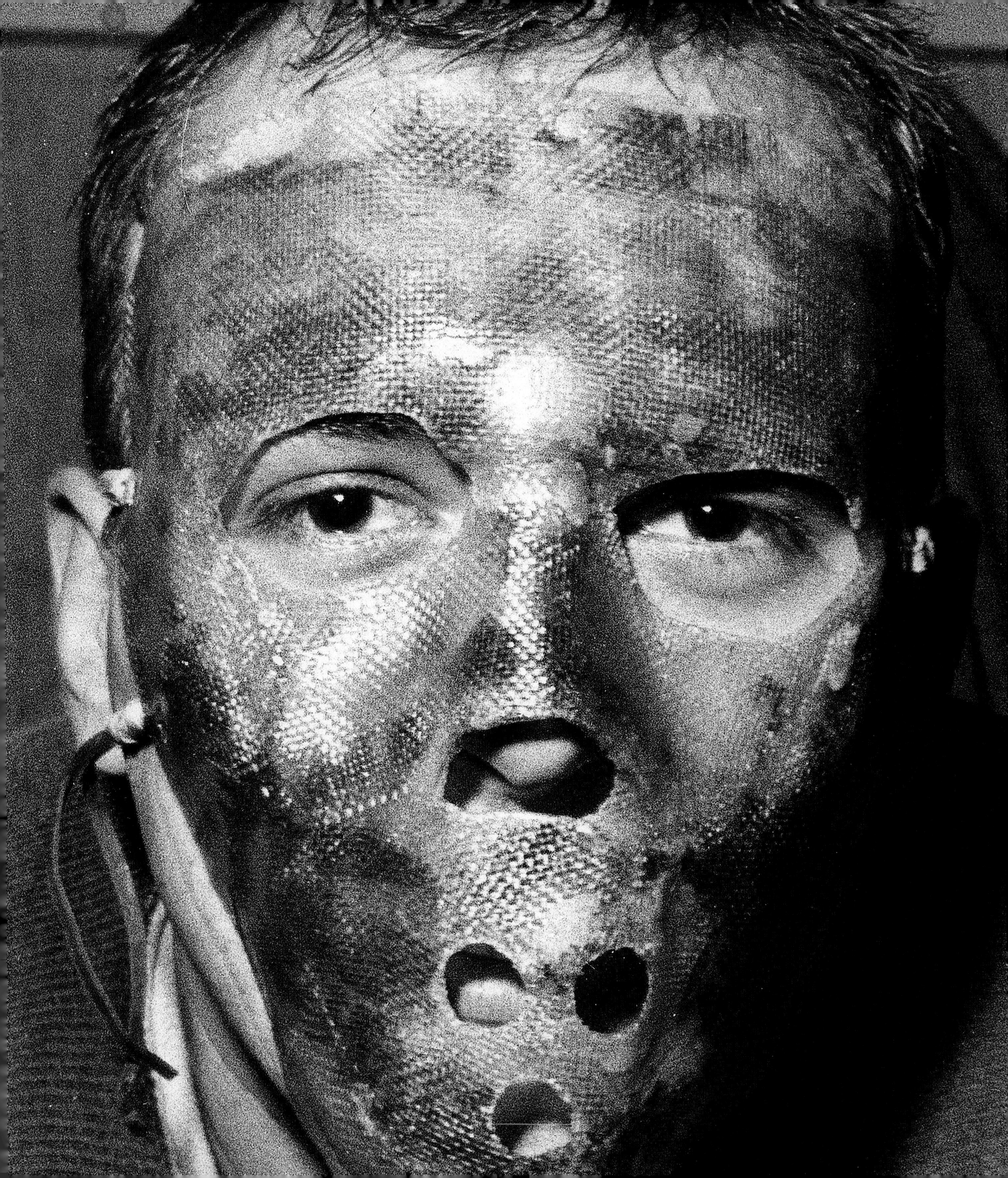

1899
Dickie Boon, Montreal HC

DAVID N. BERKWITZ: HOCKEY HALL OF FAME

> Artifacts

Evolution of The Edges

Five millennia ago Scandinavian hunters made crude skates out of animal bones to pursue their prey over frozen lakes. By the time hockey arrived the concept was more advanced: Take leather shoe, affix metal blade. These days NHL skates have features such as "hydrophobic" lining, and go for up to $700

1950–51
Bill Barilko, Toronto Maple Leafs

1972–73
Morris Mott, California Golden Seals

2008–09
Nicklas Lidstrom, Detroit Red Wings

SMOOTH OPERATOR

BY STEVE RUSHIN

Born near Los Angeles in 1949 the Zamboni became the most unassuming of superstars, putting a shine on the ice and a smile on every fan's face. —*from* SI, NOVEMBER 28, 2005

THE GEAR DADDIES HAD A cult hit singing *I Want to Drive the Zamboni*, but me, I want to be a Zamboni, the last great role model in sports.

Unhurried by the hurly-burly of modern life, Zambonis are frequently test-driven on the streets surrounding their factory in the Los Angeles suburb of Paramount, merging into traffic at the stately speed of nine miles per hour.

Nobody minds. In fact people smile at the mere mention of a Zamboni. "I can only think of one other machine whose name does that," says Richard Zamboni, the 73-year-old president of the company his father founded, "and that's a Jacuzzi." Though a Zamboni in London, Ont., has been fitted with a hot tub—an aftermarket modification—Zambonis are better than a warm bath. They're like a warm memory, resurfacing periodically.

Fifty-six years have passed since Frank J. Zamboni conjured a machine, with a Jeep chassis, to resurface the ice at his skating rink; and unlike many 56-year-old sports legends, the Zamboni has remained free of scandal—although a Zamboni jockey was busted for ZUI this summer after he erratically resurfaced the ice at the Mennen Sports Arena in Morristown, N.J., and then blew a .12 on the Breathalyzer.

Otherwise, Zambonis are timeless, immune to the tides of fashion. As the title character noted in *She's a Good Skate, Charlie Brown*, "There are three things in life people like to stare at: a flowing stream, a crackling fire and a Zamboni clearing the ice."

That mesmeric quality was precisely the problem for the owner of the Chicago Blackhawks, who purchased the second Zamboni, in 1950. "Arthur Wirtz eventually became disenchanted with it," says Zamboni, "because he thought it kept people from going to the concession stands between periods."

There is something deeply satisfying when the ice shimmers like the reflecting pool that so transfixed Narcissus. "I'm not one of those people who sit in the stands and says, 'He missed a spot,' " says Zamboni, bursting this reverie. "I sit there hoping the thing doesn't break down." (When the Zamboni broke down during the first intermission of the 1986 NCAA championship game in Providence, the game was delayed while a spare was driven—with a police escort—from across town.)

Likewise, Frank Zamboni never cared for hockey and could barely stand on skates. He dropped out of school after the ninth grade and was always self-conscious about it. That's why he wanted to call his firm the Paramount Engineering Company. "He thought that sounded sophisticated," says Richard. But the name was already taken, so this Edison of the Ice settled for the Frank J. Zamboni Co., and thank goodness he did, because nobody wants a license plate frame that says MY OTHER CAR IS A PARAMOUNT.

Today's four-cylindered Zambonis have Nissan engines and top out at 14 mph, though NHL rinks are typically resurfaced at 3 to 5 mph. This year the Zamboni Company ovaled its wagons, weathered the NHL lockout and sold its 8,000th machine, to the University of Minnesota.

Last week six Zambonis sat on the factory floor, awaiting shipment to China and Sweden and various North American cities. In a good year, only 100 new Zambonis roll off the lot. A new top-of-the-line 500-series model, the kind used in the NHL, sells for about $65,000, the same sticker price as a ZO6 Corvette.

And while Zamboni has a branch in Brantford, Ont.—serendipitously enough, Wayne Gretzky's hometown—the home office and factory remain in a series of corrugated steel garages in Paramount, directly across the Los Angeles River from Compton, the cradle of gangsta rap.

Paramount has inspired nearly as much music as neighboring Compton: Minnesota's Gear Daddies, voicing the dream of every native son, sang, *Ever since I was young, it's been my dream/That I might drive a Zamboni machine*. And a Connecticut band called The Zambonis tours arenas and plays "hockey weddings."

Yes, Zamboni general manager Paula Coony has seen little plastic Zambonis atop wedding cakes. She has also seen a Zamboni converted into a barbecue, which makes sense because most Zambonis in the NHL these days run on the kind of propane tank you have hooked to your grill.

That's right: Zambonis are environmentally friendly as well as unhurried, hypnotic hockey icons. And they continue to spread happiness like a Holiday Inn housekeeper, one clean sheet at a time.

THE ZAMBONI that cleaned the ice for the San Jose Sharks in 2010 looks different from the Model C (top, in 1953) but its assignment is the same.

ZAMBONI; CHRIS TALLEY/ICON SMI

2010 | AFTER GETTING a kneeful from forward Jayna Hefford, the U.S.'s Molly Engstrom had to stomach Canada's 2–0 win in the gold-medal game. | *Photograph by* DAVID E. KLUTHO

2003 | THOUGH TIE DOMI and the Leafs pushed past Eric Weinrich and the Flyers in Game 6, Philadelphia won the first-round playoff series. | *Photograph by* DAVE SANDFORD

CANADIAN
LOUISVILLE
MISSION
CCM

1999 | THE HURRICANES' Paul Coffey skated up a storm in an effort to keep the puck from Blues center Pavol Dimitra (38). | *Photograph by* DAVID E. KLUTHO

Shell

Original Six

1946–47 *through* 1966–67

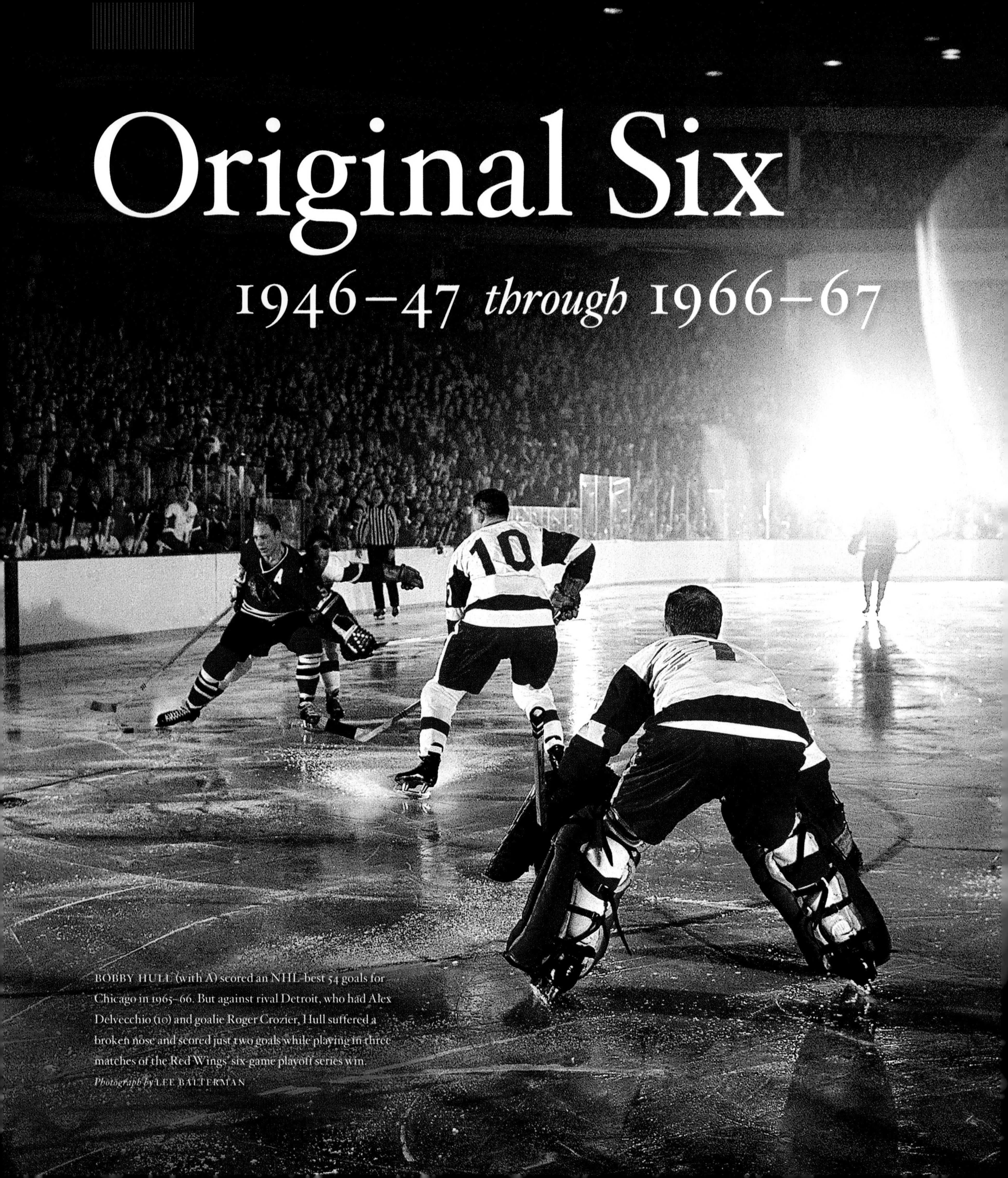

BOBBY HULL (with A) scored an NHL-best 54 goals for Chicago in 1965–66. But against rival Detroit, who had Alex Delvecchio (10) and goalie Roger Crozier, Hull suffered a broken nose and scored just two goals while playing in three matches of the Red Wings' six-game playoff series win.
Photograph by LEE BALTERMAN

> ALL-STARS OF THE ERA <

	FIRST TEAM	SECOND TEAM
LEFT WING	BOBBY HULL BLACK HAWKS	TED LINDSAY RED WINGS, BLACK HAWKS
CENTER	JEAN BÉLIVEAU CANADIENS	ALEX DELVECCHIO RED WINGS
RIGHT WING	MAURICE RICHARD CANADIENS	GORDIE HOWE RED WINGS
DEFENSEMAN	DOUG HARVEY CANADIENS, RANGERS, RED WINGS	BILL GADSBY BLACK HAWKS, RANGERS, RED WINGS
DEFENSEMAN	RED KELLY RED WINGS, MAPLE LEAFS	PIERRE PILOTE BLACK HAWKS
GOALTENDER	JACQUES PLANTE CANADIENS, RANGERS	TERRY SAWCHUK RED WINGS, BRUINS, MAPLE LEAFS

COACH
TOE BLAKE
CANADIENS

> NICKNAMES <

Harry [Apple Cheeks] Lumley ^
Charles [Syl] Apps
Larry [Little Dempsey] Aurie
Jean [le Gros Bill] Béliveau
Gordon [the Red Baron] Berenson
Modere [Mud] Bruneteau
Johnny [Chief] Bucyk
Don [Grapes] Cherry
Alex [Fats] Delvecchio
Lou [Leapin' Louie] Fontinato
Bernie [Boom Boom] Geoffrion
Bobby [the Golden Jet] Hull
Gordie [Mr. Hockey] Howe
George [Punch] Imlach
Leonard [Red] Kelly
Ted [Teeder] Kennedy
[Terrible] Ted Lindsay
Jacques [Jake the Snake] Plante
Henri [Pocket Rocket] Richard
Maurice [Rocket] Richard
Lorne [Gump] Worsley

STATISTICAL LEADERS

GOALS	
GORDIE HOWE	649
MAURICE RICHARD	430
JEAN BÉLIVEAU	399
BERNIE GEOFFRION	388
BOBBY HULL	370

ASSISTS	
GORDIE HOWE	852
ANDY BATHGATE	556
JEAN BÉLIVEAU	545
RED KELLY	542
ALEX DELVECCHIO	536

POINTS (ALL SKATERS)	
GORDIE HOWE	1,501
JEAN BÉLIVEAU	944
ANDY BATHGATE	870
ALEX DELVECCHIO	864
RED KELLY	823

POINTS (DEFENSEMEN)	
BILL GADSBY	568
DOUG HARVEY	518
DOUG MOHNS	489
PIERRE PILOTE	440
ALLAN STANLEY	402

GOALIE WINS	
TERRY SAWCHUK	430
GLENN HALL	349
JACQUES PLANTE	346
HARRY LUMLEY	286
GUMP WORSLEY	255

GOALS AGAINST AVERAGE*	
JACQUES PLANTE	2.41
TERRY SAWCHUK	2.48
GLENN HALL	2.50
JOHNNY BOWER	2.52
HARRY LUMLEY	2.69

*MINIMUM 300 NHL GAMES

>>WISH YOU WERE THERE

Maple Leafs 2, Black Hawks 1

APRIL 22, 1962 • CHICAGO STADIUM Eleven years removed from its last Stanley Cup winner, Toronto upends Bobby Hull and the defending NHL champions when Dick Duff nets a power play goal with 14:14 gone in the third period of Game 6, the first of three consecutive Cups for the Leafs.

U.S.A. 9, Czechoslovakia 4

FEBRUARY 28, 1960 • BLYTH ARENA, SQUAW VALLEY, CALIF. The underdog U.S. caps an improbable run by overwhelming the European champs in the last game of the Olympics. Led by goalie Jack McCartan and the so-called Christian brothers, Bill and Roger, the U.S. finishes with a 7-0-0 record having beaten the top four teams in the world (Canada, Sweden, the U.S.S.R. and the Czechs) en route to gold on home ice.

Red Wings 3, Canadiens 0

NOVEMBER 10, 1963 • THE OLYMPIA, DETROIT Gordie Howe scores his 545th career goal to pass Maurice Richard as the league's alltime leading goal scorer on the same night that Terry Sawchuk ties George Hainsworth's NHL record with his 94th career shutout.

Red Wings 2, Canadiens 1

APRIL 16, 1954 • THE OLYMPIA, DETROIT The Red Wings win the Stanley Cup 4:29 into overtime of Game 7 when forward Tony Leswick's flip shot as he skates to the Detroit bench is deflected by the glove of Montreal's Doug Harvey, over goalie Gerry McNeil and into the Canadiens net for the flukiest Cup winner ever. The stunned Habs leave the ice without congratulating the victors.

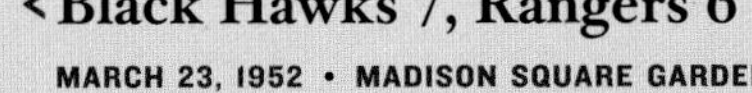

<Black Hawks 7, Rangers 6

MARCH 23, 1952 • MADISON SQUARE GARDEN, NEW YORK On the final day of the '51–52 season Chicago right wing Bill Mosienko *(left)* scores on the Rangers' rookie goalie Lorne Anderson at 6:09 of the third period, cutting the New York lead to 6–3. Eleven seconds later Mosienko strikes again, beating Anderson with another low shot. Just 10 seconds after that Mosienko skates in on Anderson, dekes him, and flips the puck into the cage for his third goal in 21 seconds—the fastest hat trick in NHL history. Continuing the wildness, Mosienko beats Anderson yet again a few seconds later with what would have been his fourth goal in half a minute had his shot not whistled just wide.

Canadiens 1, Bruins 0 (OT)

APRIL 16, 1953 • MONTREAL FORUM With Montreal leading the Stanley Cup finals three games to one, Bruins goalie Jim Henry and his Canadiens counterpart Gerry McNeil hold everyone off the scoreboard through regulation play. Then at 1:22 of overtime the Canadiens' 13-year veteran Elmer Lach, held goalless in the playoffs until then, takes a pass from Rocket Richard in the corner and fires it past Henry for the 19th (and final) playoff goal of his career.

Maple Leafs 3, Canadiens 2 (OT)

APRIL 21, 1951 • MAPLE LEAF GARDENS, TORONTO The Leafs' Tod Sloan scores with 32 seconds left in regulation to send Game 5 of the Cup finals into overtime, the teams' fifth straight OT game. When Toronto's Bill Barilko scores the game- and Cup-winner it marks the only time that each game of a finals is decided in the extra period.

>MAYHEM MOMENT

MARCH 17, 1955

Montreal Forum

Angry at NHL president Clarence Campbell who a few days earlier had suspended Maurice Richard for intentionally injuring Boston's Hal Laycoe and punching linesman Cliff Thompson, a member of a hostile Forum crowd sets off a tear gas canister near Campbell—sparking a riot that spreads to the surrounding streets, causing extensive damage and injuries.

> "I know I was wrong to hit the linesman and I would've accepted a suspension for the rest of the [regular] season. But the playoffs? That was exaggerating things."
>
> —*Maurice (Rocket) Richard, 1980*

> TEAMS OF THE ERA

MONTREAL CANADIENS

They won seven Stanley Cups in 11 seasons—including an unprecedented and never-matched five straight between 1956 and '60—and they had just two losing seasons in the entire era. Winning wasn't the only reason that the Montreal Forum felt like the center of the hockey universe. Players such as mask-wearing goalie Jacques Plante and slap shot–unleashing Boom Boom Geoffrion were changing the game.

TORONTO MAPLE LEAFS

After Conn Smythe sold the team to a consortium led by his son Stafford before the 1961–62 season, the Leafs took home three straight Stanley Cups, then won another in '66–67. Frank Mahovlich and Dave Keon were among the NHL's premier scorers but defense was Toronto's true strength with a roster that included blueliner Tim Horton and center Red Kelly as well as Vezina Trophy winners Johnny Bower and Terry Sawchuk in net.

^ DETROIT RED WINGS

The U.S.'s lone bastion of success during the Original Six era, Detroit's prowess was highlighted in 1949–50 when the first-place team employed the league's top three scorers (Ted Lindsay, Sid Abel and Gordie Howe a.k.a. The Production Line). Goaltender Terry Sawchuk arrived as a starter in '50–51 and won three Stanley Cups to help the Red Wings complete a stretch of four titles in six seasons.

[DEBUT]		[FINALE]
Gordie Howe	1946–47	Dit Clapper
Tim Horton >	1949–50	< Frank Brimsek
Jean Béliveau	1950–51	Buddy O'Connor
Dickie Moore	1951–52	Turk Broda
Johnny Bower	1953–54	Sid Abel
Norm Ullman	1955–56	Bill Quackenbush
Frank Mahovlich	1956–57	Ted Kennedy
Bobby Hull	1957–58	Sid Smith
J.C. Tremblay	1959–60	Maurice Richard
Bobby Orr	1966–67	Red Kelly

> BY THE NUMBERS

24 | Of the 25 Stanley Cups played in the years that the NHL had six teams that were won by the Canadiens (10), Maple Leafs (9) or Red Wings (5). The Black Hawks won in 1961 while the Bruins and the Rangers were shut out.

4 | Goals in 45 career games for the Bruins' Willie O'Ree, who in 1958 became the first black player in the NHL.

2 | Catching gloves (and no blocker) worn by ambidextrous Canadiens goalie Bill Durnan, the goals-against average leader in six of the seven seasons from '43–44 to '49–50.

2 | Seconds between goals by Colorado College's Tony Frasca and Omer Brandt, against Michigan Tech on Feb. 1, 1952, the shortest span between goals in NCAA history.

669 | Days that Montreal's Elmer Lach was the NHL's alltime scoring leader before his total of 623 points was passed by Maurice Richard on Dec. 12, 1953, making Lach's the shortest reign since '23.

11 | Enlargement in square feet of the goal crease for the '51–52 season, from 3'×7' to 4'×8'.

> PATRICK FACTOR

After spending 11 seasons as the general manager of the Bruins, Lynn Patrick, Lester's son, is hired in 1966 to be the G.M.–coach of the St. Louis Blues, a new team that was planning to begin NHL play the following season. Lynn taps a young scout to join the club as his assistant coach: Scotty Bowman.

PITTSBURGH PENGUINS
C
87
Winter CLASSIC
RBK
PENGUINS
CCM
VECTOR
BAUER

2008 | AFTER A flurry of activity at the NHL's Jan. 1 Winter Classic, Sidney Crosby (87) scored in a shootout to lift the Penguins over the Sabres. | *Photograph by* DAVID E. KLUTHO

1997 | PUCK BATTLES like this one between Detroit's Kirk Maltby (18) and Colorado's Eric Messier epitomized the classic Avs-Red Wings rivalry. | *Photograph by* DAVID E. KLUTHO

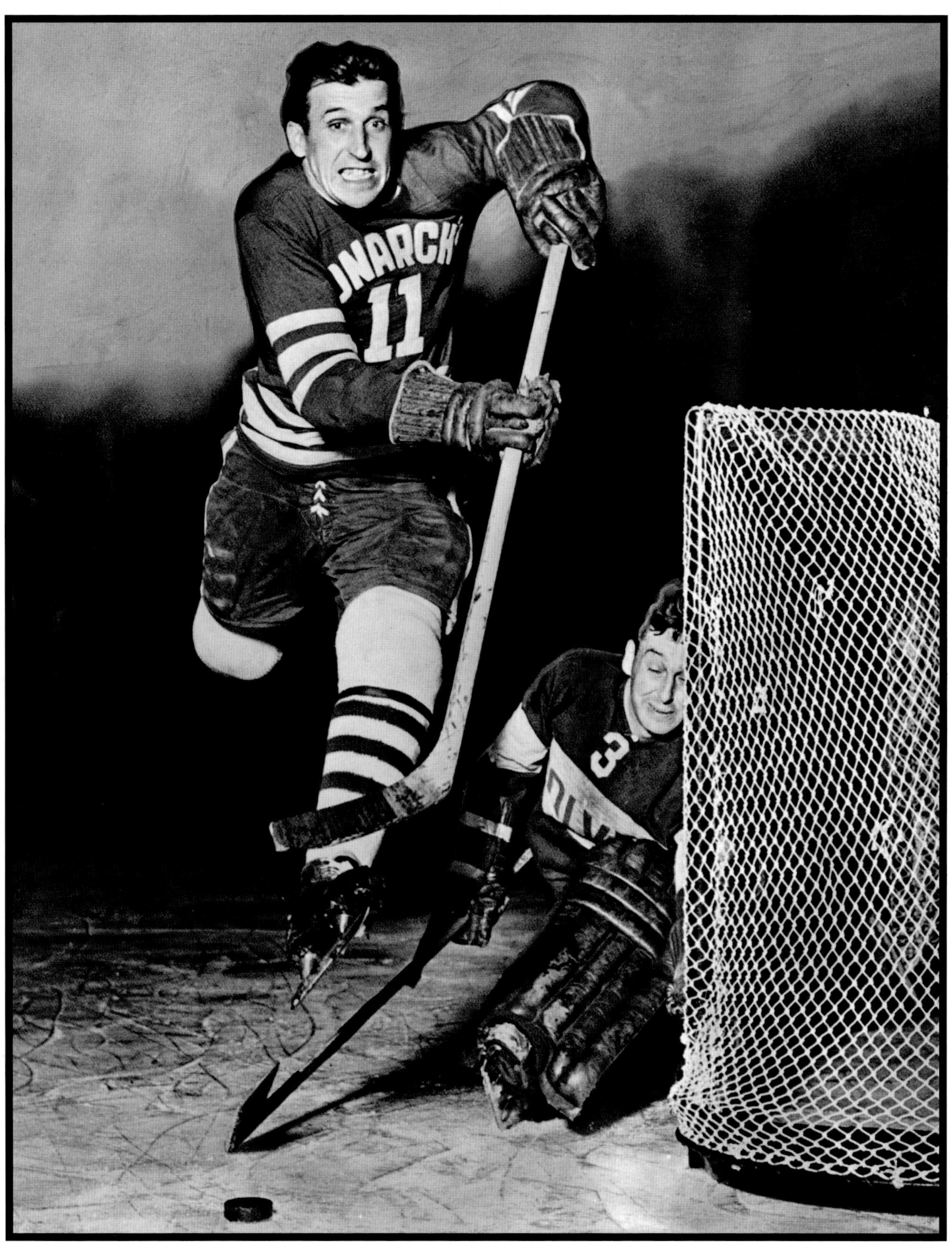

1944 | FLOAT LIKE a butterfly? Los Angeles Monarchs player-coach John Polich took flight over Hollywood Wolves goaltender Ray Biss. | *Photograph by* BROWN BROTHERS

1956 | LEAPIN' LINDSAY! Detroit captain Ted went high while Gordie Howe tried to crowd past the Canadiens' Claude Provost down low in the Cup finals. | *Photograph by* ROY BASH

SINGLE-MINDED

BY GARY SMITH

Coach Mike Keenan was ruthless and relentless in his quest for the Stanley Cup. For that, he paid a price. —*from* SI, MAY 8, 1995

PERHAPS PEOPLE WILL ALWAYS dispute who Mike Keenan really is. In Philadelphia, as he coached the Flyers to two Stanley Cup finals, players gave him fascist salutes when he turned his back. In Chicago, Mike willed an average Blackhawks team into the finals but soon lost his job and his marriage. RAT and SCOUNDREL screamed the New York headlines when he fled the Rangers weeks after leading them to the Stanley Cup last year. His mailbox was blown up.

The St. Louis Blues hired him immediately, of course, as coach and G.M., and their executive vice president called him the messiah. He drove the Blues to second place in the Central Division, but he and his new bosses had already gone to war. "The management," he seethed, "has promoted superstar status without the team concept. They produced a selfish culture."

With each new team he would sweep through the locker room, a fleet of assistant coaches, trainers, therapists, physiologists, equipment managers, video experts and carpenters trailing him as he pointed left and right, barking, "Change this. Move that. We need more space here. More light there." The room's centerpiece, of course, would be the photograph of the Stanley Cup, track lights focused on it in the way that crucifixes are illuminated behind altars. "We're going to do everything we can to bring the chalice here," he would tell fans in each city. "The Holy Grail. You have to go through hell to get it."

Part of that hell was Keenan himself. He skated straight at players who made mistakes in practice, as if he were going to knock them heels over head, then came to a halt inches away. In his office he stood over a seated player, brandishing a hockey stick and seething as the player cowered, thinking he was about to be hit. "He'd get Peter Zezel in the stick room and motivate the hell out of him," hints Flyer fitness specialist Pat Croce.... "It wasn't just me," says Zezel. "He threw sticks at other players."

"I lose my temper for a reason, to make players better," says Keenan. "People think I enjoy conflict. I *hate* it. I'd walk away from doing those things to players and I'd feel awful inside. The media thought I was arrogant. I was really just scared. I carried fear every game. Fear that it would be the last game I'd coach."

He shut off the locker room lights between periods and left his team in darkness. He called for practices at 11:59 a.m. just so players would wonder why. "Mike wouldn't tolerate one bad practice or one bad shift," says ex-Blackhawk Steve Thomas. "Not one. Not even from a superstar. Eventually, he just drove us physically and mentally insane."

His objective was to make losing so dark and confusing that his team's only choice, its one way out of the tunnel, was to win. "Teams get too cozy," he says. "You can't win with flat-liners. You go first-class, you give them clarity and comfort... and then you introduce confusion. If you feel a sigh of relief on your team, even for a moment—bang!—you shake them up. There must be a dynamic. If I'm unpredictable, the players have to stay focused. They're thinking, *When is the sonofabitch gonna call on me?*"

Yet his teams had camaraderie; his vision was so white hot, it fused them. There were delights as well as horrors around each hairpin curve. During a break in the schedule, his players were suddenly flying to a mountain resort for a retreat. He took them to musicals and movies. He'd spend hours driving around, talking with a player who had lost his father; he'd spend thousands of dollars buying everyone, even the locker room broom man, Christmas gifts. So deeply did he install himself in the psyches of his men that when they suddenly found that they were no longer part of the crusade, they were unsure whether to feel relief, sadness or rage.

Thomas: "I know what it takes to win because of Mike."

Zezel: "Things he taught me have added five goals a year."

He subordinated everything—his family, his past—to his dream. "That's why I win, I guess," Keenan says. "I pay the ultimate price. I gave up sanity." When he took the job in New York his wife, Rita, and his daughter, Gayla, didn't come along. Some nights, rather than go home to an empty house, he slept on the sofa at the Rangers' practice facility. Some nights he never slept at all. He pretended Gayla had gone away to boarding school. "Pain," he says, "beyond what you can imagine."

And then, even as he feuded with Rangers G.M. Neil Smith, the team won more games than any other team in the league, and Mike won his first Stanley Cup and the Rangers their first in 54 years. He took the Cup to that barren home and stared at it. "The goddam thing is unbelievable," he says. "It has a personality. Like it's talking to you—of all the broken hearts, the broken legs, the broken families that went into it. For a small period of time, all the heartache goes away. I just looked at it and cried."

AFTER THE FIRE: Keenan won 18 playoff series in his first 11 seasons as a coach (his Blackhawks went to the finals) but none in nine seasons after that.

PAUL BERESWILL

1959–60 | THE CANADIENS' Jacques Plante, here dishing to Henri Richard (16), was among the first goalies to play the puck outside the crease. | *Photograph by* IMPERIAL OIL–TUROFSKY

1968 | THE GREAT Terry Sawchuk, the first player taken in the 1967 NHL expansion draft, left Toronto and, at 37, played one season as an L.A. King. | *Photograph by* TONY TRIOLO

> **Artifacts**

Finger Bling

Hoisting the Stanley Cup is nice and all but, well, you can only hold on to it for so long. Championship rings—from the gold band awarded to the first Cup winner and the 1893 amateur champ, Montreal, to modern, diamond-encrusted baubles—can be a hit at parties and a family heirloom

MONTREAL HOCKEY CLUB – 1893

CHICAGO BLACK HAWKS – 1961

CALGARY FLAMES – 1989

ANAHEIM DUCKS – 2007

PITTSBURGH PENGUINS – 2009

DAVID N. BERKWITZ; COURTESY OF HOCKEY HALL OF FAME

DETROIT RED WINGS — 2008

2009 | THE CANUCKS' Daniel (far left, honest) and Henrik Sedin have a symbiotic on-ice relationship as well as eerily similar career statistics. | *Photograph by* JEFF VINNICK

2003 | BLADE RUNNER: Players sharpen their skates to about ⅛ of an inch thick, and this St. Louis Blue seemed to be losing his edge. | *Photograph by* DAVID E. KLUTHO

LEAGUE OF HIS OWN

BY MICHAEL FARBER

Less than three months into a dramatic comeback, the Penguins' Mario Lemieux was playing to sellout crowds and scoring like his younger self. —*from* SI, MARCH 12, 2001

FOR MARIO LEMIEUX THIS WASN'T a hockey game but an insult, one long Don Rickles routine at his expense. His linen-and-fine-china Pittsburgh Penguins were trailing 1–0 in the third period to the fries-with-that expansion Minnesota Wild, a team that had subdued the Penguins three days before and touched off an exchange of barbs between Lemieux and Minnesota coach Jacques Lemaire about the aesthetics of NHL hockey. The Wild embodies the trapping style of play that helped drive Lemieux out of the game in 1997. Now, with nearly 13 minutes remaining, Lemieux decided he'd had enough. He was going to take this game and shake some sense into it. He retrieved the puck deep in the Pittsburgh zone and started out four-on-four, his body language screaming, This shall not pass.

Lemieux didn't quite go coast-to-coast. He took the puck over the Penguins' blue line, and then the red line, brushing off a hook by Marian Gaborik as if Gaborik were a piece of lint on his suit. As he crossed the Wild's blue line, he curled to create extra space and rifled the puck from 30 feet. The shot, from inside the right face-off circle, handcuffed goaltender Manny Fernandez and went in. It was a goal scorer's goal—a shot that pluggers would have buried in Fernandez's glove or pads. Nine minutes later, when Lemieux fired the puck toward the net from the right half boards, it struck a skate in front and caromed past Fernandez for the game-winner. This might not have been a battle for hockey's soul, but it wasn't a bad tussle for two points: Mario 2, Minnesota 1. Who's the hockey puck now?

There's only one real story in the NHL these days. From a standing start on Dec. 27, when he came out of a 3½-year retirement with a goal and two assists, Lemieux has been weaving through the scoring list like a New York City taxi. With 24 goals and 23 assists in 28 games after a two-goal, two-assist performance in a 7–5 win over the Rangers, Lemieux had more points than anyone on Minnesota, Montreal or San Jose and more goals than the leaders of six NHL teams. Pittsburgh had averaged 1.14 more goals a game since he put the uniform back on—he'd figured in 41.6% of the Penguins' scores—and even opponents had benefited from Mario's return. He'd played in 12 road games, and not a ticket to those matches had gone unsold, not even to games played in the usual sea of indifference in New Jersey or in the NHL's Shawshank, also known as the Nassau Coliseum, home of the New York Islanders. He might as well have parted the Red Sea. "This is the best time of my life," Lemieux said recently. "I had great moments in the early 1990s, but to be back and have a chance to play one more time has been great, especially with me playing well and the team playing well."

Lemieux, whose chronic back ailment was a factor in his retirement, felt his back seize up at practice on Feb. 9, touching off a panic in Pittsburgh. But while the coccyx crowed and massage therapist Tommy Plasko worked overtime, something wonderful was happening elsewhere on Lemieux's body. His legs suddenly felt as fresh as they had in almost a decade. He was struck by an urge to grab the puck and go, to beat defenders one-on-one, to do substantially more than fill in the blanks. His legs carried him to that game-turner against Minnesota—"An old Mario goal, a late '80s-early '90s goal," Penguins defenseman Marc Bergevin called it—and to a rebound against the Devils two nights later that forced goalie Martin Brodeur, who had just foiled Jaromir Jagr on a breakaway, to make a second, spectacular save.

"My goal is to be better than I was in 1997," says Lemieux, who led the NHL in scoring in '96–97 with 122 points in 76 games. "If my back hangs in, I can get there. I could carry the puck in the neutral zone against Minnesota, and once I'm able to do that regularly, my game will go to the next level."

"You can see he's getting more comfortable, doing things now he wasn't a few weeks ago," Penguins defenseman Darius Kasparaitis says. "He's becoming the most dangerous player in the league again, maybe more than Jagr."

Lemieux, 35, won't rewrite the record books—he is thirteen 100-point seasons or so behind Gretzky's career-points mark—but he might redefine the notion that anyone who scores a point a game is a star. His 1.68-points-per-game average has forced NHL players to reconsider how good they really are. Lemieux is like the math whiz who aces every test and trashes the grading curve. "He's the only guy who can make the puck disappear for a second," says Lemaire. "Here's the puck now—oops, where is it? He still has it." Compared with Lemieux's ability to make regular-season apathy vanish, to turn the Penguins into a circus team, to make every Pittsburgh game Christmas morning, his magic with the puck is a mere parlor trick.

LEMIEUX WAS presumed to have passed the torch when he retired with a bad back. But upon his return, said a general manager, "Mario picked the torch back up."

DAVID E. KLUTHO

1998 | DUBBED THE Little Ball of Hate, Dallas's Pat Verbeek, here head-to-head with Washington's Mike Eagles, is the only NHL player with 500 goals and 2,500 penalty minutes. | *Photograph by* DAVID E. KLUTHO

THE PANTHEON >> *Defensemen*

2007 | IN WINNING six Norris trophies with the Red Wings, Lidstrom was sometimes known as Mr. Perfect for his flawless game. | *Photograph by* DAVID E. KLUTHO

SI's TOP 25

Ray Bourque

Chris Chelios

Paul Coffey

Slava Fetisov

Bill Gadsby

Herb Gardiner

Ebbie Goodfellow

Doug Harvey

Rod Langway

< Nicklas Lidstrom

Ching Johnson

Red Kelly

Brian Leetch

Al MacInnis

Scott Niedermayer

Bobby Orr

Brad Park

Pierre Pilote

Denis Potvin

Chris Pronger

Larry Robinson

Börje Salming

Serge Savard

Eddie Shore

Scott Stevens

NORTHLAND

SPORTSMAN OF THE YEAR: BOBBY ORR

BY JACK OLSEN

Orr was hockey's best player and most marketable star, and he had scored the spectacular overtime goal that won the Bruins the Stanley Cup. His real heroism, though, was in the way that he devoted himself to people in need. —*from* SI, DECEMBER 21, 1970

WHEN ROBERT GORDON Orr comes walking out of the Boston Bruins' dressing room in his halfway mod attire and head-down shy manner, you would be excused for thinking that he is the water boy or perhaps an assistant bookkeeper learning the trade of attendance-padding. He is a mere 5' 11", 185 pounds, with blue-gray eyes and a thick shock of hair that is browner than blond and blonder than brown and flops down over his forehead, producing a little-boy-lost effect that is deadly to the female. His legs are muscular, but not much more than Carol Channing's. His arms are of normal length and look strong, but not strikingly so. His hands remind one of an e. e. cummings line: "nobody, not even the rain, has such small hands." His shoulders are squared, but not with the slablike precision of Bobby Hull's. His overall physique is adequate but not impressive; he will never gain employment as a male model or appear covered with salad oil in today's versions of *Sunshine and Health*.

At 22, Orr is beginning to show the indelible facial evidences of his occupation: the thick tissue over the eye sockets, the spidery scars from interrupted pucks and sticks, the drooping lip and asymmetric nose from medical insult and injury. After five years in the bullpits of the National Hockey League, Orr's nose has been fractured three or four times and he has taken 50 or so stitches, mostly in the face. His strong, sturdy jaw remains intact, but from the way he plays hockey one can easily foresee the day when he will be wired up and sipping tomato juice through a straw.

"Look at him," says Orr's crony and roommate, assistant trainer John (Frosty) Forristall. "He's the key to everything—to the Boston Bruins, to the National Hockey League, to the whole game of hockey. And he skates like he's afraid he'll be sent back to the minors. He takes chances like a rookie."

Let it be said and done with: by acclamation Bobby Orr is the greatest player ever to don skates. Not the greatest defenseman, the greatest *player*. As an 18-year-old rookie he made the NHL's All-Star team. Last season, his fourth, he was the league's Most Valuable Player, the acknowledged star of the Stanley Cup playoffs, the league's top-ranking defenseman and the league's top scorer. To comprehend what it means to be the best both defensively and offensively in the brutal game of ice hockey, the fan must imagine a combination of Dick Butkus and Leroy Kelly, of Bob Gibson and Boog Powell, of Bill Russell and Oscar Robertson. Because of Orr, there are fewer arguments in the big hockey towns about "the good old days." He has brought a sheen to every skater, a gloss to the whole league and the whole sport.

Orr has reached the stage where the records he is shooting at are his own. Last season he scored 120 points on 33 goals and 87 assists, the most goals ever scored by a defenseman, the most assists ever scored by anyone. This year he will probably fall short of those records; other teams are bearing down on him, slowing him, clutching and grabbing.

He remains the game's pivotal figure, the charismatic personality around whom hockey will coalesce, as golf once coalesced around Arnold Palmer, baseball around Babe Ruth, football around John Unitas. Three years ago the cottage industry known as the National Hockey League became 12 teams instead of six, and this season two more clubs were added. The result has been dilutions, mismatches, distortions. Orr is the fixative that binds this unstable mess together.

"Bobby has all the tricky moves, the fakes and blocks that excite the experts. He does things that no other hockey player can do," says Bruins coach Tom Johnson. "But he also does the things that excite the newcomer: the rink-long rushes, the hard body checks and that whistling slap shot of his. He has the quality of directing the attention to himself. He *runs* things. The puck is on his stick half the time. If you're looking at your first hockey game all you do is watch Orr and you catch on fast."

BRUINS VERSUS BLUES, THIS SEASON

Orr is helping to kill a penalty. With 30 seconds left in the power play, St. Louis's Christian Bordeleau winds up to

AS A ROOKIE in 1966–67, Orr began to reveal an inimitable style. He paced Bruins defensemen with 28 assists, while his feistiness led to more than 100 penalty minutes.

JAMES DRAKE

shoot from the blue line. Out of nowhere Orr appears and lowers his stick across the line of the shot; the classic sweep check repels the puck, but Bordeleau has shot so hard that Orr's stick is knocked away. He lets it go and skates toward another St. Louis player whose stick is already on the backswing. Orr blocks the shot with his skate, chases the puck into the boards, immobilizes another St. Louis shooter and freezes the puck. One second later the teams are at equal strength. "Did you ever see a hockey player do things like that?" coach Johnson asks later. No, never.

TO STUDENTS of Bobby Orr, the spectacular has become routine. One of a defenseman's primary jobs is to get the puck out of his own end and down the ice. Some players carry out this task with all the grace and ease of a starving man eating a pomegranate through a screen door. Orr has somewhat less trouble. "As soon as Bobby gets the puck on his stick," says Johnson, "you know it's coming out. People take it for granted. They forget that this isn't automatic. At least it never used to be."

When the Bruins are on offense Orr takes up the traditional defenseman's stance, guarding the point, but it is by no means certain that he will remain there. "If he has the puck at the point and somebody takes a run at him," says a teammate, "that's the end. He'll give them that one-two-circle dance of his, that ballerina twirl, and he's moving in on the net at top speed. No other defenseman would dare do this, because meanwhile he's leaving the whole wing wide-open. But I've never seen him get caught."

"If Bobby has a problem," says Boston goaltender Gerry Cheevers, "it's just that he has no fear. No fear whatever. If nothing else will do, I swear he'll use his head to block a shot. But that's his style. He won't change. He won't play it safe."

All the talk, all the praise, seems to make Orr more demanding of himself. "Let 'em say all those nice things," he says, "but I know my mistakes, and I make plenty of them. They say practice makes perfect, and they're wrong. Practice'll make you better, but nothing'll make you perfect. At least I'll never be. I do dumb things. Once I was rushing against the Rangers, and I crossed their blue line and I heard a voice say, 'Drop it! Drop it!' So I made this drop pass and skated in to screen the goalie, and by the time I turned around Vic Hadfield was on a breakaway for New York and he scored. He was the one that was saying, 'Drop it!' Every time I start to get a swelled head I think about that play or all the other mistakes I made and I still make."

Off the ice, Orr's charitable activities have become a quiet legend in hockey, even while he does his best to keep them personal and private. "[Bobby] is a bleeding heart and a do-gooder, that's all," says his lawyer and friend, Alan Eagleson. "Every once in a while he cleans out his whole wardrobe and gives it to the priest over at the Sacred Heart in Watertown. He'll get $500 for an appearance somewhere, and he'll give it to the first charity worker he sees. I asked him what happened to his bonus check last year. He says, 'Oh, I endorsed it over to Father Chase.' You wouldn't have space to list the things he's honorary chairman of: Muscular Dystrophy Association of Canada, United Fund of Boston, March of Dimes, all kinds of things. But that isn't where his time goes. His time goes in visiting hospitals, orphan homes, poor kids. It's more than a duty with him, it's an obsession."

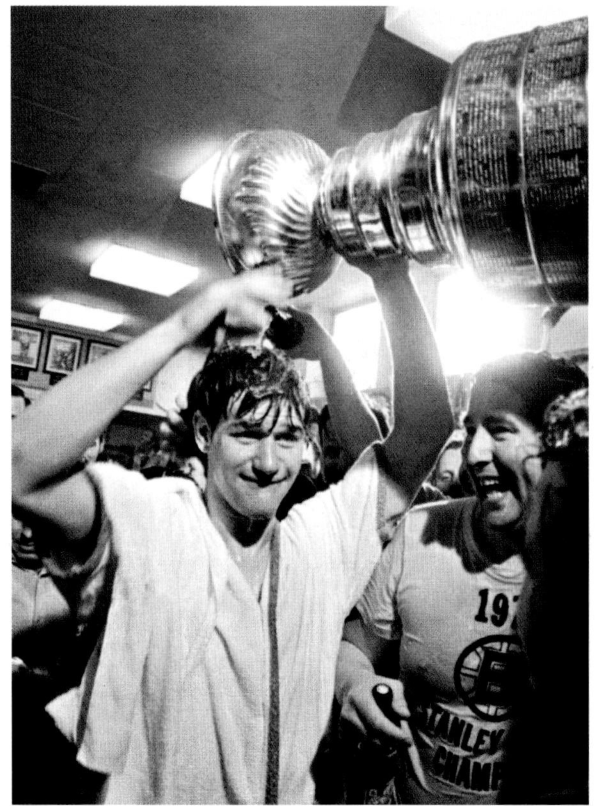

Orr turns off the subject of his generosity whenever it comes up. It takes a week of persistent questioning to elicit the following: "O.K., I'm lucky, right? I've been gifted, right? But the world is full of people who've not been gifted. Not only haven't been gifted, but have had things taken away from them. All I have to do is see one of them—a little girl who can't walk and yet she keeps on smiling at me, a lady who goes home to an iron lung every night and still gives me a kiss and a hug after every hockey game. All I have to do is see someone like that and then I don't think I'm such a big hero anymore. I think that compared to those people I'm a very small article! It knocks me down pretty bloody fast. It cuts deep into me, and I'd rather not talk about it. Ask me about broads or booze, anything else."

"It's reached the point where something's got to give," says Frosty Forristall. "It's either gotta be his play or his charities.

ORR'S CHAMPAGNE shower came after his goal delivered the Bruins their first Stanley Cup in 29 seasons. They would win again two years later.

BETTMANN/CORBIS

Every time I turn around in the apartment there's five kids from Cerebral Palsy and a photographer, and it's time to go to the game and Bobby's saying, 'No, no, no hurry, this is more important,' and he'll sit there forever with those kids."

Orr lives in a high-rise luxury apartment overlooking Boston's Back Bay and Beacon Hill. He has more luxury cars than he needs—and they cost him nothing. He drives a blue Cadillac Eldorado, allows friends to drive another freebie car that is replaced each year with a new model, and his father drives a third, a fancy station wagon. Snowmobile companies line up for the honor of giving the Orr family of Parry Sound, Ont., half a dozen of the latest models each year. A furrier offered Orr a full-length mink coat as a gift, "but I chickened out," Orr recalls. His consuming passion is anonymity. "That mink coat wouldn't have helped at all," he says, laughing.

The ease with which Orr turns dollars is probably unmatched in sport; certainly it is unmatched in hockey. Bobby Orr Enterprises Ltd., a Canadian corporation, sails blithely upward toward the multimillion level, and the only fingers that Orr must lift to earn most of the money are raised in his normal role as a hockey player. His most recent deal, for an unannounced but large sum, requires him to play golf with a few important people two or three times a year and show up at the company's Christmas party. Nothing more. Another company gave him $10,000 for doing two radio commercials and making an appearance. He has deals with Yardley of London, Bic Pens, General Motors, General Foods and others. He owns all or part of a hockey camp, a car wash, apartment projects, a farm, a condominium in Florida. A picture book about him, *Orr on Ice*, was expected to sell 5,000 copies; it sold 30,000 copies in the first three weeks. He has been offered $15,000 in advance for a book to be called *Dear Bobby: Children's Letters to Bobby Orr*, a literary motif that has heretofore been restricted to God, Santa and Art Linkletter.

"Orr is a whole 'nother ball game, a whole new breed of superstar," says an NHL official. "He brings a new image to the game. He's modest, he's restrained, he's understated. He's the opposite of a Joe Namath. Namath reached millionaire status as a kind of mixed-up antihero. Orr will reach it as a hero in the classic sense."

EARLY AFTERNOON, BOSTON

After a workout several Bruins repair to the 99 Club, a Joycean bar-and-lunchroom near the Boston Garden. One of the Bruins is Bobby Orr. He sits at a rear table eating cheeseburgers and drinking beer and he pauses every few minutes to sign an autograph or accept an outstretched hand.

The bartender comes over, bearing slips of paper for autographs and issuing instructions that Orr meticulously follows. "Write: TO EVANS, FROM YOUR PAL BOBBY ORR," the bartender says. "Here, on this one make it: TO JULIE WITH LOVE. She's 5. On this one here make it: DEAR BARRIE, HOPE YOU GET WELL SOON!"

From time to time women appear at the bar and saunter over for introductions. Orr is polite and restrained. The afternoon wears on. Orr drinks beer after beer but shows no effects. If the Chicago Black Hawks cannot knock him down, neither can Michelob.

"See that bartender?" Orr says to a visitor. "That's Tommy Maher. Watch out or he'll hit you for a five-or ten-dollar bill. A few weeks later you'll get a note from the cancer ward of some children's hospital thanking you for helping them get a color TV. He's always selling my equipment. I gave him my skates; he auctioned them off for $1,000 for a youth center. Now he wants my shirt and my sticks."

Late in the afternoon Orr and the bartender retire to a corner table—to discuss charity deals, it turns out. "Get me all the tickets you can," Maher says. "I can get $54 for expansion-game tickets and $116 for regular. When they find out it's for the youth center they get the dough up fast." The two men are talking *sotto voce*, as though planning a bank job. "Another thing," Maher says, "this year I can get $5,000 for the skates. You just decide where you want it to go." The last thing the observer hears is Orr telling Maher, "No, Tommy, you're wrong about that one. I think we get a better deal from the nun. . . ."

AS MUCH as he preferred anonymity, Orr was always the focus of attention—especially when the Bruins "drove" through Boston during the Cup parade.

BETTMANN/CORBIS

6001
CANADIEN

1982 | MIKE BOSSY swept past defenseman Colin Campbell – and Bossy's Islanders swept past these space suit–clad Canucks – in the Cup finals. | *Photograph by* TONY TRIOLO

1988–90 | THE PADS that stopped a thousand shots, and more. They were worn by Oilers Hall of Famer Grant Fuhr who made 21,623 career saves. | *Photograph by* DAVID N. BERKWITZ

2000 | WE WIN! Martin Brodeur leapt for joy after Devils teammate Jason Arnott scored the Cup-clinching double-overtime goal in Game 6 of the finals at Dallas. | *Photograph by* DAVID E. KLUTHO

QUAKER STATE
UPS
BUD LIGHT
BRODEUR
30
POWERADE

ABP MADE IN CANADA

ON AND ON AND ON...

BY E.M. SWIFT

Gordie Howe was a grandfather of two, playing in his 32nd pro season and still, at 51, a threat to score—or to rattle an opponent with one of his famous elbows. —*from* SI, JANUARY 21, 1980

GORDIE HOWE IS NOT A philosophical man. Philosophical men are forever brooding about things, mulling over the whys and wherefores of the six mad-scramble days of Creation, concocting philosophies that attempt to make order out of chaos so that they may cope. Gordie Howe does not brood. He has a philosophy, but he does not brood.

In that way he resembles, say, a farmer. Gordie Howe is not a farmer. He has never been a farmer, although before he was born his father did own a homestead in Saskatchewan and grew wheat. Still, there is something about Gordie that calls to mind that manner of man—horse sense, perhaps. Equilibrium. Farmers get it from the land, from weather that one year makes the crops fat and the next year brings a famine, from prices that fluctuate unpredictably, from things beyond a man's control. *No sense hollering about it. Make do.* Equilibrium. Who knows where Howe's comes from? But it is there. He is steady. And he has a down-to-earth way of speaking, so that the toddling grandson is "like a dog, examining every damn tree." Farmers say things like that.

One precept Howe lives by is this: Set your goals high, but not so high that you can't reach them. When you do, set new ones. The trouble is, he has attained so many that he is running out of goals to set. Today, as a Hartford Whaler, he is in his fifth *decade* as a professional hockey player. "One of my goals was longevity; I guess I've pretty much got the lock on that." he says with Gordian understatement.

The '40s, '50s, '60s, '70s and '80s. Old Gord has seen more decades in North America than the Volkswagen Beetle. You think he's old? Early in his third decade in the National Hockey League, 1961, this magazine called Howe an "ageless one-man team." So, what is 19 years beyond ageless? Eternal?

Howe has received stupendous ovations wherever he has played in this, his 32nd season. The first round of applause is for his past, for what he has given the fans over the years in hockey artistry, for he is the greatest player in the game's history. People have had to look to other sports to find suitably sublime parallels for Howe. He was said to be as effortless as DiMaggio, as well-balanced and deceptively fast as Jimmy Brown, as steady and soft-spoken as Gehrig. A great to-do was made in 1969 when Howe scored his 715th goal, passing the home run record of Babe Ruth. When, at 43, Howe retired for the first time, after 25 seasons as a Red Wing, league president Clarence Campbell said, "When Gordie came into the NHL hockey was a Canadian game. He's converted it into a North American game."

His first NHL game was on Oct. 16, 1946. The Nuremberg trials were on; Doc Blanchard was leading Army to a rout of the University of Michigan; Ted Williams and the Red Sox fell in the World Series to the Cardinals. "Gordon Howe is the squad's baby, 18 years old," wrote Paul Chandler in *The Detroit News*. "But he was one of Detroit's most valuable men last night. In his first major league game he scored a goal, skated tirelessly and had perfect poise. The goal came [when] he literally powered his way through the players from the blue line to the goalmouth."

"Power" would become Howe's nickname—the Whalers use it still when they are not calling him "Gramps." As a young man, with giant hands and a muscular back and low-slung shoulders that would be characterized hundreds of times in the next 35 years as "sloping," Howe might have been the prototype for the laborers in Thomas Hart Benton's murals. Yet his tireless skating was his most memorable trademark—along with his elbows. Says former Montreal center Jean Béliveau, "His stamina, maybe that's what you remember best when you've played against him. He just kept going and going and going."

The next wave of applause this season is for what he is doing *now*. It would be absurd to suggest Gordie Howe is the player he used to be. He will be 52 in March, and is the grandfather of two. To compare him with the greatest player of all time is silly. But it is not silly to compare him with the players coming in today, the 20-year-olds who can skate and shoot and throw their bodies around but who cannot beat Howe out of a job, or keep him from scoring. When Howe had his physical before this season, the cardiologist said, "This man could run up Mount Everest." Howe, in fact, loathes running as far as up the driveway, but his pulse rate and blood pressure remain those of a young man. "The stamina is there, the strength is there, it's the speed that goes," says Vincent Turco, the Whalers' team doctor. Howe, then, is an affirmation of the game's subtleties, succeeding with strength and savvy and guile. He has earned his position on the Whalers. The man can play.

AT 51, Howe may have been the slowest forward in the NHL, but his craftiness and vision remained. Said Jean Béliveau that year: "Gordie, he still has the instinct."

UPI/BETTMANN-CORBIS

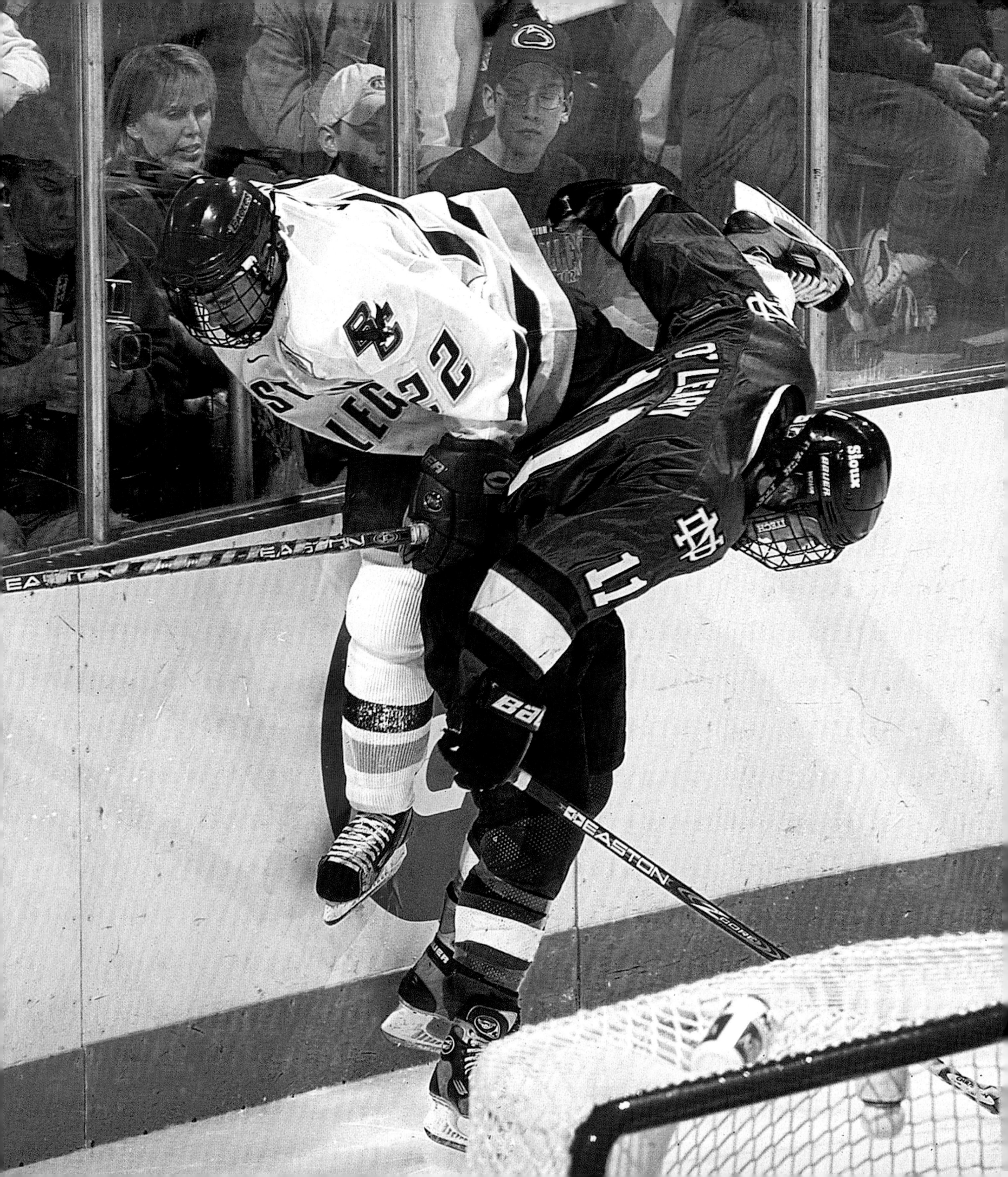
O'LEARY
11
EASTON
Sioux

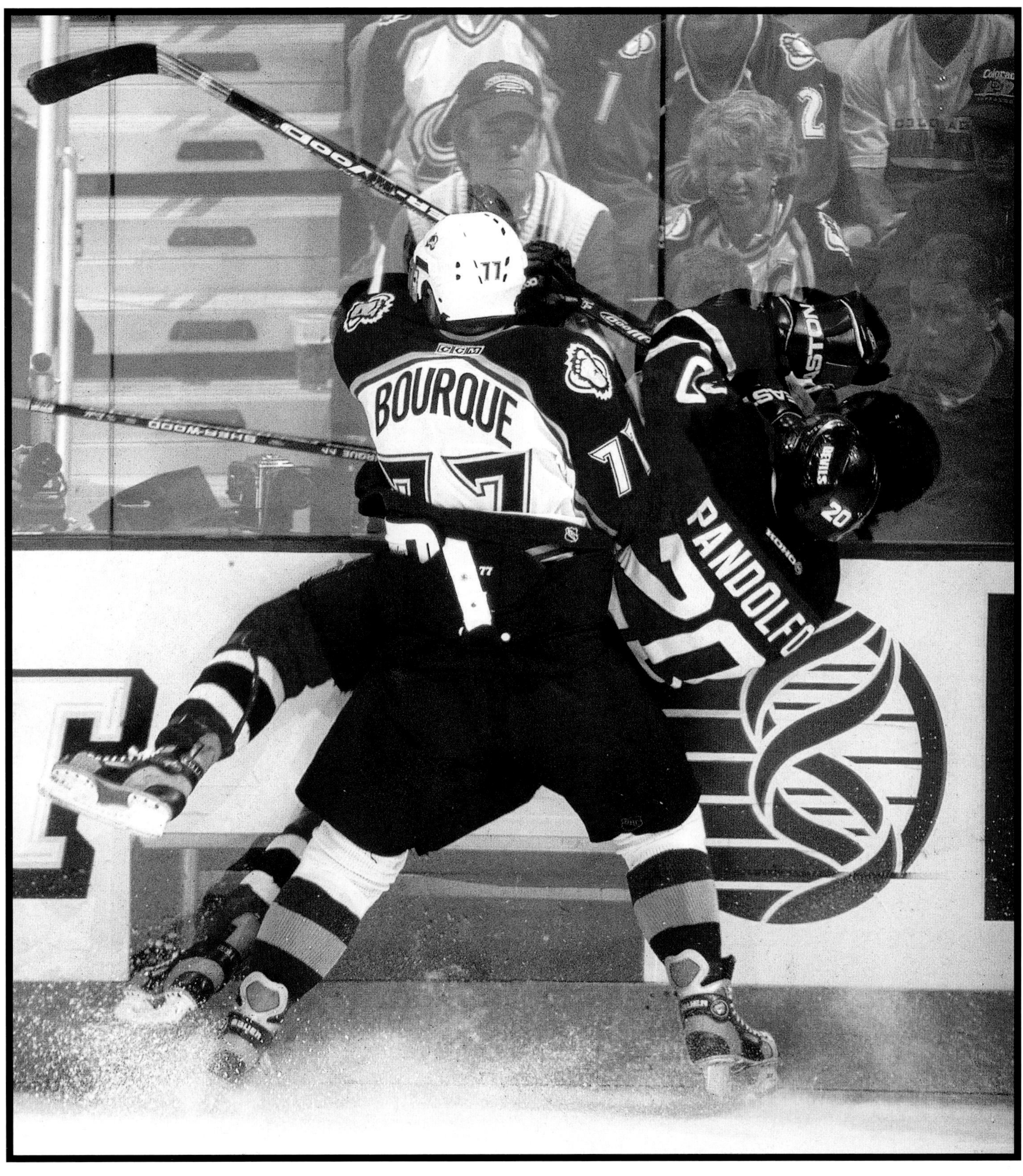

2001 | AN AVALANCHE (as in defenseman Ray Bourque) swept the Devils' Jay Pandolfo into the glass during Game 7 of the Stanley Cup finals. | *Photograph by* DAVID E. KLUTHO

2001 | COLLEGE BOARDS? North Dakota's Pat O'Leary (11) and Ben Eaves of BC were tested in the NCAA championship game. | *Photograph by* DAMIAN STROHMEYER

1971 | A SEASON *after* winning the Conn Smythe and leading Montreal to the Stanley Cup, Ken Dryden was officially a rookie—and won the Calder. | *Photograph by* TONY TRIOLO

2007 | FRESH OFF being named the Hart Trophy winner as a 19-year-old, Sidney Crosby unleashed a shot past Buffalo's Jocelyn Thibault. | *Photograph by* LOU CAPOZZOLA

41
NZA
Rbk
SHER-WOOD
87
TPS

Expansion

1967–68 *through* 1978–79

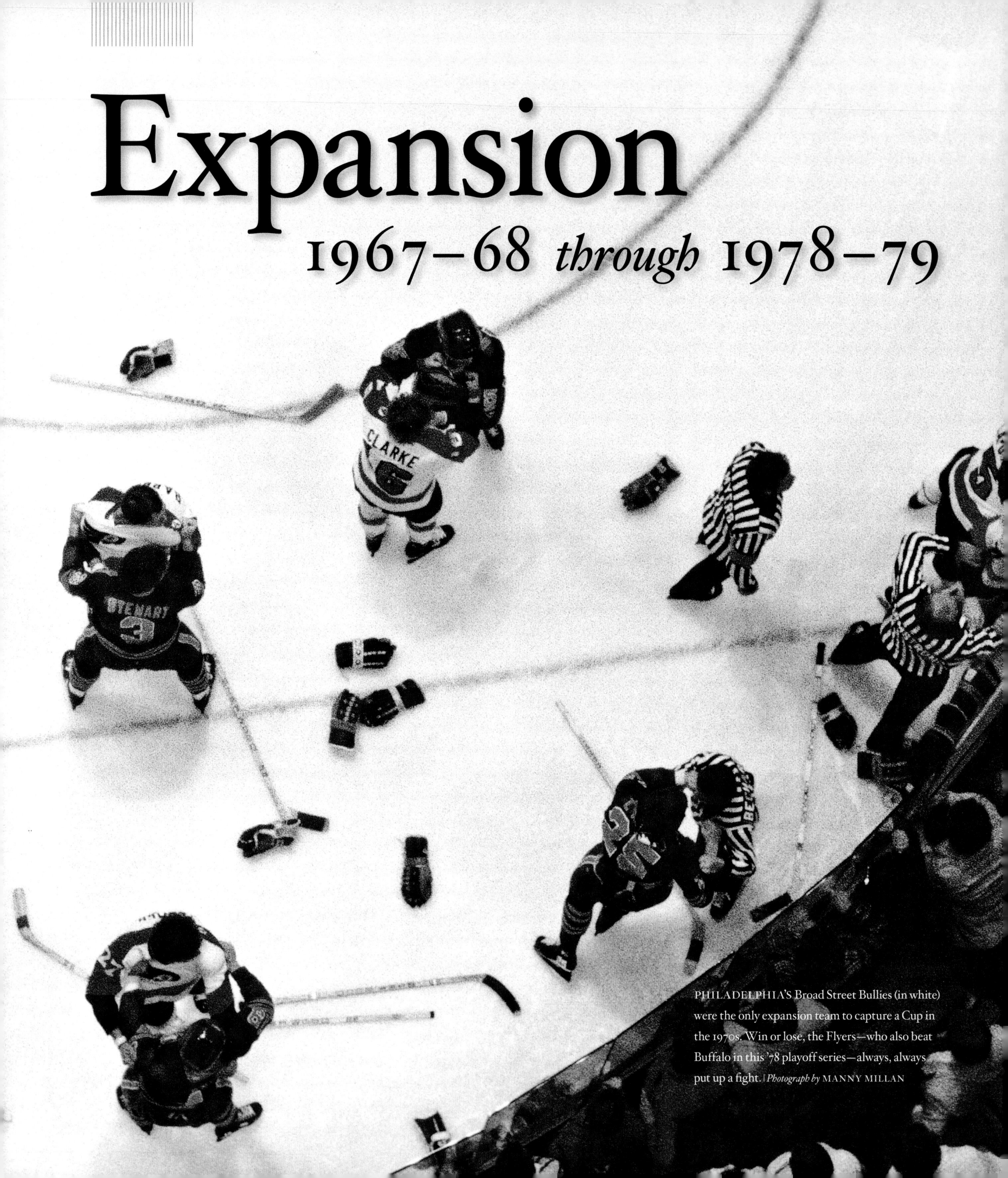

PHILADELPHIA'S Broad Street Bullies (in white) were the only expansion team to capture a Cup in the 1970s. Win or lose, the Flyers—who also beat Buffalo in this '78 playoff series—always, always put up a fight. | *Photograph by* MANNY MILLAN

> ALL-STARS OF THE ERA <

FIRST TEAM	SECOND TEAM
LEFT WING BOBBY HULL BLACK HAWKS	LEFT WING VALERI KHARLAMOV SOVIET RED ARMY
CENTER PHIL ESPOSITO BRUINS, RANGERS	CENTER BOBBY CLARKE FLYERS
RIGHT WING GUY LAFLEUR CANADIENS	RIGHT WING YVAN COURNOYER CANADIENS
DEFENSEMAN BOBBY ORR BRUINS, BLACK HAWKS	DEFENSEMAN BÖRJE SALMING MAPLE LEAFS
DEFENSEMAN DENIS POTVIN ISLANDERS	DEFENSEMAN SERGE SAVARD CANADIENS
GOALIE VLADISLAV TRETIAK SOVIET RED ARMY	GOALIE KEN DRYDEN CANADIENS

COACH
SCOTTY BOWMAN
CANADIENS, BLUES

> NICKNAMES <

Clark [Jethro] Gillies ^
Gerry [Cheesy] Cheevers
Yvan [Roadrunner] Cournoyer
Ken [the Thieving Giraffe] Dryden
Robert [Butch] Goring
Jerry [King Kong] Korab
Guy [the Flower] Lafleur
Michel [Bunny] Larocque
Reggie [the Riverton Rifle] Leach
Kenny [the Rat] Linseman
Rick [Nifty] Middleton
Don [Murder] Murdoch
Derek [Turk] Sanderson
Glen [Slats] Sather
Serge [the Senator] Savard
Dave [the Hammer] Schultz
Dave [Cementhead] Semenko
Fred [Freddie the Fog] Shero
Mario [Bionic Blueberry] Tremblay
Garry [Iron Man] Unger
Dave [Tiger] Williams

STATISTICAL LEADERS

GOALS	
PHIL ESPOSITO	602
JEAN RATELLE	394
GARRY UNGER	377
YVAN COURNOYER	374
JACQUES LEMAIRE	366

ASSISTS	
PHIL ESPOSITO	716
JEAN RATELLE	624
BOBBY ORR	617
BOBBY CLARKE	598
STAN MIKITA	552

POINTS (ALL SKATERS)	
PHIL ESPOSITO	1,318
JEAN RATELLE	1,018
STAN MIKITA	876
BOBBY ORR	874
BOBBY CLARKE	868

POINTS (DEFENSEMEN)	
BOBBY ORR	874
BRAD PARK	616
CAROL VADNAIS	518
GUY LAPOINTE	516
DENIS POTVIN	503

GOALIE WINS	
TONY ESPOSITO	316
ROGIE VACHON	280
KEN DRYDEN	258
BERNIE PARENT	256
ED GIACOMIN	251

GOALS AGAINST AVERAGE*	
KEN DRYDEN	2.24
BERNIE PARENT	2.44
TONY ESPOSITO	2.62
ED GIACOMIN	2.78
GERRY CHEEVERS	2.82

*MINIMUM 300 NHL GAMES

>>WISH YOU WERE THERE

Bruins 4, Blues 3 (OT)

MAY 10, 1970 • BOSTON GARDEN The Bruins' long wait for the Stanley Cup ends with a flair when Bobby Orr blasts a Derek Sanderson feed past goalie Glenn Hall with 40 seconds gone in sudden death for the Game 4 and Cup winner, the Bruins' first title since 1941. The goal is Orr's ninth in 14 playoff games that season but his only one during the finals.

Team Canada 6, Soviet Union 5 >

SEPTEMBER 28, 1972 • MOSCOW PALACE OF SPORT Having erased a three-goal third-period deficit in Game 8 of the Summit Series between the top two teams in the world, Canada is headed toward a tie with the U.S.S.R. That would mean a series victory for the Soviets based on goal differential. But with just 34 seconds remaining left wing Paul Henderson scores what has since been known to Canadians as "The Goal"—earning his nation hockey bragging rights over the rest of the world. Henderson's marker is the third consecutive game-winner for the previously little-known Maple Leaf from Kincardine Ont., earning him an eternal spot in Canada's, and hockey's, lore.

Canadiens 3, Black Hawks 2

MAY 18, 1971 • CHICAGO STADIUM After playing just six regular-season games first-year goalie Ken Dryden's extraordinary playoff performances lead Montreal over Boston and Minnesota and into the finals against Chicago. In this Game 7 the 23-year-old Dryden makes 31 saves, stoning Chicago snipers Bobby Hull and Stan Mikita in the waning moments to preserve the win.

Canadiens 5, Bruins 4 (OT)

MAY 10, 1979 • MONTREAL FORUM Boston takes a 4–3 lead with four minutes remaining in Game 7 of the Stanley Cup semifinals on a goal by Rick Middleton, but with just 2:34 on the clock the Bruins, coached by Don Cherry, are called for having too many men on the ice during a line change. Canadiens coach Scotty Bowman sends out a power play unit consisting of five future Hall of Famers and, with just 1:14 left, Guy Lafleur puts one past goaltender Gilles Gilbert to tie the game. Then 9:33 into overtime left wing Yvon Lambert takes a pass from Mario Tremblay and beats Gilbert, sending Montreal to the finals.

Maple Leafs 11, Bruins 4

FEBRUARY 7, 1976 • MAPLE LEAF GARDENS, TORONTO Maple Leafs captain Darryl Sittler sets an NHL standard with 10 points (six goals, four assists) in a game while becoming the first player to score hat tricks in consecutive periods. The 25-year-old center also ties the then-record for points in a period with five in the second.

WHA All Stars 4, Moscow Dynamo 2

JANUARY 2, 1979 • NORTHLANDS COLISEUM, EDMONTON Three weeks shy of his 18th birthday, Edmonton Oilers rookie phenom Wayne Gretzky centers a line that has his boyhood idol Gordie Howe of the New England Whalers on the right side and Gordie's son and New England teammate Mark on the left in the first of a three-game series against the Soviet club. Gretzky scores 35 seconds into the match on a feed from the younger Howe. The linemates wind up totaling seven points in the win.

>MAYHEM MOMENT

SEPTEMBER 21, 1969

Ottawa Civic Centre

An ugly stick fight between Boston tough guy Ted Green *(left)* and Blues enforcer Wayne Maki breaks out in an exhibition game. Maki's spear to the head results in Green's falling to the ice with a compound skull fracture. During the 2½ hour operation that follows Green has a metal plate inserted into his skull and he is forced to miss the '69–70 season.

> "Maki was under a reasonable apprehension of bodily harm. Green in my opinion was the aggressor up to the point of the [final] blow."

—Ontario Provincial Judge Edward C. Carter in his decision to dismiss criminal assault charges against Maki, March 1970

> TEAMS OF THE ERA

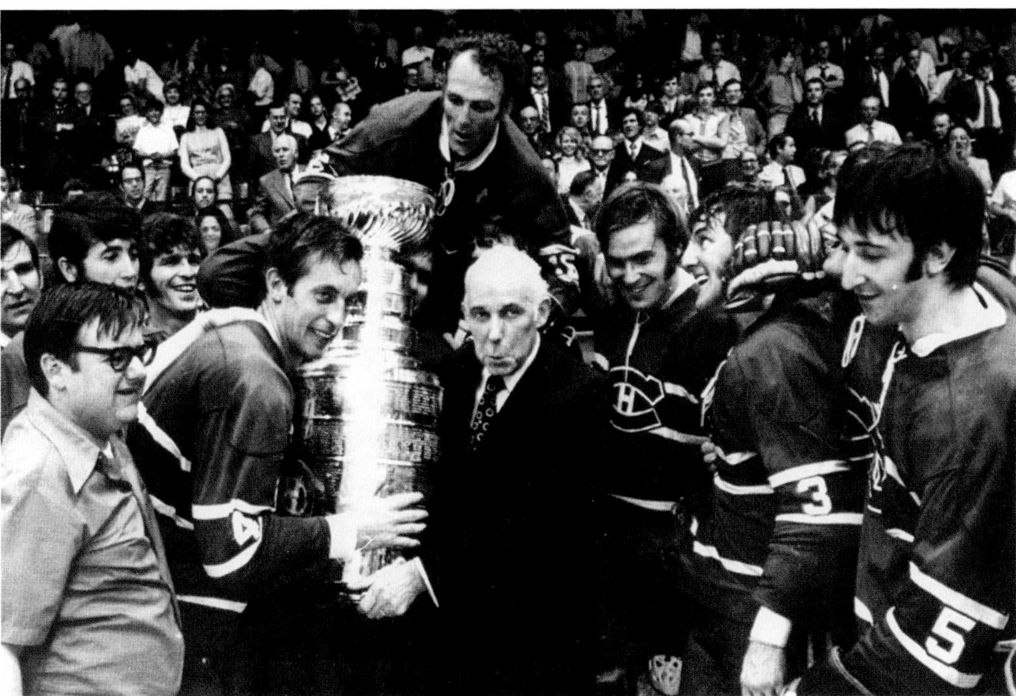

^

MONTREAL CANADIENS

Logic suggests that doubling the size of the NHL would have made it hard for the Canadiens to continue the wild success that they enjoyed in the league's first half century, but with Hall of Famers littering their roster (Jean Béliveau, Ken Dryden, Guy Lafleur, Henri Richard, Serge Savard . . .) the Habs won eight of the first 12 Stanley Cups of this era and also produced two of the four best regular-season records in NHL history.

PHILADELPHIA FLYERS

The poster children for the rough and tumble style of 1970s life in the NHL, this swashbuckling band of largely toothless Bullies was as likely to be involved in a full-scale brawl as in a goal celebration. Then, in '74, just two years removed from missing the playoffs altogether, a team led by Bobby Clarke, Bill Barber and Rick MacLeish beat the Bruins in the Stanley Cup finals—and then repeated as champs a year later.

TEAM CANADA

Having withdrawn from major international competition in 1970 due to the IIHF's inclusion of non-NHL professionals, Canada fielded a team of its top pros to take on the Soviet Union's best team in an eight game "Summit Series" in '72. The Canadians won the final three matches to defeat the U.S.S.R. 4-3-1. Four years later Canada's finest beat Czechoslovakia in the final of the inaugural Canada Cup.

[DEBUT] [FINALE]

DEBUT	Season	FINALE
Jacques Lemaire	1967–68	Bernie Geoffrion
Tony Esposito	1968–69	Doug Harvey
Bobby Clarke	1969–70	Terry Sawchuk
Ken Dryden	1970–71	Jean Beliveau
Guy Lafleur	1971–72	Dick Duff
Larry Robinson	1972–73	Jacques Plante
Denis Potvin	1973–74	Frank Mahovlich
Clark Gillies	1974–75	Henri Richard
Bryan Trottier	1975–76	Glen Sather
Mike Bossy >	1977–78	< John Bucyk

> BY THE NUMBERS

29.9 | Percent by which Bruins center Phil Esposito raised the NHL single-season scoring mark in 1968–69. His 126 points shattered the old standard of 97 points held by Bobby Hull and Stan Mikita.

750 | Amount in hundreds of thousands of dollars of the five-year contract given to Maple Leafs goalie Bernie Parent by the WHA's Miami Screaming Eagles, making Parent the first star poached by the upstart league.

28 | Amount in millions of dollars grossed at U.S. box offices by the 1977 motion picture, *Slap Shot*.

48 | Penalty minutes assessed to Toronto defenseman Jim Dorey in his first game, Oct. 16, 1968, a record for NHL debuts. Only three other Leafs players received more penalty minutes that entire season.

63 | Consecutive wins for Cornell from Jan. 14, 1967 to Jan. 29, 1972, an NCAA record that still stands.

37 | Straight away-game losses, an NHL record, for the expansion Washington Capitals in their first season, 1974–75.

> PATRICK FACTOR

The NHL divided into four divisions before the 1974–75 season, and names were chosen to honor the great builders of the league. Originally consisting of the Islanders, Flames, Flyers and Rangers, the Patrick Division was so-titled to salute the late, and great, Lester Patrick.

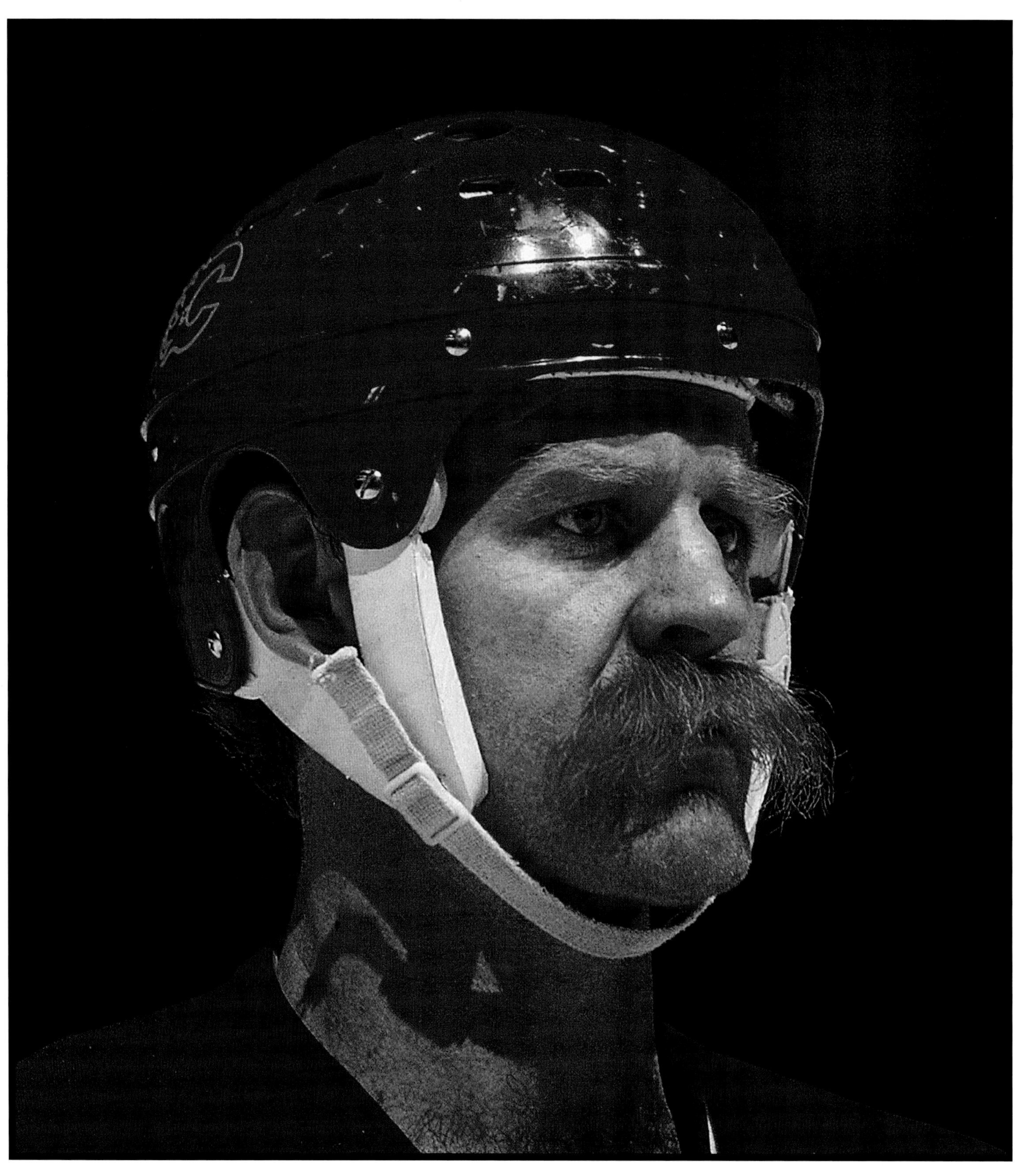

1980s | WITH HIS trademark blazing red mustache complementing his Flames jersey, future Hall of Famer Lanny McDonald stood out in Calgary. | *Photograph by* BRUCE BENNETT STUDIOS

c. 1970 | EVEN INTO his 40s, Gordie Howe, here barking instructions to Wings' teammate Alex Delvecchio, commanded a goalie's watchful eye. | *Photograph by* DENIS BRODEUR

VICTORIAVILL

Cooper
CUSTOM PRO
25

WHEN HELL FROZE OVER

BY ALLEN ABEL

The sometimes zany, sometimes dismal, always original WHA wasn't just a league that enriched stars like Bobby Hull and (very briefly) Derek Sanderson. It also altered the NHL in ways that 25 years later were still being felt. —*from* SI, APRIL 6, 1998

THIS IS THE HOUR TO CELEBRATE hockey's great pretender: a league where Bobby Hull soared, Gordie Howe scored and Maurice Richard coached (for a week). Where Wayne Gretzky arrived, Frank Mahovlich thrived, and Derek Sanderson—when his team's first home game was canceled because the Zamboni crashed through the ice—was pelted with pucks by irate fans.

Mark Messier played here, and scored one goal all season. Harry Neale coached a team, but it folded. Twice. The league's championship trophy was sponsored by a finance company. The Dayton and Miami franchises never played a game. The Ottawa team, in its second incarnation, lasted only two nights. The league's most memorable moment came when a brawler yanked the toupee off the No. 1 star. Yet the league endured—and, in places, flourished—for seven unforgettable years.

This was the World Hockey Association, created in the Watergate autumn of 1972 by a marriage of California confidence men and giddy millionaires with major league dreams. The new league didn't just change the face of hockey; it drew a mustache and beard on the portrait of a fossilized sport. The WHA terrorized the NHL's fraternity of plantation slaveholders, blithely kidnapped teenage prospects, crusaded bravely into the Sun Belt, enriched a few headliners and an underclass of ordinary puck chasers beyond their wildest nightmares, and went head-to-head with the NHL in every major city—and lost every time.

In its brief and addled existence, the WHA spanned the continent from Boston to Vancouver, from St. Paul to Birmingham. Its rosters included some of the icons of the sport: Howe, Hull, Mahovlich, Gerry Cheevers, Paul Henderson, Dave Keon, Bernie Parent and Jacques Plante. The league sent its All-Stars to Moscow as the proxies of Canada's national pride—and won one game out of eight. It enlisted some of the fiercest goons in hockey history, yet it embraced Europe's daintiest pros and welcomed the U.S. collegians and Russian militiamen whose kind would rise to rule the game today.

Twenty-five years after the first blue WHA pucks were dropped, the Chicago Cougars and Minnesota Fighting Saints, the Michigan Stags and New York Golden Blades are ancient history. But the legacy of the WHA—from Gretzky and Messier to the explosion of U.S. and European players—remains vibrant. "We gave entertainment to a lot of people," says Hull, the superstar who in 1972 jumped from the Black Hawks to the WHA's Winnipeg Jets for a $1 million payday—one of numerous NHL players lured by money to the WHA. "And the year after the leagues merged [in 1979–80] a lot of the top scorers in the NHL had come from the WHA."

The Bruins Derek Sanderson went from the NHL to the WHA in 1977, signed by the Philadelphia Blazers for a stint that lasted eight games. "We were in Sherbrooke, Quebec, for an exhibition," Sanderson recalls. "There were 58 people in the stands, and 45 of them were on free tickets from one of our players who came from there. Bernie Parent, our goalie, looks around and says, 'What are they? Politely late?' Then he disappears into the dressing room. I go in there [after him] and Bernie is taking his equipment off. He says, 'I don't risk my life for no people.' He talked me out of it too! I didn't play either."

Sanderson had signed with Philadelphia for $2.65 million, over five years, a sum that made him, a talented but unexceptional playmaker, the highest-paid athlete in the world. He didn't want to jump to the WHA—nobody did, really. He just wanted to wake up the Boston management and to be a Bruin forever; the penthouse playboy of mod-squad New England; Joe Namath's partner in a chain of saloons; drunk and oversexed and a walking Walgreen's, addicted to a variety of prescription drugs. Sanderson would gladly have stayed in Boston had the Bruins offered him a piddling 80 grand. But they didn't.

Playing the Crusaders in Cleveland, Sanderson scored two goals against his old Boston netminder, Cheevers—another astonished new millionaire—before suffering the injury that would, much to his delight, end his WHA career. "I was in the penalty box, and the fans were throwing stuff at me," Sanderson says. "I said, 'I don't need this s---,' and I jumped out. I landed on a piece of garbage and slipped a disk in my back."

A week or so later, it was over. Sanderson went to the owners of the Blazers, begged to be allowed to return to the Bruins, and made a settlement. "The WHA was like buying a motor home," says Sanderson. "There are only two great days—the day you buy it and the day you sell it."

DESPITE HIS record-setting Blazers contract, Sanderson never felt comfortable wearing what he called, "the most hideous uniform in the world."

TONY TRIOLO

ROY
44

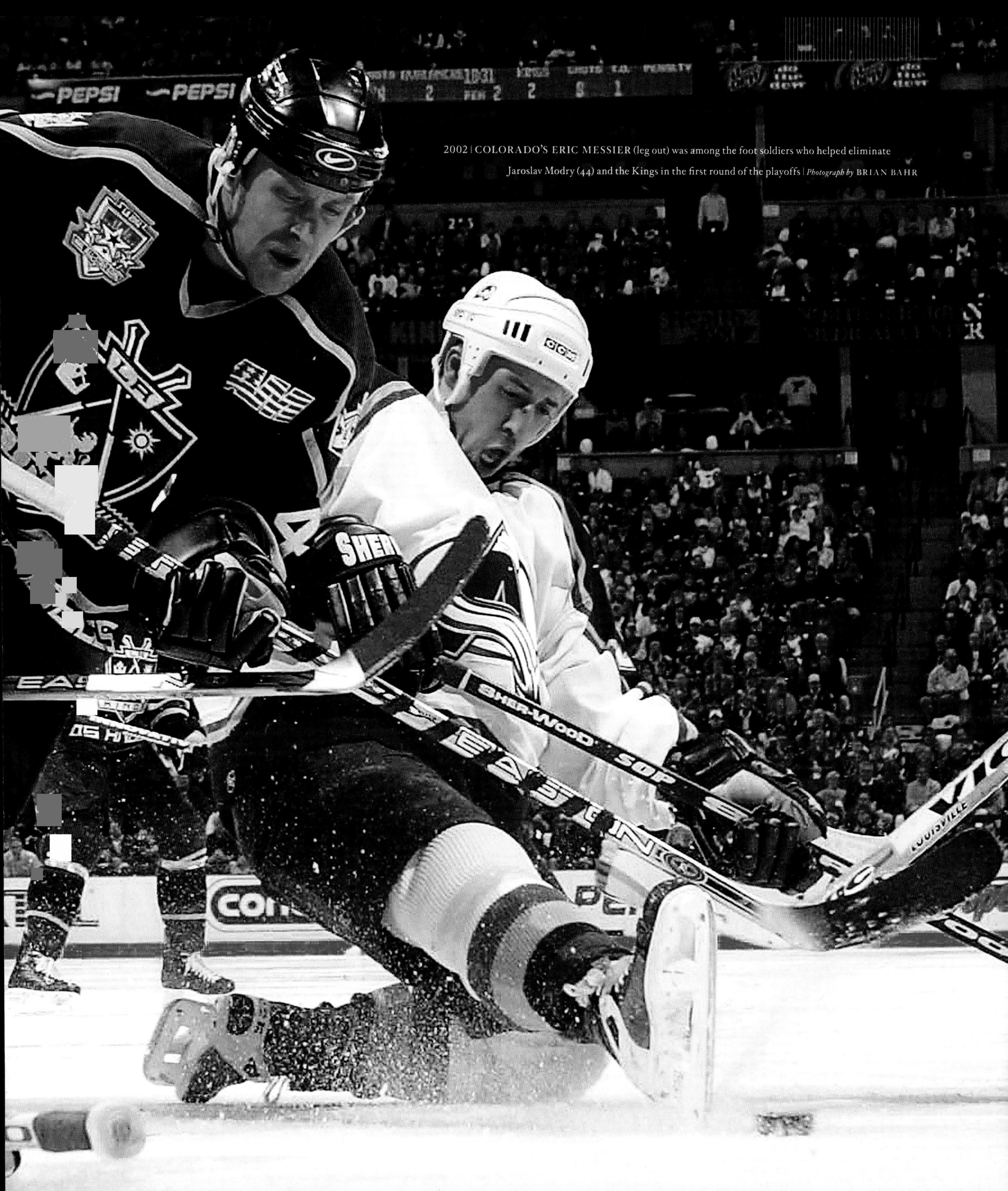

2002 | COLORADO'S ERIC MESSIER (leg out) was among the foot soldiers who helped eliminate Jaroslav Modry (44) and the Kings in the first round of the playoffs | *Photograph by* BRIAN BAHR

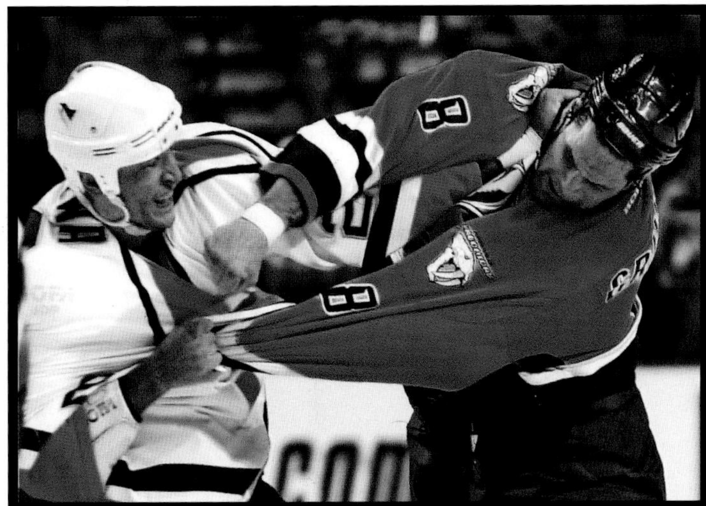

2001 | PENGUINS' KRZYSZTOF OLIWA *vs.* PREDATORS' STU GRIMSON

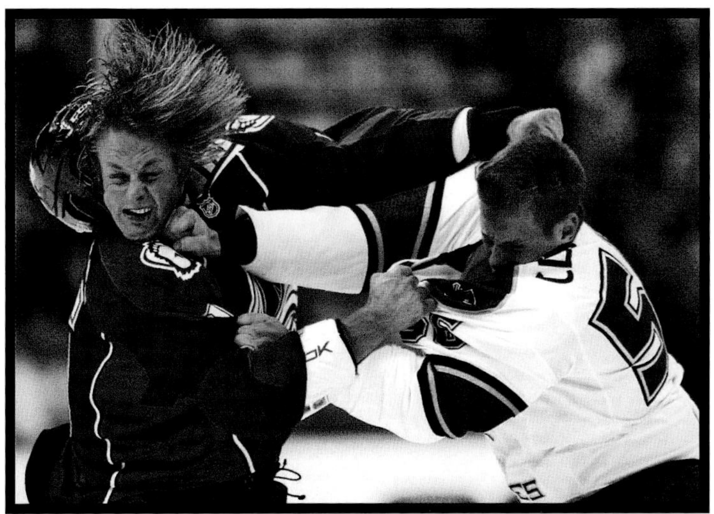

2009 | AVALANCHE'S MATT HENDRICKS *vs.* KINGS' RICH CLUNE

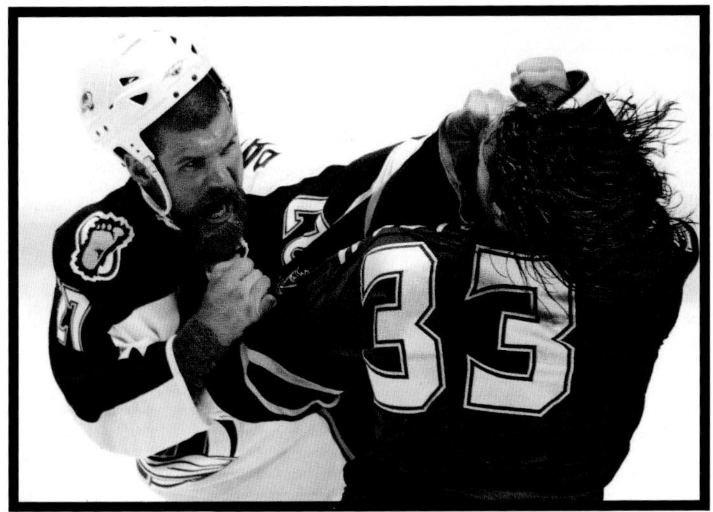

2008 | AVALANCHE'S SCOTT PARKER *vs.* KINGS' KEVIN WESTGARTH

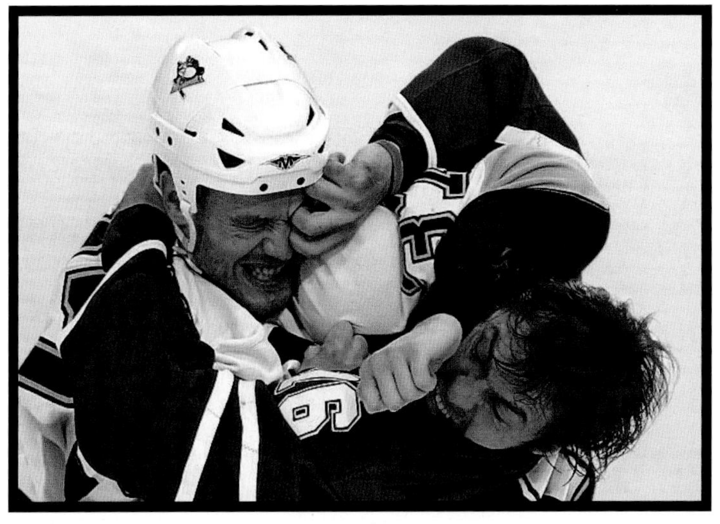

2008 | PENGUINS' JARKKO RUUTU *vs.* LEAFS' DARCY TUCKER

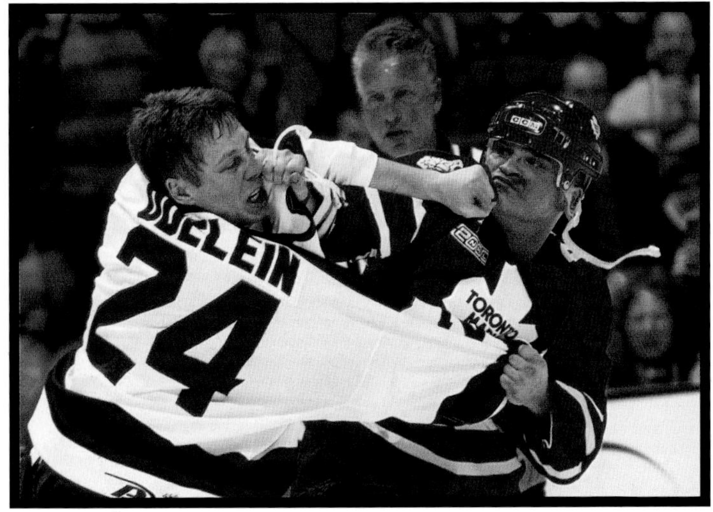

2000 | DEVILS' LYLE ODELEIN *vs.* LEAFS' TIE DOMI

2008 | HAWKS' DUSTIN BYFUGLIEN *vs.* BLUES' KEITH TKACHUK

CLOCKWISE FROM TOP LEFT: MARK HUMPHREY/AP; J. NEIL PRATHER/ICON SMI; GENE J. PUSKAR/AP; NAM Y. HUH/AP; DAMIAN STROHMEYER; ISAAC BREKKEN/AP

2008 | AFTER ARRIVING from Pittsburgh, Ottawa's Jarkko Ruutu (73) was the object of Francis Bouillon's aggression—and the refs' attention. | *Photograph by* ED WOLFSTEIN

NHL
73

BOZO THE BRUIN

BY GEORGE PLIMPTON

Possessing only minimal skating ability—but a good deal of wit—the writer strapped on the equipment to play goal for the Bruins against the Flyers. He lived to tell the tale in a two-part series.

—*from* SI, JANUARY 30 *and* FEBRUARY 6, 1978

I WENT THROUGH SOME FRIGHTENING indignities during practice. The ultimate occurred in an afternoon scrimmage when a puck emerged from a melee at the blue line and came down the ice toward me—not so much a shot as a push, moving about 4 mph. I glared at it; my intent was to sweep it into the corner for the defensemen to pick up, but as I swiped at the puck I lifted my stick just enough for the puck to slide underneath and between my skates. As I turned, I could see the puck sliding slowly across the red line at the goalmouth, now moving about 1 mph—indeed, it barely had enough momentum to reach the back of the net. Laughter echoed all around the rink; the players could not contain themselves. Within the cage of my helmet I produced a high cry of dismay. Subsequently, I wrote in my notebook, I was "utterly devastated."

When a scrimmage was whistled over, the squad lined up along the boards for 10 minutes of wind sprints—racing across the width of the rink and back. I skated with the goalies, invariably in their wake after three or four strides, and thus was left out in the open for the Bruins to contemplate my strange skating style, in which I appeared to be traveling on my anklebones. They were especially taken by my attempts at bringing myself to a stop—which was to skate full tilt into the boards, my hands outstretched like a horror-movie monster's. Thus brought to an abrupt halt, I could turn myself around to set off again. As one of the Bruins remarked, I was one of the few players he had ever seen in an NHL uniform who checked himself into the boards.

For me, the surface of the ice seemed to have a tendency to tilt and slip, like a tabletop in a séance; my goalie's stick, even in my moments of repose, seemed to have a disposition of its own. Once when I was housecleaning during a scrimmage, sweeping the ice shavings from in front of the crease and being very nonchalant and cool because the puck was at the other end of the rink, the stick slipped from my grasp and clattered out across the ice toward the blue line. In grabbing for it, I felt my skates go out from under me, and I landed belly down, arms outstretched, with a considerable thump, the goalie's stick still sliding out in front of me. I pulled myself up, laboriously, and skated out to get it. No harm done, because the puck was still at the other end, but I heard a voice from the stands call out—a teenager's by the sound of it—"All right. Great moves out there, Bozo, great moves!"

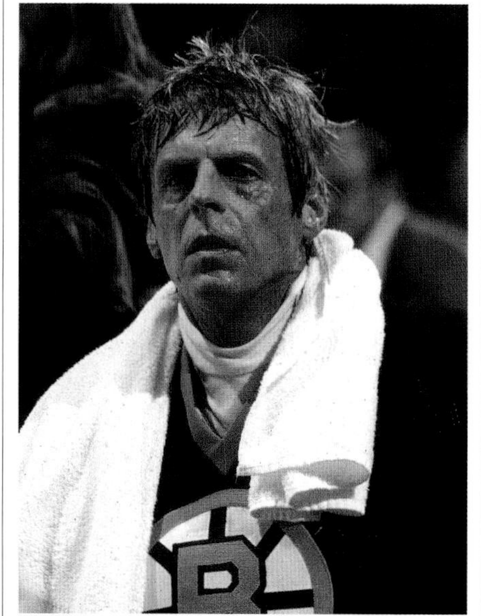

A few days later came the game, a five-minute-exhibition against the Philadelphia Flyers, and for the first two minutes the Bruins kept the puck in the Flyers' end. Well, this wasn't bad at all, I thought. There can be nothing easier in sport than being a hockey goalie when the puck is at the opposite end. It occurred to me it was not unlike standing at the edge of a millpond, looking out across a quiet expanse at some vague activity at the opposite end almost too far away to be discernible. Could they be fishing down there? But then, suddenly, the distant, aimless, waterbug scurrying becomes an oncoming surge of movement as everything starts approaching on a direct line, almost as if a tsunami had suddenly materialized at the far end of the millpond and was beginning to sweep down toward one. There's a great encroaching wave full of things being borne along at full-tilt—hockey sticks, helmets, faces with no teeth in them, those black, barrel-like hockey pants, the skates and, somewhere in there, that awful puck. And then, of course, the noise. The crowd roars as the players come down the ice, and so the noise seems as if it were being generated by the wave itself.

The first shot that the Flyers took went in. I had only the briefest peek at the puck as it sped in from the point to my right,

PLIMPTON'S FORAY in the nets was one of a series of groundbreaking participatory ventures in which he boxed, pitched and played QB for the NFL's Lions.

JOHN IACONO (2)

a zinger, and was tipped in on the fly by a Philadelphia player named Orest Kindrachuk who was standing just off the crease. I yelled loudly and beat the side of my helmet with my blocking pad. "I didn't see the damn thing!" I cried.

Then, soon after the face-off following that Philadelphia goal, my teammate Bobby Schmautz was sent to the penalty box for tripping. With the Bruins a man short, the Flyers employed their power play, and for the remainder of the action the puck stayed in the Bruin zone. I have seen a film of those minutes, much of it in slow-motion, so that the inadequacies of my curious goaltending style are apparent, especially my delayed reactions to the puck's whereabouts. The big mitt rises and flaps slowly, long after the puck has passed. If there is any design to my goaltending, the film discloses that it is a near-studied attempt to keep my back to the puck. One sequence shows a puck coming in over my shoulder and hitting the crossbar. As it rebounds, a reaction finally begins: The mitt flaps, and my body begins to pirouette, as if I wished to discover what had made the noise behind me. While the players struggle over the puck, now back out in front of the crease, my back is to them, and the camera catches me leaning over and staring into the depths of the goal, my posture that of a man peering under the hood of his car. I seem completely oblivious to the melee immediately behind me.

The film also shows that I spend a great deal of time flat on the ice. It does not take much to put me down. Once, a hard shot missed the far post, and as if blown over by the passage of the puck, I collapsed weirdly and sprawled on the ice. My efforts to get back up—the puck sailing around like an attendant bumblebee—use up a lot of footage as well, including an odd tableau in the crease in which I am seen grasping one of my defensemen around his legs, his stick and skates locked in my grasp, as I try to haul myself upright, using him the way a drunk uses a lamppost.

What was most astonishing about those hectic moments, however, was that the Flyers did not score. Six Flyer shots were actually on the goal. One of them ricocheted off my mask in a high arc out to the blue line. My own contribution to such feats was negligible. By chance my body seemed to be in the right place when the puck appeared; it would whack into me, my conscious reaction to its incoming about akin to a tree's in the line of flight of a golf ball.

My most spectacular save was made when I was prostrate on the ice. Quite inexplicably the puck appeared under my nose and I was able to slap my glove on it. I could hear the Bruins breathing and chortling as they clustered over me to protect the puck from probing Flyer sticks. I lifted my glove and peeked, just to make sure.

A few seconds before my five-minute stint was up, Mike Milbury threw a stick across the path of an oncoming Flyer wing and a penalty shot was assessed. No doubt Milbury had been put up to it by my other teammates so that I could experience a goalie's most nightmarish challenge—defending against a shooter coming in at him unencumbered. The Flyers picked Reggie Leach, who scored 61 goals two seasons ago, to take the shot. I heard his name over the public-address system, and the crowd began to roar. I watched the other players withdraw. There were just the two of us on that vast expanse. Then I saw Leach begin to pick up speed. As he crossed the blue line, I skated hastily out to meet him, and as we converged I threw myself sideways onto the ice. (Someone said later it looked like the collapse of an ancient sofa.) As I slid up to him, I closed my eyes. Leach took his shot; it hit the edge of one of my skates and skidded away.

I heard the tumult from the stands. The Bruins came off the bench to assist me off. I saw their big grins, and their gloves cuffed me around. Halfway to the Boston bench I tripped, or perhaps I was knocked over by one of the congratulatory backslaps, and I half slipped to the ice before the Bruins hauled me up like a sack of potatoes and skated me over to the bench. I beamed at the Bruins seated alongside.

"How many saves?"

"Oh, 30 or 40 at least. You were really in the barrel."

"Was that really Leach who took the penalty shot?"

"Yeah, Leach. He's finished. He's a psychological ruin to have missed a penalty shot against you. You've won us the Stanley Cup."

Later, after the regular Bruins-Flyers game was over, I started to dress. I noticed that the room had quieted and the Bruins were looking over. I discovered why. They had carved up my clothing: my tie was chopped in half, the toes were snipped from my socks, the seat was gone from my underpants. As I pulled on one of these ruined items, the Bruins rocked back and forth in their stalls, pounding on the wooden seats and roaring with laughter.

The Bruins coach Don Cherry looked on. "Well," he said, "you've been initiated."

HAVING PLAYED pond hockey as a boy in New England, Plimpton imagined he'd retained enough basic skill to move smoothly around the ice. He was wrong.

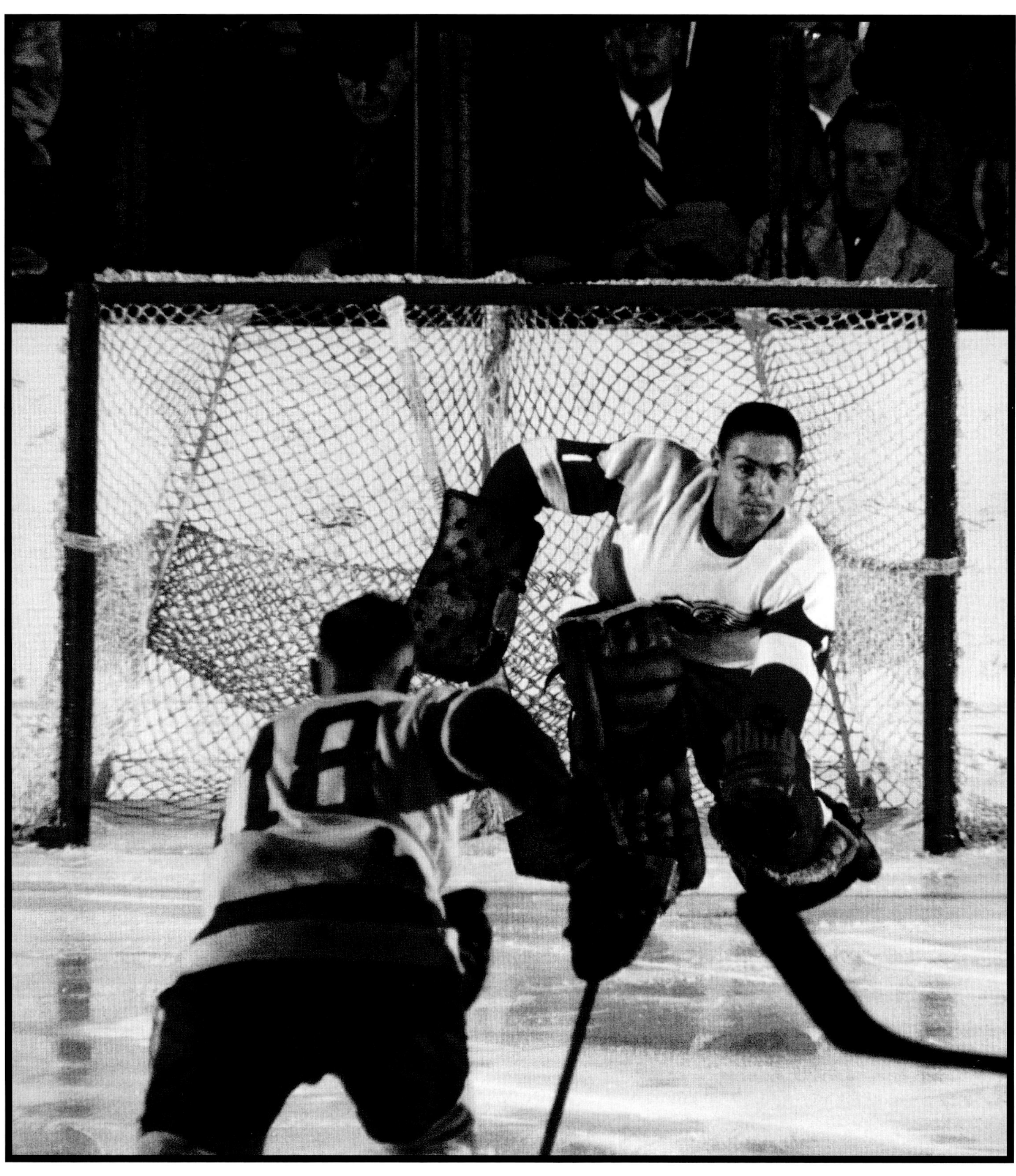

1960 | DETROIT SIGNED Terry Sawchuk as a teenager. Nice catch. He played 14 of his 21 seasons and won three Vezinas with the Wings. | *Photograph by* JOHN G. ZIMMERMAN

1966 | DOUBLE BARREL: Against Chicago, the Maple Leafs had to contend with the elusive Bobby Hull (9) and the sharpshooting Phil Esposito (7). | *Photograph by* JAMES DRAKE

1924 | IN THE FIRST Winter Games, held in Chamonix, France, the Toronto Granites took gold for Canada with this 6–1 win over the U.S. | *Photograph by* HOCKEY HALL OF FAME

THE HANDSOME HERO OF THE HAWKS

BY KENNETH RUDEEN

Blond forward Bobby Hull, one of the NHL's brightest young stars, had brought Chicago hockey fans something they had not had in years: hope. —*from* SI, NOVEMBER 14, 1960

ROBERT MARVIN HULL MAY turn out to be one of the world's great hockey players. At 21, he is among the truly unusual athletes who leapt to the top after the briefest apprenticeship. He came directly from amateur hockey to the big time and last spring, in his third NHL season, became the second-youngest player ever to win the scoring championship. Hull's slashing skill in the service of the Hawks has brought light and hope to a team that, over the years, has dwelt in a state of almost unrelieved darkness and despair.

Not only one of hockey's finest, Hull is also its handsomest player. His hair is blond, his eyes blue and his smile uncommonly forthright. From the neck down he has the sculptured musculature of a Muscle Beach playboy. Hockey is not a game of giants, and at 5 feet 10 and 190 pounds Hull is literally a big man on the ice. Game pads, jersey and bulky shorts give him a tanklike look, but he moves with the grace and fluency of a figure skater. There is a cheerful, vivid, freewheeling recklessness about him. He picks up the puck and sprints toward the enemy goal with a kind of jackrabbit acceleration. Head up, eyes unblinking and calculating, he seems almost visibly deciding whether to try to roughhouse past the defense or feed a linemate. When he has a chance to shoot, and also a little room, he takes a big backswing and gives the puck a tremendous swat. His shot is "heavy" as well as hard—that is, not easily deflected. One goalie says it feels like lead when it chunks against him.

In a game in which tempers flare, skulls are sometimes cracked and blood is frequently drawn, Hull is a live-and-let-live player. He lost his front teeth at the hands of an opposing player early in his career, but he is incapable of the wild rage that used to erupt in Rocket Richard, nor does he have the executioner's touch of Gordie Howe, who exacts the traditional eye for an eye and tooth for a tooth when officials are looking elsewhere.

Happy-go-lucky, genial, a little cocky, Bobby Hull is essentially the same gleeful kid who had more energy to expend than anyone else in Point Anne, Ont., where he was born on Jan. 3, 1939. Point Anne is a company town tacked on to a local cement plant. Its fat twin smokestacks dominate the north, or mainland, shore of the Bay of Quinte. "The population is about a thousand if you count the dogs," says Hull's 14-year-old sister, Judy, "about a hundred if you don't."

As the son of a cement company foreman, Bobby Hull grew up in a succession of company houses around the town. Bigger houses were needed as new Hulls arrived (Bobby is the fifth-oldest of 11 brothers and sisters). Today, a look at his father, Robert Edward Hull, is a clue to Bobby Hull's heft. The elder Hull is a thick-chested 225 pounder with a booming voice and faded blond hair. When he had more of it, some years ago, he too was a well-known local hockey player called The Blond Flash.

It was on the ice of the Bay of Quinte that Bobby learned to skate, to whack a puck straight and hard toward a makeshift goal and to use the strength he found in his stocky legs. "We gave Robert a pair of skates for Christmas when he wasn't quite 3," said Hull Sr. "I took him over to a frozen pond near home, and I'll be darned if he wasn't taking a few strides within a half hour."

At 18 he took the giant stride from juniors to Chicago, and he was a sensational rookie, delighting the crowds and scoring a solid 47 points. But he was still inexperienced enough to think he had to do it all himself. It was only last year, playing exhibition games in Europe, that Hull went from a merely good to a potentially great player, one who uses his head as well as his stick. Though his schedule called for 23 games in 25 nights, Bobby was determined not to miss a thing. He saw all the sights between London and Vienna, walked through every museum and climbed every recommended staircase, including the one that leads to the top of Paris's Eiffel Tower. "After that," says Bobby, "I was so tired I couldn't have taken the puck down the ice alone and put it in if I'd wanted to. I had to pass it off. The best part was that I still came out the leading scorer." His lesson learned, Hull deemphasized his rhinoceros charges and spruced up his team play so remarkably last season that he collected 39 goals and 42 assists.

Now, all over the league, coaches are praying and searching for signs of greatness in their youngsters. But none of them has what Chicago has, for Chicago has Hull, and Hull has everything.

AT AGE 22 Hull led the Blackhawks to the Stanley Cup in 1961; five years later he scored 54 goals, the highest single-season total of the Original Six era.

ART RICKERBY

2010 | THE SHARKS got called for interfering with Avs goalie Craig Anderson *(below)* during this playoff mosh, but Devin Setoguchi (16) later rose up to score the game-winner. | *Photograph by* ROBERT BECK

2007 | WHILE ISLANDERS goaltender Rick DiPietro *(opposite)* laid low, his teammates provided crease protection against Sabres forward Jochen Hecht. | *Photograph by* JIM McISAAC

SUTTON
25
HECHT
55
GERVAIS
8

> Collectibles

Trade Bait

Let's hope no one's mom threw out their 1911 Georges Vézina rookie card (below). One of these little dandies (it measures 2½ by 1½ inches and first came in a cigarette pack) sold, in 2007, for $100,000. The rest of the cards here may be less pricey, but, in the hearts of those who collected and swapped 'em, highly valuable nonetheless

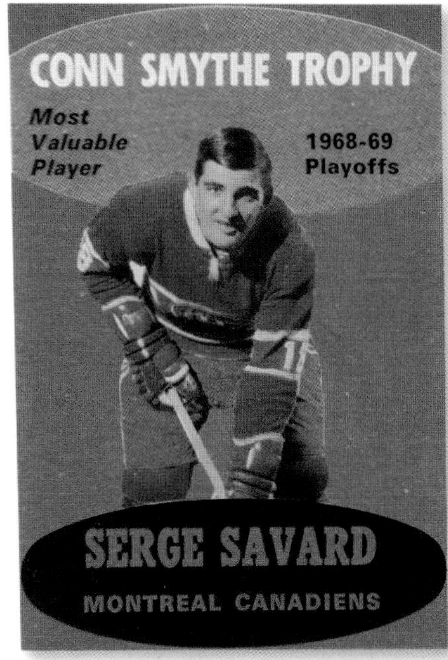

CONN SMYTHE TROPHY
Most Valuable Player
1968-69 Playoffs
SERGE SAVARD
MONTREAL CANADIENS

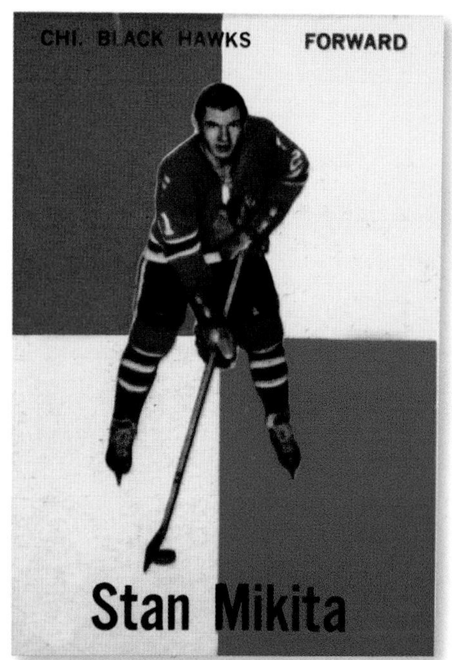

HOCKEY PICTURE GUM
CHARLIE (CHUCK) GARDINER
"SAVE THESE LETTERS
Fascinating Home Hockey Game FREE for collecting Hockey Picture Card letters. See reverse side.
G
CONSERVEZ CES LETTRES
Jeu de Hockey pour la maison GRATIS pour collection des lettres des Cartes Images de Hockey. Voir au verso.

DAVID N. BERKWITZ; COURTESY OF HOCKEY HALL OF FAME

ELEVEN SECONDS

BY E.M. SWIFT

Boston University freshman Travis Roy had just fulfilled his dream of playing Division I hockey when a terrible accident on the ice changed his life forever. —*from* SI, NOVEMBER 20, 1995

THERE WAS AN UNWRITTEN rule in the Roy household: No lying down on the ice. Ever since Travis was three, a towheaded bug of a kid playing for his father's Mite team, he was taught that if he got knocked down, or if he tumbled into the boards, or if he got whacked in the ankle by a puck, he should bounce back up. His dad, Lee, a former MVP at the University of Vermont, wouldn't stand for the theatrics some kids pulled, collapsing at the first sting of pain as if they'd been felled by a splitting maul. "Get up, you're not hurt," Lee would say, a Yankee accent flavoring the reproach, a smile creasing his gentle face.

Lee was famous for these words in Maine, where for the last 20-plus years he has been Mr. Youth Hockey, helping to found the Portland Youth Hockey Association in 1972, managing four different rinks in the southern part of the state, coaching kids from Mite to college age. *Get up, you're not hurt.* It was right there in Travis Matthew Roy's scrapbook, a city phone book–sized compilation of hockey clippings, programs, photos and award certificates. Travis had pasted in a picture of his dad with a cartoon balloon coming out of his mouth that read, "Get up, you're not hurt. Get up."

And Travis always did. One time, when he was about 12, he skated past the bench during a game and yanked off a glove so his dad could see the blood dripping from the tip of one of his fingers. "What do I do?" Travis asked.

"What do you mean?" Lee replied, having ascertained that the wound was a long way from the boy's heart. "There's a shift going on." Travis slid the glove back on and kept playing.

Which was why, on Friday, Oct. 20, as Travis lay motionless on the ice of Boston University's Walter Brown Arena, just 1:56 into the opening period of the season, those who knew him felt a cold wave of panic. Travis had never lain on the ice. No coach who'd ever had him—not his father, not any of his three high school mentors and certainly not BU coach Jack Parker—had ever had to go out onto the ice to help Travis Roy to his feet. Never. But 11 seconds into his first shift of his first college game with his family in the stands, Travis lost his balance while trying to put a little something extra into a check. He hit the end boards with the top of his helmet and fell to the ice like a rag doll, utterly inert.

"It looked scary," says Tim Pratt, Travis's coach for two years at Tabor Academy in Marion, Mass. Pratt had driven up to see his former star player's first Division I game. "But I've been around hockey my whole life. You're used to scary moments that turn out all right. But the longer it went on, the scarier it became."

"I thought it was a shoulder or an arm," says Brenda Roy, Travis's mother, an assistant high school principal. "We're trained after all these years that if the boy goes down, you sit. Lee never panics. But Lee went down to the ice fairly quickly. I thought, If it's a shoulder, darn, he'll miss a few games. Maybe the season. After all that hard work. Then my daughter, Tobi, said she wasn't going to sit there any longer, and she went down. I told her I'd wait. I was still thinking, He'll roll over. Then Lee called me down, and I knew it must really be something."

One of Travis's roommates, defenseman Dan Ronan, was on the ice when the accident happened. "He was lying so still, I automatically thought he'd been KO'd, because his chin was flat on the ice," Ronan says. "That ice is cold. I was thinking, If he were conscious, he'd get his chin off the ice. But when I finally went over to him, I saw his eyes were wide-open."

Lee Roy had walked down to the end of the rink. He replayed the missed check in his mind. Travis had wanted to pop somebody right off, to show that he belonged. Someone came up to Lee and said, "Are you Mr. Roy? Travis wants to talk to you."

Lee shuffled onto the ice, hoping his son had suffered a broken arm or a separated shoulder. Deep down, though, he must have known. "I think Travis was looking for a friendly face," he says. "I wanted to sound upbeat, so I said, 'Hey, boy, let's get going. There's a hockey game to play.' But when I got down on the ice next to him, he said, 'Dad, I'm in deep ----. I can't feel my arms or legs. My neck hurts.' I was trying to think of something positive to say back. Then Travis looked me right in the eyes and said, 'But Dad. I made it.'" Lee's pale blue eyes fill with tears as he recounts this, and shaking his head, he starts to weep. "I said, 'You're right, son. You did.' It didn't last long. Eleven seconds. But he made it."

CRACKED VERTEBRAE left Roy—known as a small kid who played big—paralyzed from the neck down. His foundation now benefits victims of spinal cord injuries.

BILL BELKNAP/THE BOSTON HERALD

1963 | THE RED WINGS' Floyd Smith had an inside track on this loose puck; more than a decade later he engaged in another spirited chase—to the Stanley Cup finals as coach of the Sabres. | *Photograph by* JOHN G. ZIMMERMAN

3
37
64
BAUER
BAUER
BAUER
EASTON
Reebok

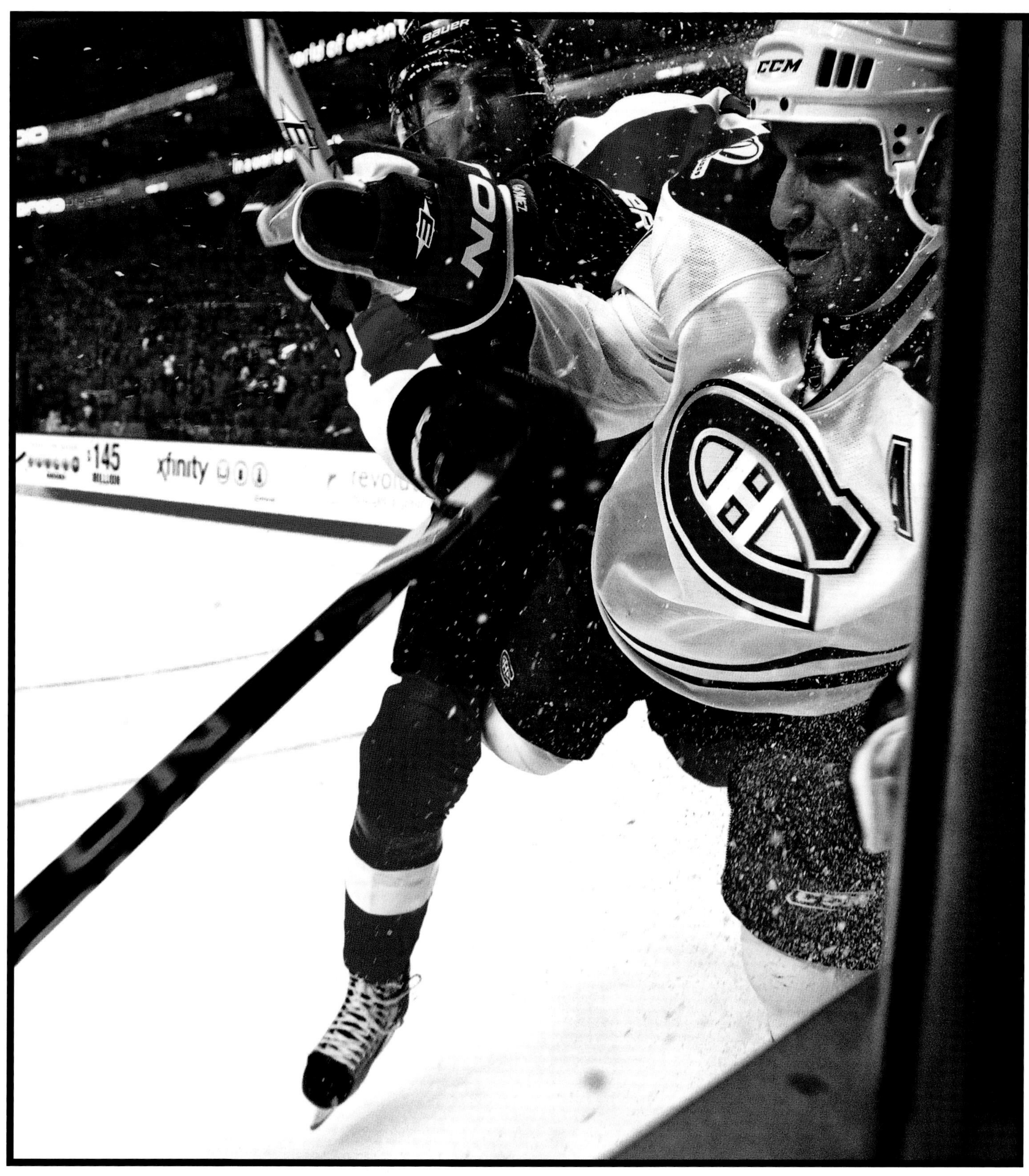

2010 | CORNER LAYOUT Braydon Coburn and the Flyers pushed aside Scott Gomez and the Canadiens in the Eastern Conference finals. | *Photograph by* LOU CAPOZZOLA

2010 | SHARK SANDWICH Though San Jose closed in on Chicago's Ben Eager (55), he and the Hawks easily escaped—with a playoff sweep. | *Photograph by* ROBERT BECK

Gretzky

1979–80 *through* 1990–91

AT AGE 19, in 1979–80, Wayne Gretzky had 137 points as an NHL rookie. At 23 he won the first of his four Stanley Cups with the inimitable Oilers. At 27 he was sent to L.A. where he would lift the Kings and soon help put the NHL on the map, literally, across the southern U.S.A.

Photograph by PAUL KENNEDY

>ALL-STARS OF THE ERA<

	FIRST TEAM	SECOND TEAM
LEFT WING	MARK MESSIER (OILERS, RANGERS)	MICHEL GOULET (NORDIQUES, BLACKHAWKS)
CENTER	WAYNE GRETZKY (OILERS, KINGS)	MARIO LEMIEUX (PENGUINS)
RIGHT WING	MIKE BOSSY (ISLANDERS)	BRETT HULL (BLUES, FLAMES)
DEFENSEMAN	LARRY ROBINSON (CANADIENS, KINGS)	PAUL COFFEY (OILERS, PENGUINS, KINGS)
DEFENSEMAN	RAY BOURQUE (BRUINS)	SLAVA FETISOV (CSKA MOSCOW, SOVIET RED ARMY, DEVILS)
GOALIE	GRANT FUHR (OILERS, MAPLE LEAFS)	BILLY SMITH (ISLANDERS)

COACH
GLEN SATHER
OILERS

>NICKNAMES<

Brett [the Golden Brett] Hull ^
Eddie [the Eagle] Belfour
Tahir [Tie] Domi
Bob [Frosty] Froese
Doug [Killer] Gilmour
Wayne [the Great One] Gretzky
Stu [the Grim Reaper] Grimson
Ed [Boxcar] Hospodar
Al [Wild Thing] Iafrate
[Super] Mario Lemieux
[Captain] Kirk McLean
Mark [Moose] Messier
Ken [Wolfman] Morrow
Mats [le Petit Viking] Naslund
Chris [Knuckles] Nilan
Glenn [Chico] Resch
[Lucky] Luc Robitaille
Teemu [the Finnish Flash] Selanne
Brent [Pup] Sutter
Duane [Dog] Sutter
Pat [Little Ball of Hate] Verbeek

STATISTICAL LEADERS

GOALS	
WAYNE GRETZKY	718
MIKE GARTNER	498
MICHEL GOULET	487
JARI KURRI	474
MIKE BOSSY	451

ASSISTS	
WAYNE GRETZKY	1,424
PAUL COFFEY	738
PETER STASTNY	716
DENIS SAVARD	693
RAY BOURQUE	683

POINTS (ALL SKATERS)	
WAYNE GRETZKY	2,142
PETER STASTNY	1,119
DENIS SAVARD	1,072
PAUL COFFEY	1,045
JARI KURRI	1,043

POINTS (DEFENSEMEN)	
PAUL COFFEY	1,045
RAY BOURQUE	934
DOUG WILSON	719
LARRY MURPHY	672
MARK HOWE	653

GOALIE WINS	
MIKE LIUT	283
PETE PEETERS	245
GRANT FUHR	226
REGGIE LEMELIN	218
ANDY MOOG	214

GOALS AGAINST AVERAGE*	
PETE PEETERS	3.08
RICK WAMSLEY	3.29
BILLY SMITH	3.34
ANDY MOOG	3.37
PAT RIGGIN	3.43

*MINIMUM 300 NHL GAMES

>>WISH YOU WERE THERE

U.S.A. 4, Soviet Union 3 >

FEBRUARY 22, 1980 • OLYMPIC FIELD HOUSE, LAKE PLACID, N.Y. The Cold War plays backdrop for what is expected to be a lopsided Olympic semifinal, but U.S. captain Mike Eruzione scores the go-ahead goal with 10 minutes left in the third period. Then goalie Jim Craig stops an onslaught of shots by the U.S.S.R., preserving the most unlikely upset in hockey history for a group of upstart collegians.

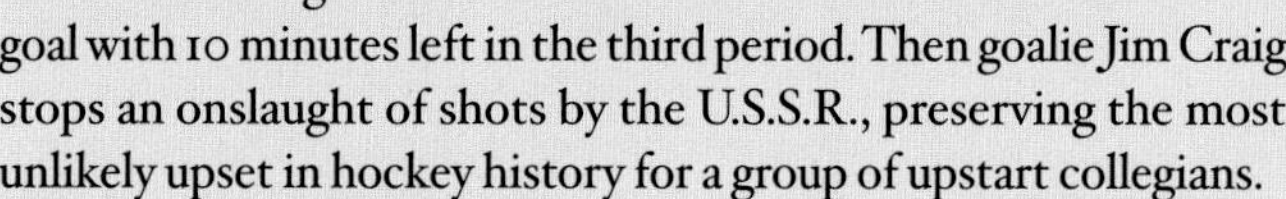

Islanders 5, Flyers 4 (OT)

MAY 24, 1980 • NASSAU COLISEUM, UNIONDALE, N.Y. Bobby Nystrom redirects a pass from John Tonelli to beat Flyers goalie Pete Peeters with 7:11 gone in overtime in a deciding Game 6 of the 1980 Stanley Cup finals—the first of four straight Cups for the Islanders.

Canada 6, Soviet Union 5 (2OT)

SEPTEMBER 13, 1987 • COPPS COLISEUM, HAMILTON, ONT. With Canada down a game in the best-of-three Canada Cup series Wayne Gretzky puts his homeland on his back, racking up five assists including a setup at 10:07 of a second extra session for fellow icon Mario Lemieux—his third goal of the game—to force a Game 3. Canada won that one 6–5 too.

Islanders 3, Capitals 2 (4OT)

APRIL 18 & 19, 1987 • CAPITAL CENTRE, LANDOVER, MD. Kelly Hrudey stops 73 shots and Pat LaFontaine's 35-foot turnaround shot ends the longest NHL game in 44 years (128 minutes, 47 seconds), in the Islanders' Game 7 Patrick Division semifinal victory.

Oilers 7, Flyers 5

DECEMBER 30, 1981 • NORTHLANDS COLISEUM, EDMONTON Wayne Gretzky's empty-netter, his fifth goal of the evening, gives him 50 for the season in just the Oilers' 39th game. That obliterates the NHL record of 50 goals in 50 games set by Maurice Richard in 1944–45 and matched by Mike Bossy in '80–81.

Penguins 8, Devils 6

DECEMBER 31, 1988 • CIVIC ARENA, PITTSBURGH Mario Lemieux becomes the first and still only NHL player in history to score a goal five different ways: at even-strength, shorthanded, on the power play, on a penalty shot and into an empty net.

Flyers 5, Bruins 2

DECEMBER 8, 1987 • THE SPECTRUM, PHILADELPHIA Philadelphia's Ron Hextall makes history as the first NHL goalie to shoot and score a goal when his length-of-the-ice flip slides into Boston's empty net.

Kings 6, Oilers 5 (OT)

APRIL 10, 1982 • THE FORUM, LOS ANGELES The heavily favored Gretzky-led Oilers go up 5–0 on the Kings after two periods in Game 3 of a first-round playoff series. But L.A. comes alive, getting goals from five players to tie the game when Steve Bozek knocks a rebound past Grant Fuhr with five seconds left in regulation. Winger Daryl Evans completes the greatest comeback in NHL playoff history by blasting a 30-footer past Fuhr with 2:35 gone in overtime. L.A. then ousts the Oilers in five games.

>MAYHEM MOMENT

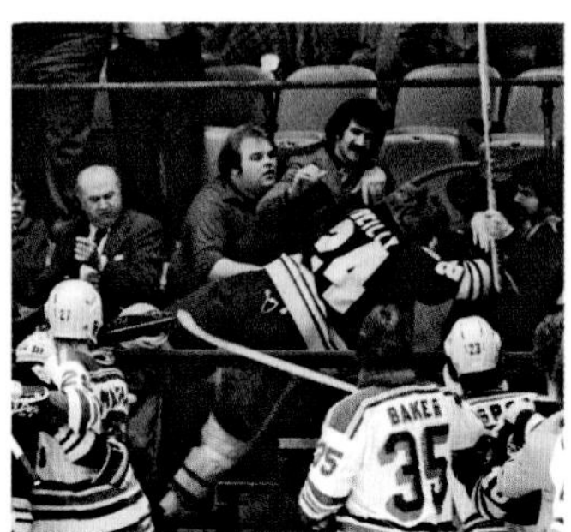

DECEMBER 23, 1979

Madison Square Garden, N.Y.C.

Led by captain Terry O'Reilly (24) members of the Bruins vault over the glass and into the Madison Square Garden seats after a spectator grabs Boston forward Stan Jonathan's stick and hits him with it. Defenseman Mike Milbury, who is in the locker room when the melee begins, emerges, joins in and winds up beating a man with the man's own shoe.

> "It's unbelievable that after more than 30 years in the game, pummeling a guy with his loafer will be my legacy. But I guess it's better than having no legacy at all."
>
> —*Mike Milbury, 2004*

> TEAMS OF THE ERA

^

EDMONTON OILERS

Featuring the NHL's alltime greatest scorer, Wayne Gretzky, the former WHA franchise was more than just the most explosive goal-scoring team the NHL had ever seen. They were champions, winning five Stanley Cups in seven years, including in 1989–90 after Gretzky had been traded to L.A. Gretzky (with Cup) and Mark Messier won 10 of 11 Hart Trophies awarded between '79–80 and '89–90, while Paul Coffey won two Norrises.

NEW YORK ISLANDERS

Built through the amateur draft by general manager Bill Torrey and coach Al Arbour, the Islanders made a meteoric rise after joining the NHL in 1972, quickly becoming competitive and then becoming dominant. The team won four straight Stanley Cups from 1980 to '83. The first line of Bryan Trottier, Mike Bossy and Clark Gillies are all members of the Hall of Fame as are goalie Billy Smith and defenseman Denis Potvin.

1980 U.S. OLYMPIC TEAM

Although only together for about six months, the ragtag bunch assembled by coach Herb Brooks club achieved the most monumental and least anticipated upset in hockey history. Amateurs at the time of the Lake Placid Games, 13 of the U.S. heroes went on to NHL careers, including defenseman Ken Morrow who immediately followed up his gold medal with four consecutive Stanley Cups as a member of the Islanders.

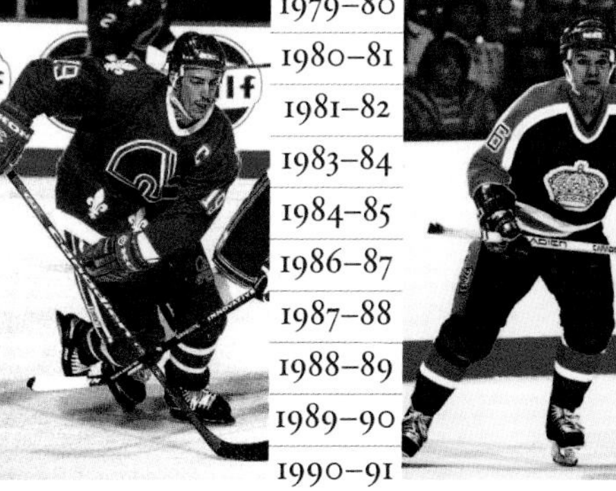

[DEBUT]		[FINALE]
Wayne Gretzky	1979–80	Gordie Howe
Paul Coffey	1980–81	Phil Esposito
Ron Francis	1981–82	Dave Keon
Steve Yzerman	1983–84	Bobby Clarke
Mario Lemieux	1984–85	Darryl Sittler
Luc Robitaille	1986–87	Mike Bossy
Brian Leetch	1987–88	Denis Potvin
Joe Sakic >	1988–89	< Marcel Dionne
Mike Modano	1989–90	Bernie Federko
Jaromir Jagr	1990–91	Guy Lafleur

> BY THE NUMBERS

3 | Overall draft position for St. John's Prep's (Mass.) center Bobby Carpenter, taken by the Washington Capitals in the 1981 entry draft as the first-ever U.S.–born first-round pick.

964 | Consecutive games played by forward Doug Jarvis, an NHL record. His streak started in 1975 with the Canadiens and ended in '87 with the Hartford Whalers.

35 | Consecutive games without a loss for the 1979–80 Flyers, an NHL record. Philadelphia went 25-0-10 between Oct. 14 and Jan. 6.

116 | NCAA single-season record points total (46 goals, 70 assists) scored by North Dakota's Tony Hrkac in 48 games in 1986–87.

234 | Points scored (104 goals, 130 assists) by Pat LaFontaine of Verdun in the QMJHL in the 1982–83 season, a total bettered only by Mario Lemieux and Pierre Larouche.

3 | Straight years (1989 through '91) that the Quebec Nordiques made the No. 1 selection in the entry draft. They chose Mats Sundin, Owen Nolan and Eric Lindros.

> PATRICK FACTOR

In 1982 Dick Patrick, the son of Muzz and the grandson of Lester, becomes president of the Capitals, a team that has had no playoff berths in its eight seasons of existence. Under Dick's watch, however, the Caps make the playoffs 21 times in 27 years. He would go on to become part-owner in '99.

1989–96 | BRIAN LEETCH, one of the NHL's swiftest defensemen, wore these skates while winning the Conn Smythe with the Rangers in '94. | *Photograph by* DAVID N. BERKWITZ

2002 | SCOTT STEVENS, the '00 Conn Smythe winner with the Devils, went blades up in this playoff collision with Carolina's Rod Brind'Amour. | *Photograph by* KENT SMITH

COURTESY OF HOCKEY HALL OF FAME

OMPUWARE
Energy
HESPE
BAUER
EAST

THE PANTHEON >> *Goaltenders*

SI's TOP 25

Ed Belfour
Frank Brimsek
Turk Broda
Alex Connell
Clint Benedict
Johnny Bower
Martin Brodeur
Ken Dryden
Bill Durnan
Tony Esposito
Grant Fuhr
Ed Giacomin
George Hainsworth
Glenn Hall
Dominik Hasek
Harry Lumley
Bernie Parent >
Jacques Plante
Patrick Roy
Terry Sawchuk
Billy Smith
Tiny Thompson
Vladislav Tretiak
Georges Vézina
Gump Worsley

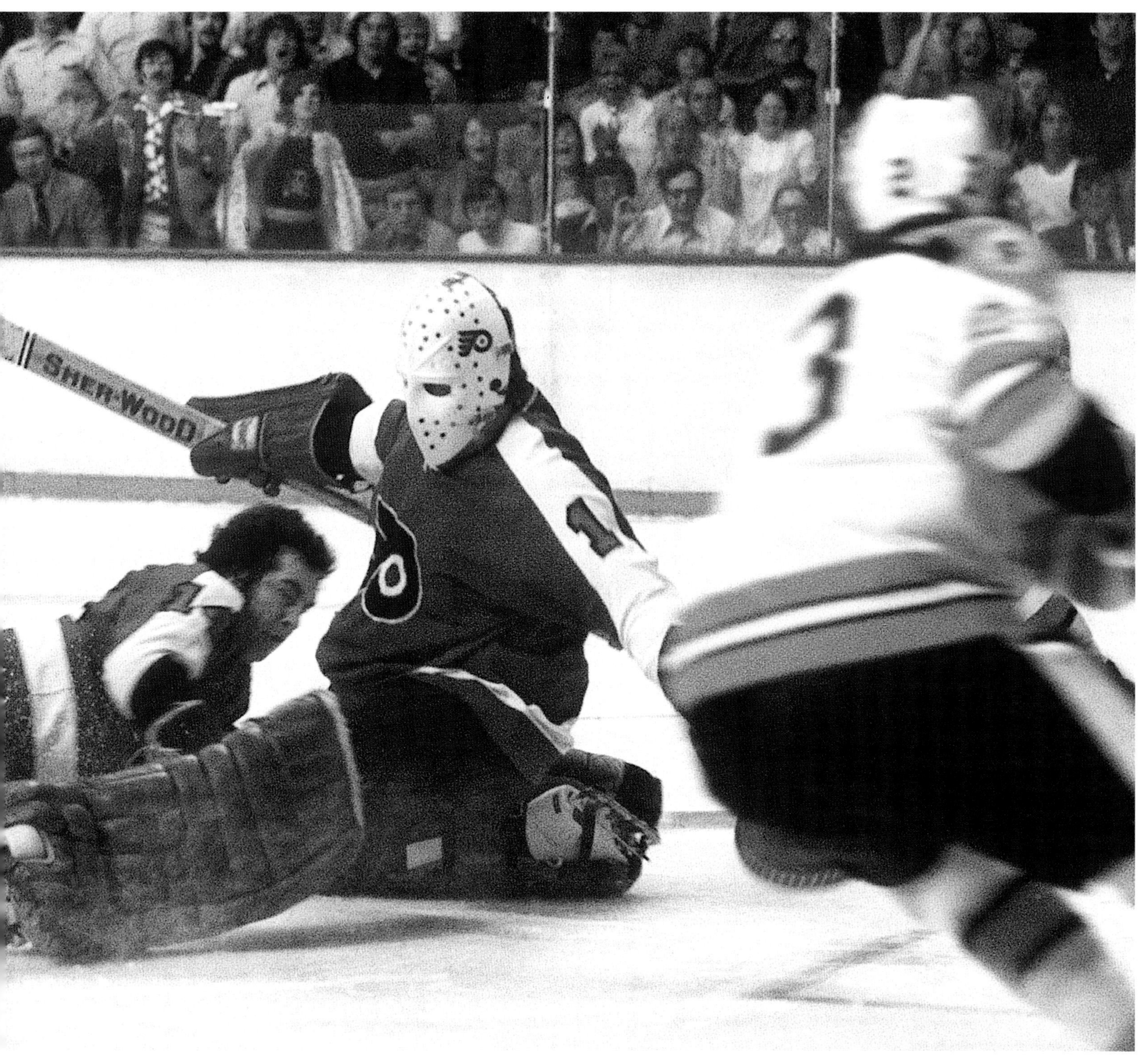

1974 | PHILADELPHIA'S PARENT kicked aside Boston in the finals and won the first of two Cups, two Conn Smythe awards and two Vezina trophies. | *Photograph by* TONY TRIOLO

THE PIONEER...

BY MICHAEL FARBER

Still dominant in his 17th season, Patrick Roy had changed the face of modern goaltending. —*from* SI, APRIL 8, 2002

THE HOUR WAS LATE, THE TAB was open, and, as he gazed across a New York City saloon at Patrick Roy earlier this season, Greg de Vries uttered the type of declarative statement often heard in that kind of place and at that time of night. "We are playing with the greatest goalie who ever lived," De Vries announced to fellow Colorado Avalanche defenseman Rob Blake.

This is a wonderful bar-stool debate: Who is the best NHL netminder of all time? There's no indisputable proof, not even 86 proof. Roy's numbers are staggering—the 36-year-old Avalanche goalie has a record 514 NHL regular-season victories, having zoomed past Terry Sawchuck last season. Roy's four Stanley Cups, three Conn Smythe Trophies and three Vezina Trophies merely make his case robust, not bulletproof. Capitals general manager George McPhee says Roy, who is also the career leader in playoff wins (137), "could be the top money goalie ever," but to pronounce Roy the no-doubt-about-it best is to invite a whiskey rebellion from backers of a pair who starred 40 years ago: the pugnacious Sawchuk, whose 103 shutouts led Roy by 43, and the eccentric Jacques Plante, who won seven Vezina Trophies. No, we're taking this argument outside—outside the box of numbers and awards—by saying that Roy is the most important goalie in history.

Roy didn't write the book on goaltending. Plante did. And like most netminders of his generation, Roy read *Devant le Filet* (or: *In Front of the Net*), by the goaltender who popularized the use of the mask. But Roy redefined the position. He conquered the game with his pioneering butterfly style and he helped change goalie gear by working with Koho, which manufactures his pads, to make them lighter. "Roy revolutionized equipment," says Anaheim Mighty Ducks G.M. Pierre Gauthier. "Goalies are so good now because the equipment is better. Patrick did that."

Any goalkeeper who drops to his knees to cover the bottom of the net wearing six-pound leg pads rather than the old nine-pounders should genuflect to Roy. He was not the original butterfly goalie—Hall of Famers Glenn Hall and Tony Esposito used variations of the butterfly decades ago—but Roy made it the standard. He plays the percentages by taking away shots along the ice and forcing shooters to beat him top shelf. Roy has moved goaltending from the realm of artistry to that of science. He is, in that sense, the first modern goalie. "People mirror him," says Calgary Flames netminder Mike Vernon. "You can try to mirror someone's style, but it's what's inside that makes the player. With Patty, it's determination and will."

In the Colorado dressing room there have also been confirmed sightings of full-blown smiles and even dressing-room guffaws this season. "That's something you never saw before," says Avalanche winger Mike Keane, who has played with Roy for nine seasons in two cities. "This is a different Patrick. He's at the back end of his career and he doesn't want to be remembered just as the a------ who thought winning was the only thing."

The possibility that this is Roy's last year seems remote. Colorado will pay him $8.5 million next season, and his health, other than the occasional flare-up of arthritis in his hips, is good. There is no urgency for Roy to hang around to put the record for career victories out of the reach of 29-year-old Devils goalie Martin Brodeur, who trails Roy by 195, but there is no urgency to leave because of a decline in his play. This has been a career season for Roy. His goals-against average, which has dropped in each of the past five years, was 1.97 and his save percentage was .924. Any loss of quickness that has accompanied his advancing age has been fought to a stalemate by enhanced knowledge and a feral desire to compete.

Roy still seizes a moment. When he heard last June about a remark that Brodeur's wife, Melanie, had made about the Devils being close to winning the Cup after Game 5, Roy told Colorado coach Bob Hartley, "It's your job to figure out how to get us a goal [in Game 6] because I'm not letting in any." The Avalanche won that match 4–0 and the next 3–1 to close out the series.

The goalie who some thought wouldn't last a decade—"We figured with all the up and down, his knees would be shot," says Minnesota Wild G.M. Doug Risebrough—is better in his 17th season than his seventh. Roy, Plante, Sawchuk. Rock, paper, scissors. There is no correct answer to who among them is the alltime best, but the last word goes to Blake, who greeted De Vries's barroom proclamation with a sagacious nod. "In a must-win game," Blake said, "there'd be no goalie you'd take ahead of Patrick."

BEHIND ROY'S icy stare burns a fiery temper, as well as the unmatched will of a man who became the winningest playoff goalie of all time.

DAVID E. KLUTHO

33

...THE RECORD-BREAKER

BY MICHAEL FARBER

As he put up stats that no goalie—not even his rival Patrick Roy—had put up before, Martin Brodeur did it with a calmness and a style all his own. —*from* SI, MARCH 16, 2009

CONNECTIVE THREADS TIE the generations of the world's best goaltenders. The greats have played with masks on and without; they've faced shots that hugged the ice in the straight-bladed era and have parried today's high-tech slappers; they've played stand-up and butterfly. But these goalies, with rare exceptions, share a checklist of attributes: flexibility, hockey sense, a wellspring of fearlessness and, well, eccentricity. They also form a rogue's gallery of the maladjusted, as suited to *Psychology Today* as to *The Hockey News*. Jacques Plante, the backbone of the Canadiens' 1950s dynasty, was fretful and liked to knit. It was never really Happy Hour when Red Wings goalie Terry Sawchuk, who died in 1970 at age 40 from complications sustained in an alcohol-fueled fight with a teammate, walked into a bar. Glenn Hall, who played 502 straight games from 1955 to '62 and had 407 career wins, felt better when he was physically ill and threw up before games. The tempestuous Patrick Roy, who has an record 151 playoff wins, asked the Canadiens president during a 1995 game to trade him; three years later in Colorado he smashed TVs in a coach's office after being yanked from a game and missing out on a win.

Then there is the goalie who may go down as the Greatest of All Time. Three shy of Roy's record of 551 regular-season wins and three shutouts behind Sawchuk's record of 103, the Devils' Martin Brodeur is the most balanced of the men who rank among the elite. He is garrulous and engaging and he appears more than, in hockey's favorite phrase, "normal . . . for a goalie." He seems normal for almost anybody. "There's Marty after the second period, having his Sprite and half a bagel, working on a shutout, and talking and joking with the guys in the room," says former New Jersey teammate Sheldon Souray. "Then he'll go out and stop 10 shots in the third. There's a calmness about him."

As victories and shutouts add up, the issue is not whether a seemingly nice guy will finish first but how high on the top shelf Brodeur will store those records. His contract takes him through 2011–12, when he will turn 40 during the playoffs. Assuming good health, he is capable of creating a statistical case that has enough weight to crush any challenger. All Brodeur may be missing is a career-defining moment—something akin to Roy's 10 straight overtime playoff wins in 1993.

"A rivalry between two French guys," is how a former NHL goalie describes the relationship between Brodeur and Roy, and while that contains some truth, it barely hints at the complexity. To posit that they dislike each other is no more illuminating because they really don't, at least not in a Carolina-Duke kind of way. "My relationship with Patrick is good," Brodeur says. "If we see each other, we'll take the time to say 'Hi.' But I don't have his number and he doesn't have mine."

Case A in the Brodeur-Roy Passive-Aggressive Handbook: When Roy was asked after his 2003 retirement to name the next great goalies, he mentioned Anaheim's Jean-Sébastien Giguère and Florida's Roberto Luongo but not Brodeur. "The reason," Roy says now, "is I thought Marty was already there." Brodeur claims not to recall the incident, but a former teammate insists the goalie was stung by the perceived slight.

Case B: Brodeur often expresses disdain for the butterfly, a technique that allows a splay-legged goalie to cover the lower part of the net. Brodeur is the antibutterflyer, tracking the puck and standing up, dropping to one knee or even stacking his pads to stop it. Of course, whenever Brodeur, who as a teenager bolted the goalie school run by Roy's guru, François Allaire, dismisses the butterfly style, he is also prodding its progenitor, Roy.

The origins of the distant relationship are not clear but probably date to the 1998 Nagano Olympics. Brodeur says that on the flight to Japan, Team Canada coach Marc Crawford, who was also Roy's coach in Colorado, told Brodeur that he would not play in the Games. "I'll never do that to a guy," says Brodeur. He's referring to Roy, not Crawford. "I don't know if he said it or his coach . . . but the decision was made before we even skated."

Still, Brodeur says, "It's hard not to appreciate Patrick. For me, he's the top goalie, the guy I looked up to. . . . We're just two competitors. He was there first. I was just the one trying to push him off some of the records."

Roy and Brodeur—or should it be Brodeur and Roy?—will soon converge at 551. And then Brodeur will wave goodbye, taking goaltending numbers to places over the horizon.

UNFLINCHING in the face of pressure (as his three Stanley Cups attest), Brodeur amassed his monumental NHL statistics playing for one team, the Devils.

AL BELLO/GETTY IMAGES

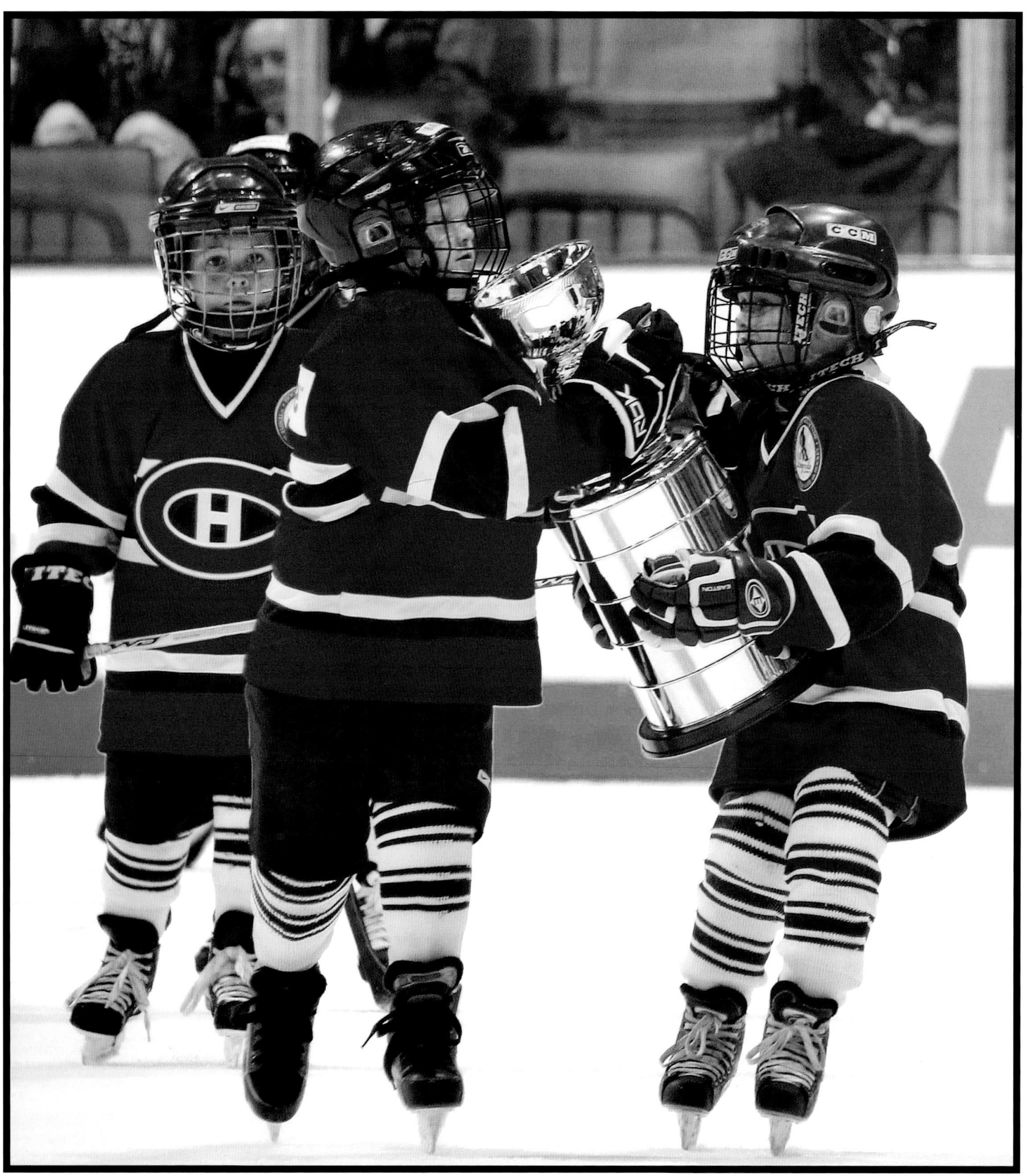

2008 | SOMEDAY THESE MITES, here at the Legends Classic in Toronto, may be wearing real Habs jerseys—and clutching the real Stanley Cup. | *Photograph by* BRUCE BENNETT

1980 | IT NEVER GETS OLD: Denis Potvin revels in the Islanders' first Stanley Cup win. The team would capture three more in a row. | *Photograph by* BRUCE BENNETT STUDIOS

NY
ISLANDERS
NY
ISLANDERS

c. 1943 | BRUINS CENTER Norm Calladine (7) played 63 games over three seasons, in which time he learned to brave even the heaviest New York traffic. | *Photograph by* BROWN BROTHERS

KINGS
A
33
KOHO

OVER THE EDGE

BY KOSTYA KENNEDY

Marty McSorley was vilified and given an unprecedented ban for his slash to the head of Donald Brashear. In the NHL, were such moments inevitable? —*from* SI, NOVEMBER 20, 2000

THE EMBODIMENT OF NHL evil has blue eyes, blond hair and cheeks that are pink from the sun. He wears a silver ring on the little finger of his right hand, and he lunches on salad and quiche. He's 37 years old, stands 6' 1", weighs 235 pounds, and his name is Martin James McSorley, though he's better known to fans, league executives and Canadian prosecutors as Marty.

You've seen the footage. The video clip of the blow led not only sports highlights shows but also late news telecasts across North America after the Feb. 21 game. The Bruins' McSorley, skating through the neutral zone, approaches the Canucks' Donald Brashear, who is gliding without the puck, from behind. With a quick, hard swing of his stick, McSorley clubs Brashear on the side of his face. Brashear's 6' 2", 225-pound body drops like a sack of stones. His helmet springs loose and, upon landing, the back of his skull hits the ice. Brashear lies motionless for a moment and then begins to convulse. He would be carried off on a stretcher, spend the night in a hospital and miss 20 games.

The moment Brashear went down, the slash became the defining moment of McSorley's long career. He was suspended indefinitely and last week, responding to McSorley's petition for reinstatement, NHL commissioner Gary Bettman extended that ban to "one calendar year," by far the longest in NHL history. British Columbia prosecutors felt strongly enough to charge him with assault with a weapon. Judge William Kitchen's finding of guilt—McSorley received a "conditional discharge" and his only punishment was being forbidden to play in a sporting event against Brashear for 18 months—rested in his judgment that "Brashear was struck as intended."

McSorley hates that. He says he never meant to hit Brashear in the head. He says he was aiming for the shoulder in an attempt to goad Brashear into a fight. (The two enforcers had fought earlier in the game and afterward Brashear had taunted McSorley and the Bruins.) In fact McSorley's stick brushed the top of Brashear's right shoulder before crashing into his face. "I take responsibility for what happened," says McSorley. "I feel bad Donald got hurt. But when somebody says that I intentionally struck him in the head with my stick, I have an issue . . . that goes to the core of who I am and the player I've been."

McSorley's 3,381 career penalty minutes are the third most in NHL history. Before the Brashear incident he had been suspended seven times for acts ranging from cross-checking an opponent in the forehead to gouging a rival's eye during a fight to spearing. "I have no halo," he says.

Yet in the vigilante world of the NHL it is no paradox that many coaches and players still respect McSorley. During his prime he was one of the game's best fighters. As Wayne Gretzky's teammate for three seasons with the Oilers and another eight with the Kings, he regularly punched out players who dared rough up the Great One. McSorley also taught himself to play well. Though he possessed marginal talent and was never drafted, he developed into one of the league's better defensemen. Would he have reached the NHL without his fighting ability? "I would not have made Junior A," he says.

"Marty plays on the edge," says the Flyers' Rick Tocchet. "That's his role. He got too close to the edge, and a bad thing happened. It was bad, but anyone who says those kind of things never happen in hockey, well, that's just bull."

For all the impact that hockey's culture of violence had upon that night, the event, finally, comes to this: Intentionally or not, McSorley bludgeoned Brashear, who might have died. "I still get headaches; I still get tired," Brashear says. "This thing keeps following me."

While several NHL general managers speak favorably of McSorley and his ability, they stop short of saying that they would sign him. "I'd love to play again," McSorley says, "but if I can't, I'll go on. I believe that my peers and the people in the game understand what happened that night. What anyone else thinks, I can't control."

YEARS BEFORE the Brashear hit, McSorley guarded Gretzky in L.A., where in '92–93 McSorley had 15 goals and 399 penalty minutes, and the Kings got to the Cup final.

ROBERT BECK

> Wayne's World

Prelude to Greatness

At age two Wayne Gretzky slipped on his first pair of skates (below) and was on his way. By 11 he was a prolific scorer and a captain. By the time he was a young Oiler he was an icon

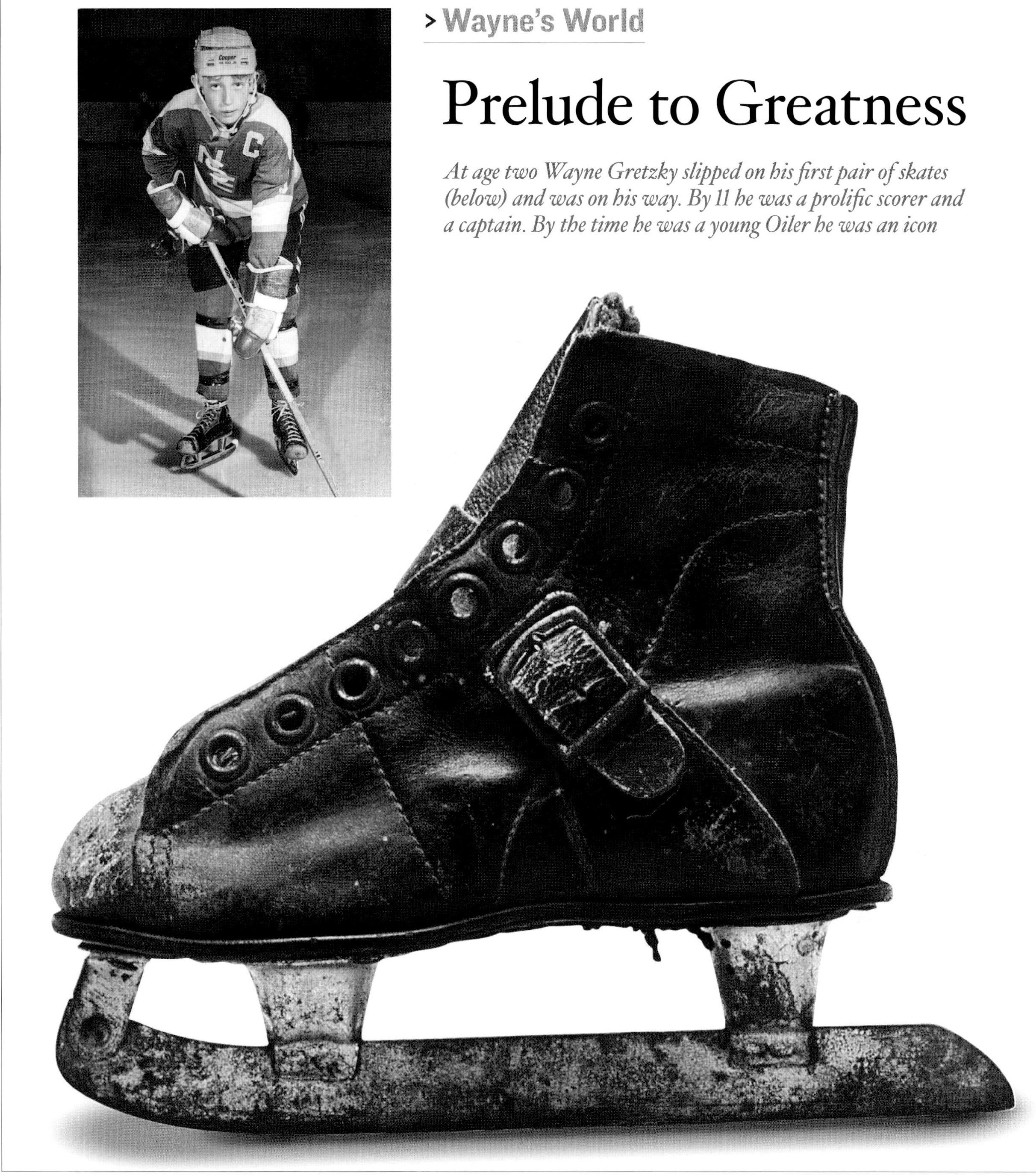

PETER SIBBALD (SKATES); AP (AS CHILD); PAUL BERESWILL (AS OILER)

JOFA

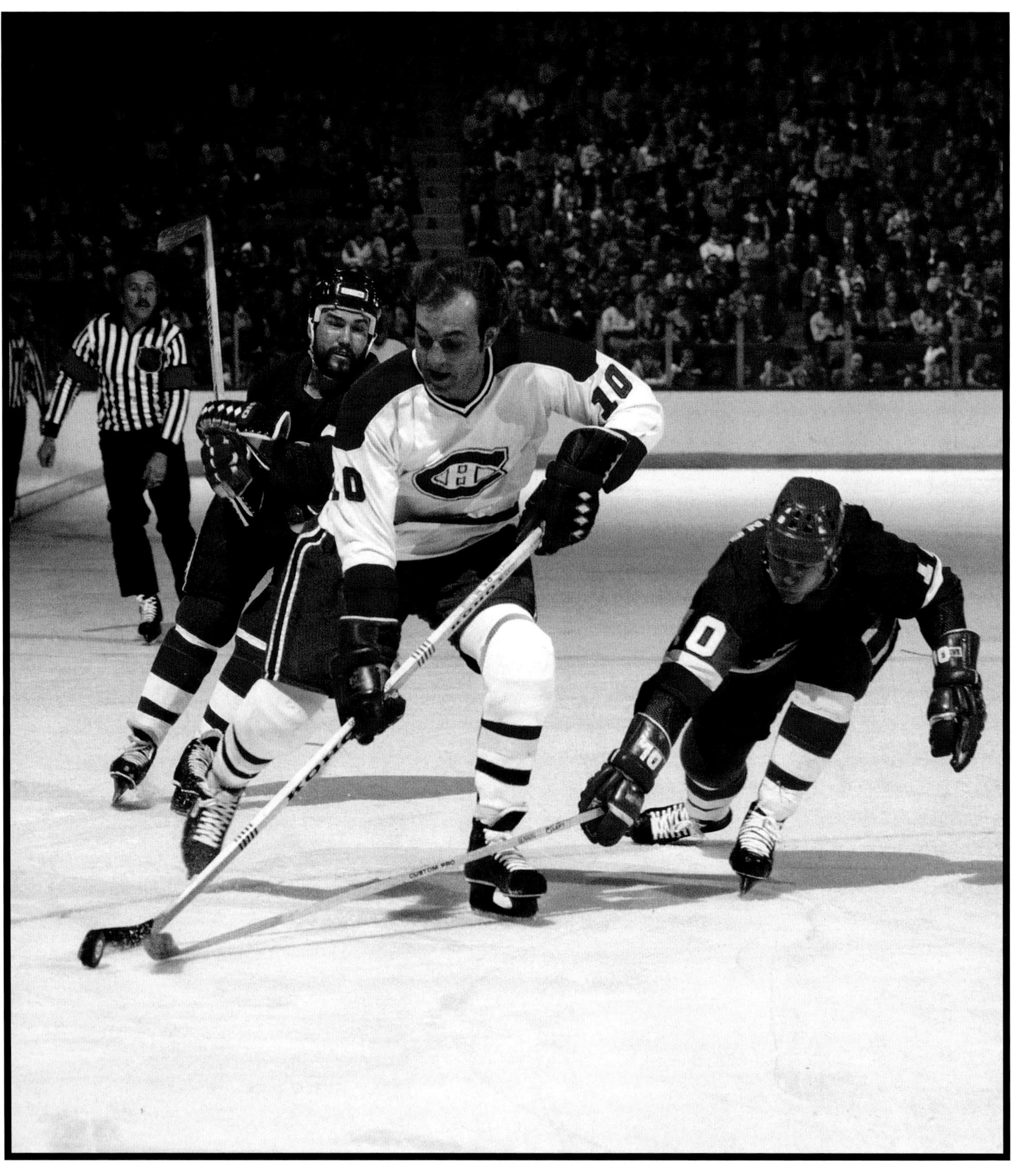

1978 | IN FULL BLOOM. Guy Lafleur had just won the Hart Trophy and was en route to scoring 52 goals, his fifth straight season with 50 or more. | *Photograph by* MANNY MILLAN

1970 | ON-ICE ESPOS. As if they were back home in Sault Ste. Marie, Phil Esposito, a Bruin, tries to score on brother Tony, a butterflying Black Hawk. | *Photograph by* DICK RAPHAEL

SUTTER CLUTTER

BY LEIGH MONTVILLE

Six brothers. One NHL game. Zero horsing around. There had never been anything like it. —*from* SI, NOVEMBER, 25, 1991

Q. *Can we go through this slowly?*
A. O.K., from the top. Brian Sutter is the head coach of the St. Louis Blues. Darryl Sutter is the associate coach of the Chicago Blackhawks. Rich and Ron Sutter play for the Blues. Brent Sutter plays for the Blackhawks. All five brothers were working in one NHL game at Chicago Stadium, a 5–1 win for the Blackhawks. A sixth brother, Duane, also is employed by Chicago as a scout.

Q. *So six Sutters were involved, in some way, in the same game?*
A. Six.

Q. *Is this an NHL Sutter record?*
A. This is the record. It will be listed as Most Sutters Involved, One Game: Six. The previous record was Most Sutters Involved, One Game: Five. That was set Oct. 19 when Chicago played at St. Louis. Brent has joined the Blackhawks since that game as part of a trade with the New York Islanders.

Q. *Can you tell us about the Sutters playing careers?*
A. Sutters have played in 4,294 NHL games. That is more than 50 seasons. Sutters have scored 1,265 goals and 2,736 points and spent more than 120 hours in the penalty box. There is no data on how many skates they have worn out or sticks they have broken. The biggest scorer, Brian, had 303 goals, 636 points, but Brent should pass him in both categories by the end of the season.

Q. *Brian is the oldest?*
A. Brian is the oldest of the hockey players. There is a seventh brother, Gary, who did not play pro hockey. He works for the highway commission back home in Viking, Alberta. Brian played 12 seasons for the Blues and was named their coach when he retired in 1988. He was the NHL Coach of the Year last season.

Q. *The others simply followed Brian?*
A. The brothers are close in age, all seven (there are no girls) born within 10 years on a 640-acre farm near Viking. Brian set a no-nonsense standard. These are not exactly the Marx Brothers, giving each other hotfoots or honking horns and spraying seltzer water. They don't smile a lot. They work hockey as if they were working on the farm. Brian showed that work could bring results. Darryl remembers thinking for the first time that he possibly could play in the NHL when Brian made the NHL.

Q. *They all play the same way?*
A. Ron Caron, the G.M. of the Blues, was asked if he would like a team of, say, 20 Sutters. "Well," he said, "you'd probably want some speed somewhere . . . and some puckhandling . . . ." The Sutter game has been to bump and disrupt, to knock people from the other team off the puck and give it to people on the Sutter team. No Sutters have been stylists. They are hockey workers.

Q. *How did they act, all involved in the one game? Were they excited?*
A. Not really. They feel as if they have been playing on the same team or against each other forever. There might have been a jolt of excitement back in 1984 when the youngest brothers, the twins, Rich and Ron, played for the Philadelphia Flyers and Brent and Duane played for the Islanders (Most Sutters On Ice, One Game: Four), but that was long ago. Ron said one bad part of a hockey job is that you lose the hockey fun, that there can be no joking around, that "hockey is a business and you have to play each game as if you might never play another one."

Q. *They didn't talk to each other on the ice? Stuff like that?*
A. Hardly. Ron and Brent are centers so they played against each other the most. They played the way most brothers play against each other in the backyard. They raised their sticks and looked like they gladly would have taken each other's head off. Ron said that he has patterned everything he does on the ice after Brent. Brent was his model, a fact he has never mentioned to Brent.

Q. *How would you like to broadcast one of these games?*
A. Here's a sample: Sutter sends Sutter out to replace Sutter to try to stop Sutter. What will Sutter do? Will he leave Sutter on the ice or make his own change? Sutter was doing all right against Sutter, but now he has to play against Sutter. How about the stars at the end of a game? First star, Sutter. Second star, Sutter. Third star, Sutter. Actually, none of the stars in this game were Sutter. Brent had the Sutters' only point, an assist in the third period.

Q. *Will the Most Sutters Involved record stand forever?*
A. Hard to say.

Q. *Hard to say?*
A. Brian is 35 and a head coach. Darryl, 33, and Duane, 31, look as if they'll stay in the game in some way. Brent is 29. The twins are 27. They're young, all of them married, and among them they already have 10 children. You look at their future and you realize that the league is expanding and . . . hard to say. Stocking a franchise would not seem out of the question. Maybe two.

ALL TOGETHER NOW: Pictured in their 1982–83 team jerseys, top row from left, Ron, Rich, Brent. Bottom row: Duane, Brian, Darryl.

NY
ISLANDERS
NY
ISLANDERS
C

1970 | A 21-YEAR-OLD Bobby Orr's attempt to help goalie Gerry Cheevers clear the puck from the Bruins' crease was a sweeping success. | *Photograph by* JOHN G. ZIMMERMAN

VISITOR
HOME
1 2 2
PENALTY TIME
10 1:20
14:53

JOHN ROSS ROACH *(right)*
Toronto St. Patricks 1921–22

CHARLIE GARDINER
Chicago Black Hawks 1927–1934

PATRICK LALIME
Ottawa Senators 1999–2004

HOCKEY HALL OF FAME

DAVID N. BERKWITZ; HOCKEY HALL OF FAME

> Artifacts

Stick Figures

Once made of maple or ash, now made of cutting-edge composites, these are the real shooting (and parrying) stars of the game

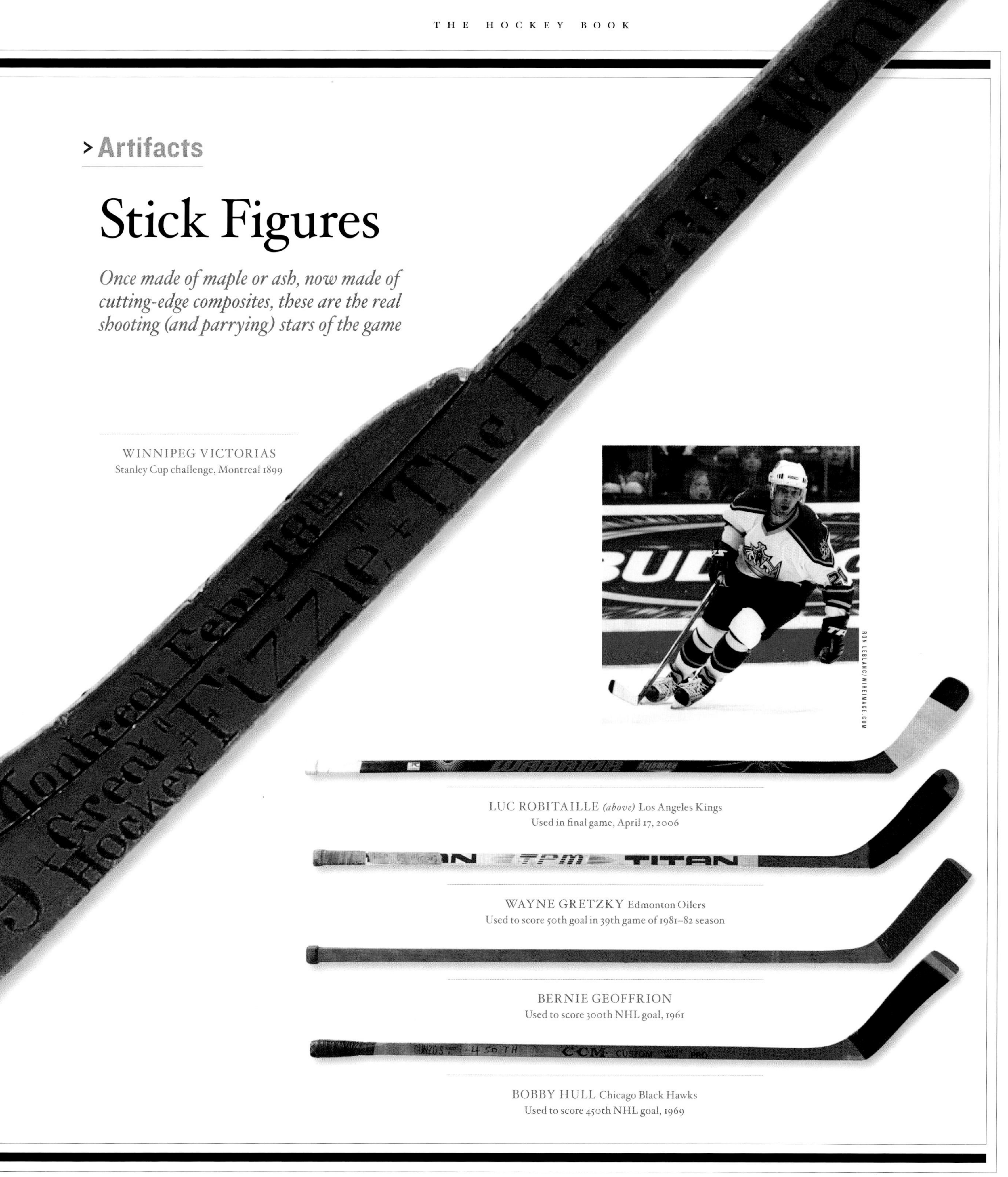

WINNIPEG VICTORIAS
Stanley Cup challenge, Montreal 1899

RON LEBLANC/WIREIMAGE.COM

LUC ROBITAILLE *(above)* Los Angeles Kings
Used in final game, April 17, 2006

WAYNE GRETZKY Edmonton Oilers
Used to score 50th goal in 39th game of 1981–82 season

BERNIE GEOFFRION
Used to score 300th NHL goal, 1961

BOBBY HULL Chicago Black Hawks
Used to score 450th NHL goal, 1969

FIRE ON ICE

BY HERBERT WARREN WIND

Of all the great athletes of our time none played his game with more skill, more color, more competitiveness and more heart than Maurice (Rocket) Richard. —*from* SI, DECEMBER 6, 1954

HOCKEY IS DEEP IN THE Montrealer's blood. After a fine play by a member of the home team or, for that matter, of the visiting team, the Forum reverberates from the rinkside to the rafters with sharp, enthusiastic applause. But many volts above this in feeling and many decibels above in volume is the singular and sudden pandemonium that shatters the Forum, like thunder and lightning, whenever the incomparable star of Les Canadiens, Maurice (Rocket) Richard, fights his way through the enemy defense and blasts the puck past the goalie. There is no sound quite like it in the whole world of sport.

A powerfully built athlete of 33 who stands 5' 10" and weighs 180 pounds, having put on about a pound a year since breaking in with Les Canadiens in 1942, Joseph Henri Maurice Richard, Gallicly handsome and eternally intense, is regarded by most aficionados, be they Montrealers or *étrangers*, as the greatest player in the history of hockey. Whether he is or not, of course, finally boils down to a matter of opinion. Yet as Richard's supporters invariably point out, hockey is in essence a game of scoring, and here there can be no argument: The Rocket stands in a class by himself, the outstanding scorer of all time. Flip through the pages of the record book: Most Goals—384, set by Maurice Richard in 12 seasons (with the next man, Nels Stewart, a full 60 goals away); Most Goals in One Season—50, set by Maurice Richard in a 50-game schedule in 1944–45; Most Goals in a Playoff Series—12, Maurice Richard; and so on and on.

It is not simply the multiplicity of Richard's goals nor their timeliness but, rather, the chronically spectacular manner in which he scores them that has made the fiery rightwinger the acknowledged Babe Ruth of hockey. "There are goals and there are Richard goals," remarked Dick Irvin, the old "Silver Fox" who has coached the Canadiens the length of Richard's career. "He doesn't get lucky goals. Let's see, he's scored over 390 now. Of these, 370 have had a flair. He can get to a puck and do things to it quicker than any man I've ever seen—even if he has to lug two defensemen with him. And his shots! They go in with such velocity that all of the net bulges."

One of the popular year-round pastimes in Montreal is talking over old Richard goals—which one you thought was the most neatly set up, which one stirred you the most, etc., much in the way Americans used to hot-stove about Ruth's home runs and do today about Willie Mays's catches. In Irvin's opinion—and Hector (Toe) Blake and Elmer Lach, Richard's teammates on the famous Punch Line also feel this way—the Rocket's most sensational goal was "the Seibert goal," in the 1945–46 season. Earl Seibert, a strapping 225-pound Detroit defenseman, hurled himself at Richard as he swept into the Red Wings zone. Richard occasionally will bend his head and neck very low when he is trying to outmaneuver a defenseman. He did on this play. The two collided with a thud, and as they straightened up, there was Richard, still on his feet, still controlling the puck, and, sitting on top of his shoulders, the burly Seibert. Richard not only carried Seibert with him on the way to the net, a tour de force in itself, but with that tremendous extra effort of which he is capable, faked the goalie out of position and with his one free hand somehow managed to hoist the puck into the far corner of the cage.

How does Le Rocket react to the adulation he receives after one of his goals? While the referee waits for the clamor to subside Richard cruises solemnly in slow circles, somewhat embarrassed by the ovation, his normally expressive dark eyes fixed on the ice. The slow circles add up to a brief moment of uncoiling, one of the few he ever allows himself. He is a terribly intense man, forever driving himself to come up to the almost impossible high standard of performance he sets.

For 10 years, because of his courage, his skill, and that magical uncultivatable quality, true magnetism, Richard has reigned in Montreal and throughout the province of Quebec as a hero whose hold on the public has no parallel in sport, unless it be the adoration that the people of Spain have from time to time heaped on their master matadors. The fact that 75% of the citizens of Montreal and a similar percentage of the Forum regulars are French-Canadians—a hero-hungry people who think of themselves not as the majority group in their province but as the minority group in Canada—goes quite a distance in explaining their idolatry of Richard. "Maurice Richard personifies French Canada and all that is great about it," an English-Canadian Richard follower declared last month. "But you know, you only have to be a lover of hockey to admire him."

RICHARD'S GOALS were often scored in spectacular, logic-defying fashion, building his legend and deflating opponents like the Red Wings.

HY PESKIN

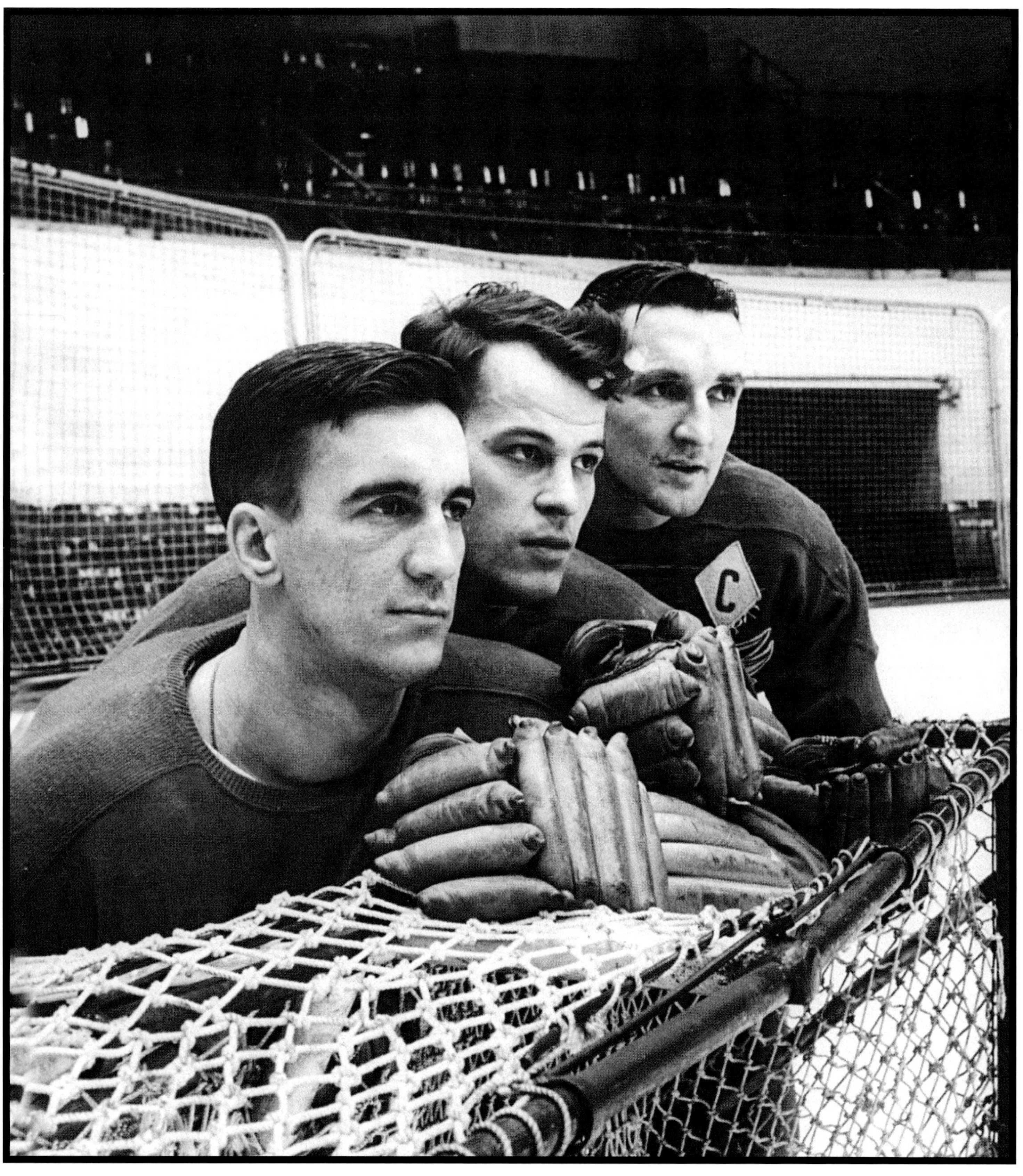

c. 1950 | DETROIT'S FAMED Production Line of (from left) Ted Lindsey, Gordie Howe and Sid Abel once again found the back of the net. | *Photograph by* HOWARD SOCHUREK

1967 | THE RANGERS' Jean Ratelle (19) and Rod Gilbert tried to cut off Henri Richard, whose Canadiens would cruise through this playoff series. | *Photograph by* JAMES DRAKE

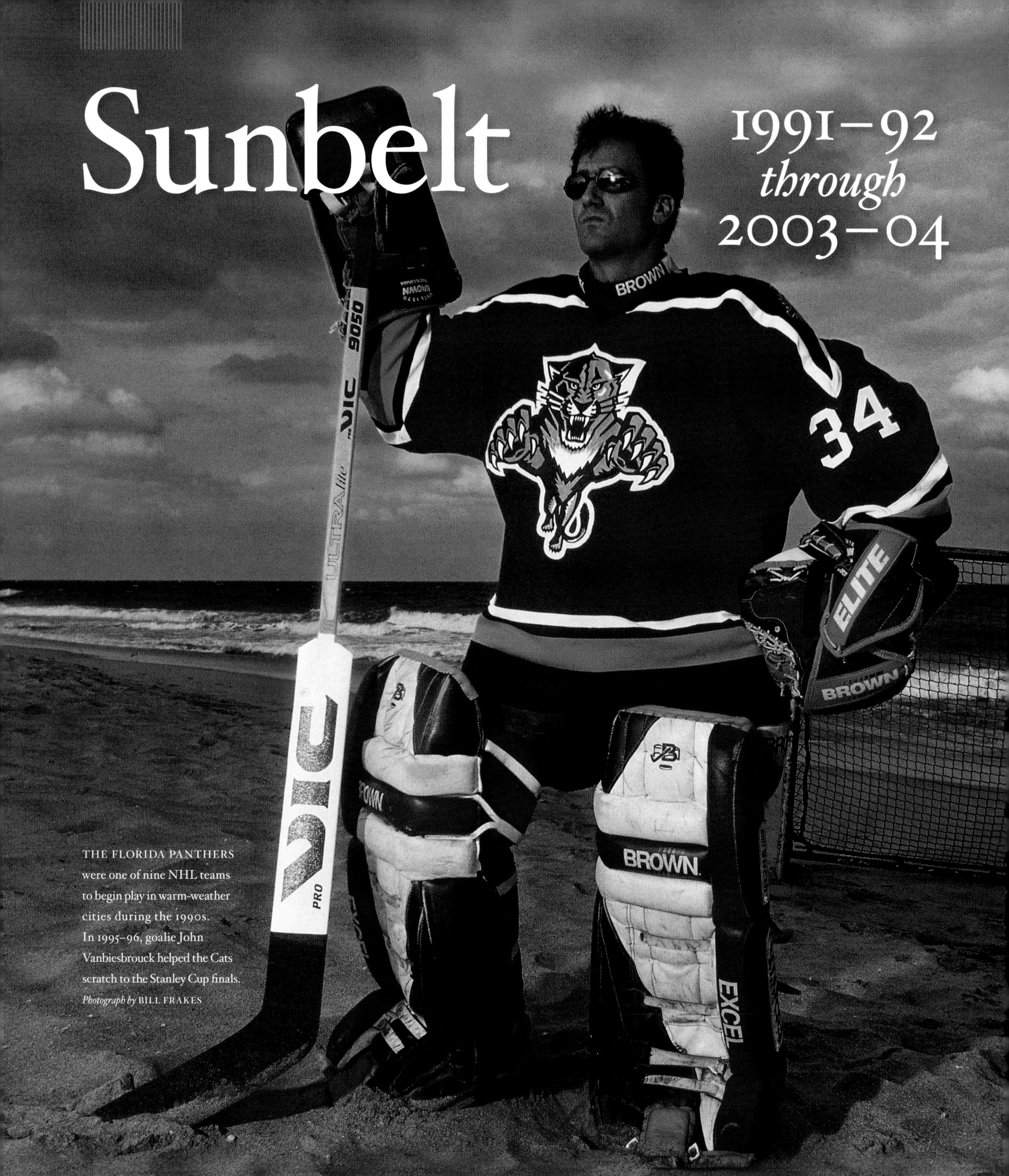

Sunbelt

1991–92 *through* 2003–04

THE FLORIDA PANTHERS were one of nine NHL teams to begin play in warm-weather cities during the 1990s. In 1995–96, goalie John Vanbiesbrouck helped the Cats scratch to the Stanley Cup finals.
Photograph by BILL FRAKES

> ALL-STARS OF THE ERA <

FIRST TEAM

LEFT WING
BRENDAN SHANAHAN
BLUES, WHALERS, RED WINGS

CENTER
MARIO LEMIEUX
PENGUINS

RIGHT WING
JAROMIR JAGR
PENGUINS, CAPITALS, RANGERS

DEFENSEMAN
NICKLAS LIDSTROM
RED WINGS

DEFENSEMAN
CHRIS CHELIOS
BLACKHAWKS, RED WINGS

GOALIE
DOMINIK HASEK
SABRES, RED WINGS

SECOND TEAM

LEFT WING
LUC ROBITAILLE
KINGS, PENGUINS, RANGERS, RED WINGS

CENTER
JOE SAKIC
NORDIQUES, AVALANCHE

RIGHT WING
PAVEL BURE
CANUCKS, PANTHERS, RANGERS

DEFENSEMAN
SCOTT STEVENS
DEVILS

DEFENSEMAN
BRIAN LEETCH
RANGERS, MAPLE LEAFS

GOALIE
PATRICK ROY
CANADIENS, AVALANCHE

COACH
SCOTTY BOWMAN
PENGUINS, RED WINGS

> NICKNAMES <

Paul [Mighty Mouse] Kariya ^
Pavel [the Russian Rocket] Bure
Rob [Cinco] DiMaio
Chris [Captain Clutch] Drury
Peter [Foppa] Forsberg
Dominik [Dominator] Hasek
Steve Heinze [Fifty-Seven]
Jaromir [Jägrmeister] Jagr
Curtis [Cujo] Joseph
Ed [Jovocop] Jovanovski
Nikolai [the Bulin Wall] Khabibulin
Alexei [AK-27] Kovalev
Igor [the Professor] Larionov
Scott [Rat Boy] Mellanby
Chris [the Wizard of Oz] Osgood
Felix [the Cat] Potvin
Mark [the Wrecking Ball] Recchi
Mike [Suitcase] Sillinger
Scott [Captain Crunch] Stevens
Mats [Sudden] Sundin
Tim [the Tool Man] Taylor

STATISTICAL LEADERS

GOALS	
JAROMIR JAGR	510
BRETT HULL	509
BRENDAN SHANAHAN	470
PETER BONDRA	465
TEEMU SELANNE	452
ASSISTS	
ADAM OATES	765
JAROMIR JAGR	742
JOE SAKIC	697
RON FRANCIS	683
MARK RECCHI	634

POINTS (ALL SKATERS)	
JAROMIR JAGR	1,252
JOE SAKIC	1,129
MATS SUNDIN	1,030
MARK RECCHI	1,019
ADAM OATES	1,004
POINTS (DEFENSEMEN)	
BRIAN LEETCH	767
NICKLAS LIDSTROM	726
AL MacINNIS	665
RAY BOURQUE	645
SERGEI ZUBOV	607

GOALIE WINS	
MARTIN BRODEUR	403
PATRICK ROY	393
ED BELFOUR	388
CURTIS JOSEPH	371
CHRIS OSGOOD	305
GOALS AGAINST AVERAGE*	
MARTIN BRODEUR	2.08
DOMINIK HASEK	2.23
ED BELFOUR	2.39
PATRICK ROY	2.44
CHRIS OSGOOD	2.44

*MINIMUM 330 NHL GAMES

>>WISH YOU WERE THERE

Rangers 4, Devils 2

MAY 25, 1994 • BRENDAN BYRNE ARENA, EAST RUTHERFORD, N.J.
With the favored Rangers trailing in the Eastern Conference semifinals three-games-to-two and heading back to New Jersey for Game 6, New York captain Mark Messier guarantees a victory. The Rangers trail 2–1 through two periods, before Messier scores a third-period hat trick to deliver on his vow.

Michigan 3, Michigan State 3 >

OCTOBER 6, 2001 • SPARTAN STADIUM, EAST LANSING, MICH.
Billed as the Cold War, the game pits the in-state and CCHA rivals in the first major outdoor hockey match since 1957. A record crowd of 74,554 sees the tie between the Wolverines, who are coached by longtime NHL player Red Berenson, and the Spartans, who are backstopped by future NHL and Olympic standout Ryan Miller *(right)*. The game inspires a rash of outdoor hockey matchups including the NHL's Heritage Classic in 2003 between the Canadiens and Oilers, and the NHL's now annual Winter Classic played outside each New Year's Day.

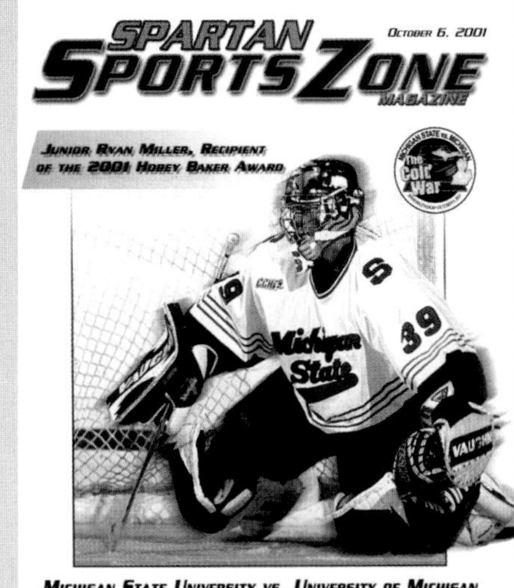

October 6, 2001
SPARTAN
SPORTS ZONE
MAGAZINE
Junior Ryan Miller, Recipient of the 2001 Hobey Baker Award
Michigan State University vs. University of Michigan
72,027 WORLD RECORD HOCKEY ATTENDANCE
- Collector's Limited Edition Program -

Team Sweden 3, Team Canada 2 (SO)

FEBRUARY 27, 1994 • HÅKONS HALL, LILLEHAMMER, NORWAY Deadlocked through overtime (Sweden tied the game with two minutes left in the third period), Canada and Sweden go to a shootout to determine the Olympic gold medal. On the 13th penalty shot Sweden's Peter Forsberg beats Corey Hirsch. Then goalie Tommy Salo stones Paul Kariya to give Sweden the win. The next year an image of Forsberg's goal is depicted on a Swedish postage stamp.

Team Canada 5, Team USA 2

FEBRUARY 24, 2002 • E CENTER, SALT LAKE CITY
With the spiritual help of a "lucky loonie" that was secretly buried under the E Center's ice by a Canadian icemaker, Joe Sakic scores twice and adds two assists as Canada pulls away to win the Olympic final and end a 50-year gold-medal drought

Stars 2, Sabres 1 (3OT)

JUNE 19, 1999 • MARINE MIDLAND ARENA, BUFFALO Brett Hull's controversial rebound goal with his left skate in Dominik Hasek's goal crease ends Game 6 of the Cup finals and gives Dallas a 4–2 series win. The Stars become the first team representing a city in the southern half of the U.S. to win the Cup.

Penguins 5, Maple Leafs 0

DECEMBER 27, 2000 • MELLON ARENA, PITTSBURGH Having retired and been inducted into the Hockey Hall of Fame in 1997, Mario Lemieux makes a startling comeback. Just 33 seconds into his first shift it's as if he never left: He sets up longtime sidekick Jaromir Jagr for the game's first goal. Lemieux adds a goal and another assist and would go on to lead the league in points-per-game for the season.

Canucks 6, Kings 3

MARCH 23, 1994 • GREAT WESTERN FORUM, INGLEWOOD, CALIF. Having eclipsed his boyhood idol in points five years earlier, Wayne Gretzky passes Gordie Howe to take the NHL's alltime goal-scoring lead when he fires a pass from longtime protector Marty McSorley past Vancouver's Kirk McLean for No. 802 of his career.

>MAYHEM MOMENT

MARCH 8, 2004

General Motors Place, Vancouver

Retaliating for a hit that had injured Canucks star Markus Naslund weeks earlier, Vancouver's Todd Bertuzzi tries to fight Colorado's Steve Moore. When Moore skates away, Bertuzzi grabs him, sucker-punches him in the back of the head and throws him to the ice causing injuries—a broken neck, concussion and ligament damage—that would end Moore's career.

> "If I'm ever able to play again, I would ask that Todd Bertuzzi never be permitted to play in any sporting activity I'm involved in."

—Steve Moore, 2005, before Bertuzzi's sentencing in Vancouver criminal court. Bertuzzi received one year probation and 80 hours of community service.

> TEAMS OF THE ERA

DETROIT RED WINGS

With Steve Yzerman, Nicklas Lidstrom and a heavy influx of dazzling Russian talent playing for the NHL's alltime winningest coach, Scotty Bowman, in the 1990s and early 2000s, the Red Wings won three Stanley Cups and made four trips to the finals. That doesn't include the 1995–96 team that set the NHL record for wins in a season with 62 but lost in the Western Conference finals to the archrival Avalanche.

COLORADO AVALANCHE

It didn't take long for the former Quebec Nordiques to ascend to the top of the NHL after moving to Denver before the 1995–96 campaign. The Joe Sakic and Peter Forsberg–led Avalanche made the playoffs in each of its first 10 seasons, winning eight division titles, two Presidents' Trophies and two Stanley Cups, including one in its first season. The 2000–01 title had added meaning; it was the only one in Ray Bourque's illustrious career.

^ NEW YORK RANGERS

In what amounted to an Oilers reunion, seven former members of Edmonton's Stanley Cup dynasty of the 1980s—including Mark Messier, Adam Graves and Esa Tikkanen—joined forces with Mike Richter and Brian Leetch *(holding Cup)* on Broadway to end New York's 54-year Cup drought. The Rangers did not reach another finals in the era, but the one magical and curse-shattering season gave the team an aura of greatness.

[DEBUT] [FINALE]

DEBUT		FINALE
Niklas Lidstrom	1991–92	Larry Robinson
Paul Kariya	1994–95	Peter Stastny
Saku Koivu	1995–96	Cam Neely
Jarome Iginla >	1996–97	< Dale Hawerchuk
Joe Thornton	1997–98	Pat LaFontaine
Vincent Lecavalier	1998–99	Wayne Gretzky
Roberto Luongo	1999–00	Grant Fuhr
Daniel & Henrik Sedin	2000–01	Ray Bourque
Henrik Zetterberg	2002–03	Theo Fleury
Eric Staal	2003–04	Mark Messier

> BY THE NUMBERS

17 | Years that Craig MacTavish played helmetless after the NHL mandated use of protective headgear. MacTavish was exempted from the rule because he was signed before it took effect in 1979.

1992 | NHL record regular-season and postseason games played by Mark Messier.

7 | Saves (on nine shots) made in a 1992 preseason game against the Blues by Lightning goalie Manon Rheaume, the only woman to play in the NHL.

6 | Former members of CSKA Moscow, a.k.a. the Soviet Red Army Team who were members of the '98 Stanley Cup champion Detroit Red Wings.

54 | Years between when Gordie Howe first tried out for the New York Rangers in 1943 at age 15, and his final pro shift, for the IHL's Detroit Vipers in '97 at age 69.

7 | Game-winning goals for Lightning center Brad Richards in the 2004 playoffs, a postseason record. Richards won the Conn Smythe Trophy; Tampa Bay won the Cup.

> PATRICK FACTOR

Joining his father Lynn, grandpa Lester and great-uncle Frank, Penguins G.M. Craig Patrick, a two-time Stanley Cup winner and the assistant coach–G.M. of the 1980 Olympics gold-medal team, enters the Hall of Fame in '01; that year Craig's brother Glenn coaches the Pens' AHL team to the Calder Cup finals.

KOHO
KOHO
KOHO

2003 | THERE WAS no masking the cold for Oilers goalie Ty Conklin during the NHL's first outdoor game, a 4–3 loss to Montreal, in Edmonton. | *Photograph by* ANDY CLARK

2003 | AFTER THREE seasons as Patrick Roy's backup, David Aebischer emerged from that considerable shadow to become Colorado's starting goalie. | *Photograph by* DAVID ZALUBOWSKI

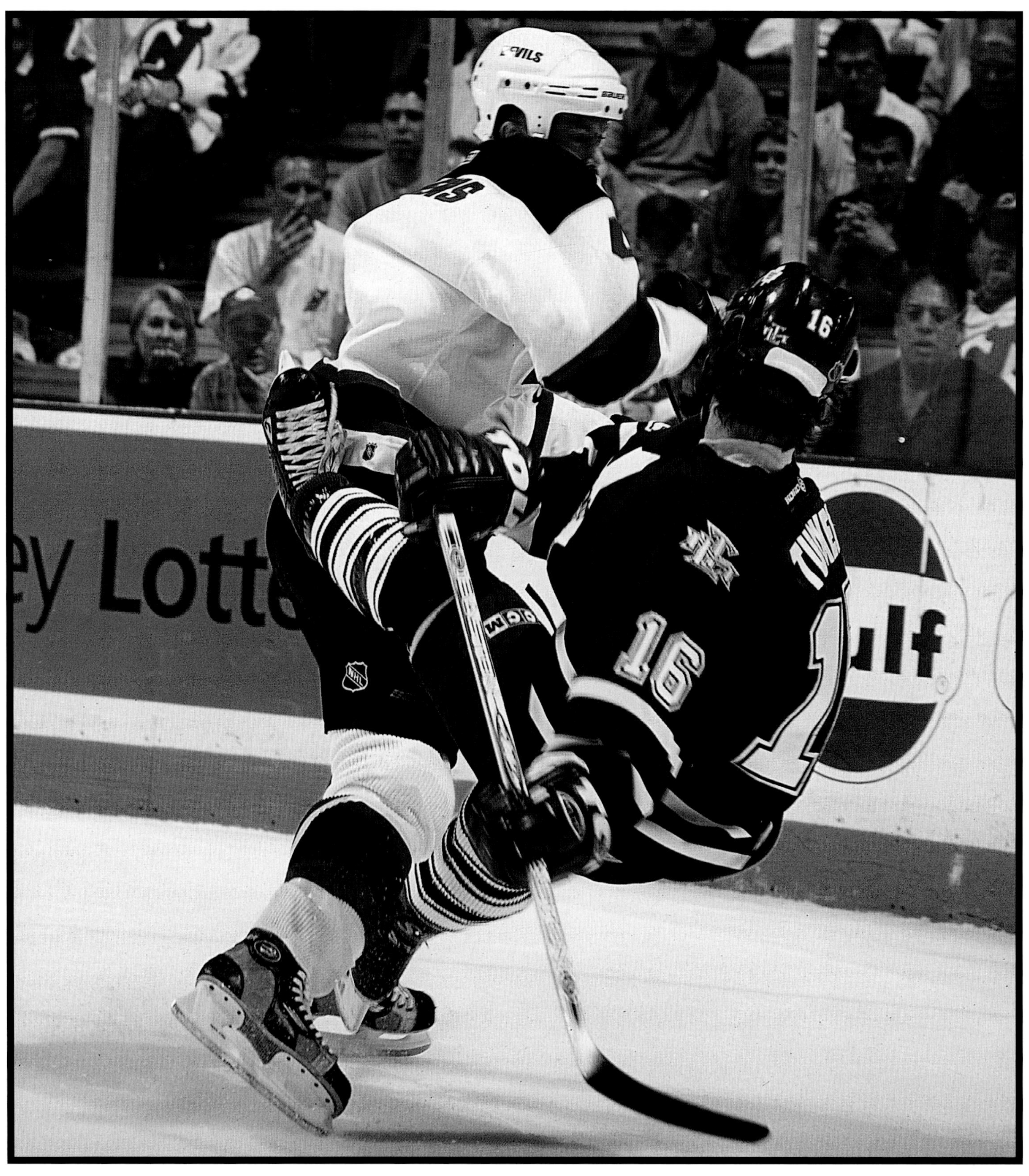

2001 | THE LEAFS' Darcy Tucker took one on the chin from New Jersey's Scott Stevens, the most menacing open-ice hitter of his time. | *Photograph by* LOU CAPPOZOLA

2010 | RUSSIA'S ALEXANDER OVECHKIN helped his team knock off the Czech Republic by laying out Jaromir Jagr at the Vancouver Games. | *Photograph by* ROBERT BECK

8
CCM

BORIS AND HIS BOYS PLAY A FEW FRIENDLIES

BY MARK MULVOY

A U.S. tour showcased Lieutenant-and-Goaltender Vladislav Tretiak and his teammates and gave a glimpse into the vaunted Soviet hockey machine. —*from* SI, JANUARY 5, 1976

CHIEF COACH BORIS KULAGIN'S party line for the historic hockey games now under way between club teams of the U.S.S.R.'s Major League and the National Hockey League is that they are "true friendlies." No way, Boris. The NHL does not pay you $200,000 and pick up your expenses—including all those pre- and postgame vodka toasts—just for some cozy games between buddies; there's also the little matter of an expected 130,824 paying guests and an intercontinental television hookup involved with the socializing.

"Pro teams do not play friendlies," admits Russian star Alexander Yakushev, Bobby Hull's choice as the best left wing in the world and currently on loan from the Spartak team to Krylya Sovetov (Wings of the Soviets) for its matches with Pittsburgh, Buffalo, Chicago and the New York Islanders. "We have been told it would be very bad for us not to win," says Valery Kharlamov, probably the No. 2 left wing in the world, who is with his regular Central Army Club mates for their games against the New York Rangers, Montreal, Boston and Philadelphia.

There are 10 teams in what the Soviet Hockey Federation calls the Major League of the U.S.S.R. Hockey Championship, with another 14 in the First Division and 28 more in the Second Division. Major League franchises cost exactly $6 million less than the $6 million that the Washington Capitals paid for the privilege of joining the NHL. And, in Russia, Washington might not always finish in last place; in fact, each season the worst team in the Major League is dropped to the minors and replaced by the champion of the First Division.

As in most Russian sports, the 10 teams in the Major League represent various trade unions or arms of the Soviet military. For example, Spartak is sponsored by a union of textile and light-industry workers in combination with public servants. Dynamo has two clubs in the league—one from Moscow, the other from Riga in Latvia—and both operate under government subsidy as affiliates of the home affairs section, which includes the militia and the KGB. Khimik represents the chemical industries in Voskresnsk, Traktor the tractor factory in Chelyabinsk and Sibir the machine works in Novosibirsk.

There are also two army teams: the Central Army Club in Moscow, which has won 19 of the 29 U.S.S.R. championships, and the Army Sports Club of Leningrad, which has never won a national title because, Muscovites joke, its best players always seem to be transferred to headquarters in Moscow. Although the Army Club players all hold rank, from private to major, they do not muster for 5 a.m. roll call, peel potatoes or spit shine their skate boots. "When I'm not in training with my teams," says Lieutenant-and-Goaltender Vladislav Tretiak, "I help instruct the young recruits here at the Central Army Club."

The U.S.S.R. schedule began in September and ends in March. Each team plays 36 Major League games; there are breaks in the schedule so that teams can compete in international events as well as those financially lucrative "friendlies." Amid the latest U.S. tour, the honorable chief coach Kulagin, who oversees all the international games and also coaches the Wings of the Soviets, was asked if he could stop popping stomach pills long enough for a brief interview.

"Of course," mumbled Kulagin, popping another pill. "You'd have a jumpy stomach and high blood pressure if you had my troubles. The Wings are only in fourth place now. I've got five newly marrieds on the team, and they spend too much time with their wives and not enough time with their hockey. We have the games against the North American professionals, then the Olympics in February, and I only hope that my stomach and my blood pressure don't crack."

It was pointed out to Kulagin that in the Major League, the most penalized team, his Wings, had 8.3 penalty minutes per game, but that the Central Army team would be playing the Flyers, who average a little more than 25 minutes a game. Kulagin shrugged. "These games are friendlies for us," he said.

"Bobby Clarke's team," he is told of the Flyers, "does not play friendlies with anyone."

"Ah, excuse me, please. I've got to see the trainer. I must get some more little pills."

FOUR-TIME OLYMPIAN (and three-time gold medalist) Tretiak starred in goal for the Central Red Army Club and became the fearsome face of Soviet hockey.

MELCHIOR DIGIACOMO

MONTREAL
20
20
PRO
Cooper
Cooper

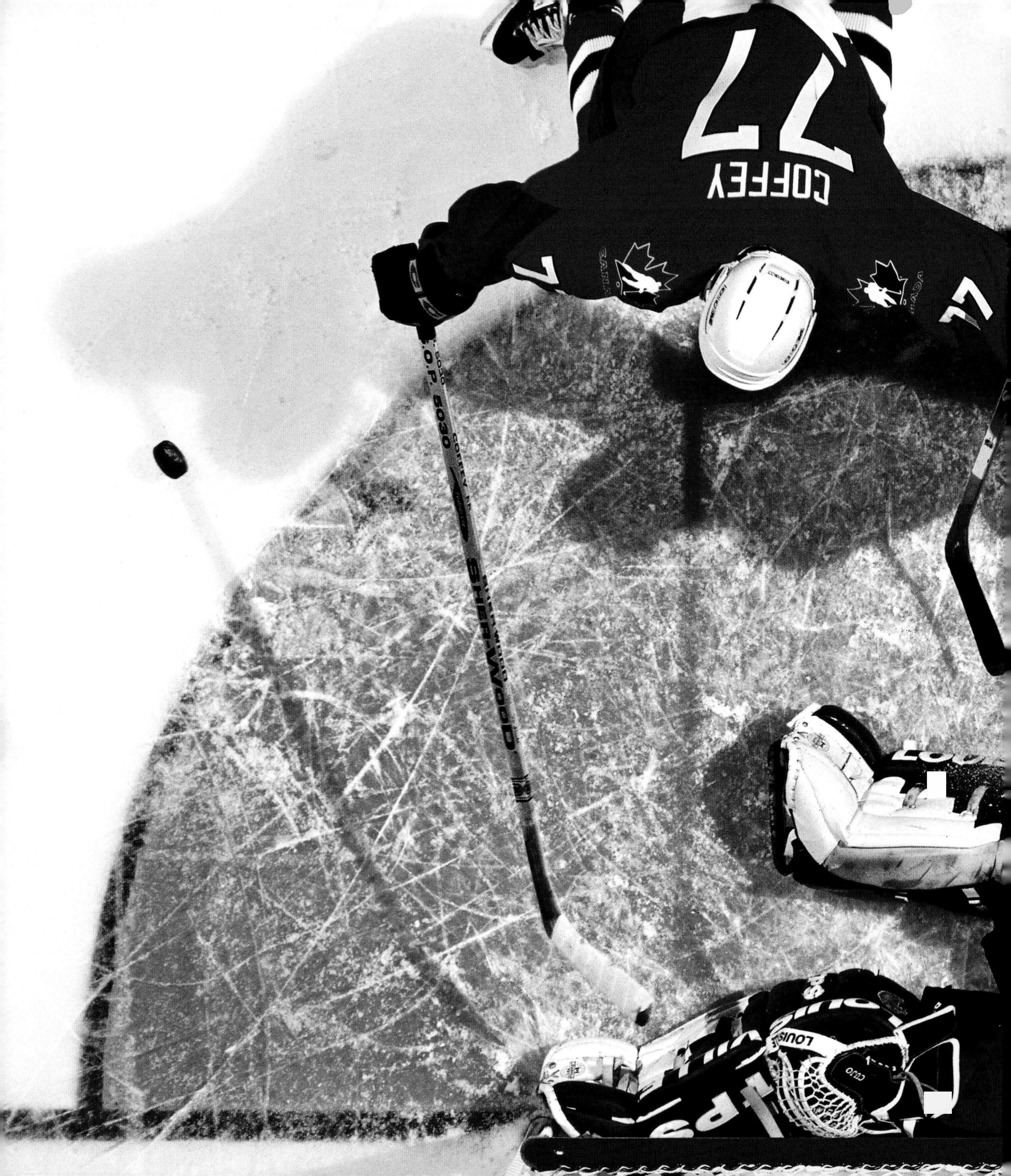
77
COFFEY
SHERWOOD
5030

1996 | CREASE CRASHER Keith Tkachuk wasn't slowed by defensemen Paul Coffey, Adam Foote or goalie Curtis Joseph as Team USA upset Canada in the three-game finals of the inaugural World Cup. | *Photograph by* DAVID E. KLUTHO

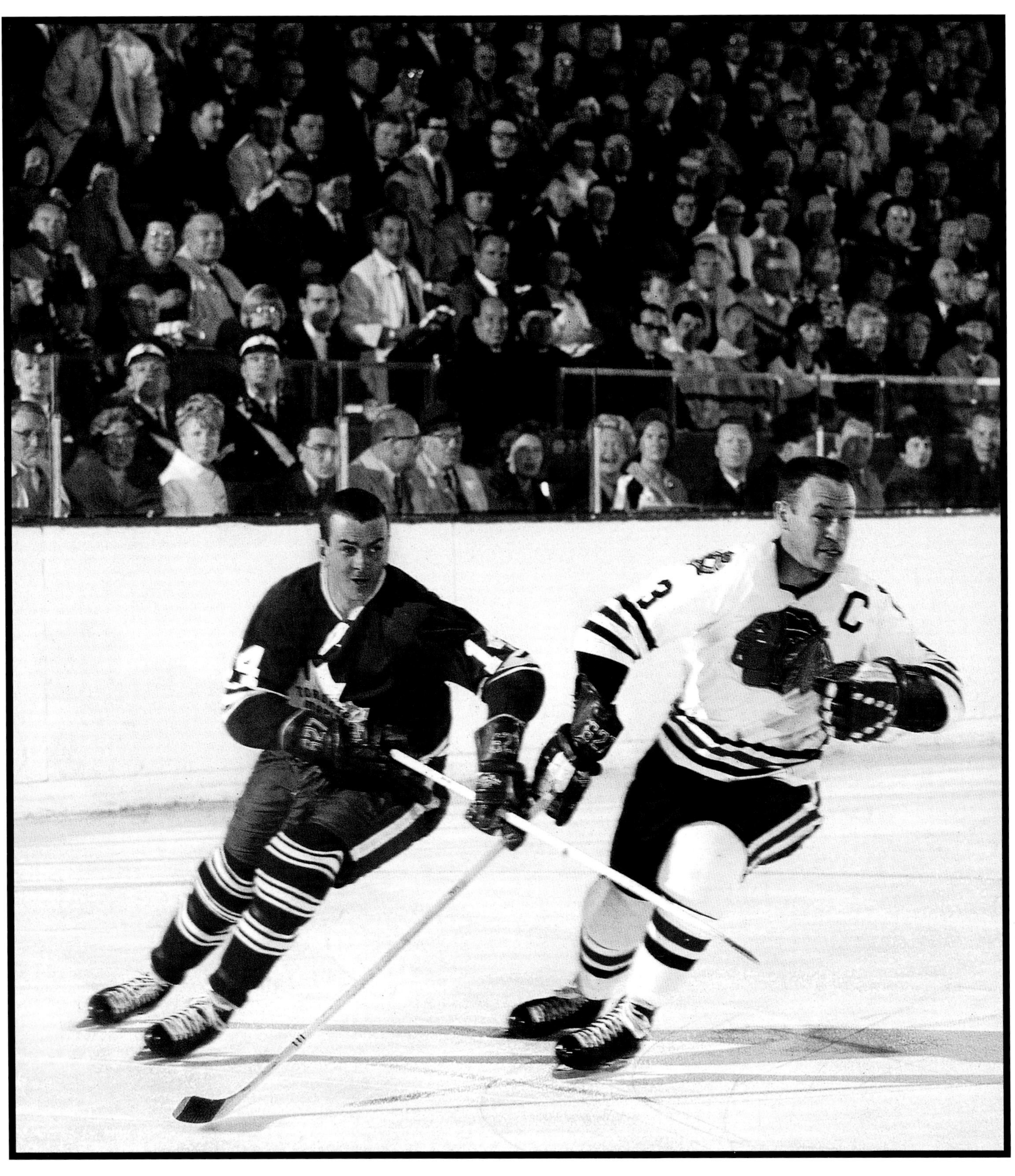

1967 | FUTURE HALL OF FAMERS Dave Keon of Toronto and Pierre Pilote of Chicago crossed sticks in the Stanley Cup semis, which the Leafs won. | *Photograph by* JAMES DRAKE

1959 | RANGERS GOALIE Marcel Paille never had to flinch: Norris Trophy winner Harry Howell got down to block the shot against Toronto. | *Photograph by* TUROFSKY

TORONTO
MAPLE
RANGE
1
3
3
NORTHLAND

87
A
Reebok
CROSBY

DESTINY'S CHILD

BY S.L. PRICE

He'd delivered on his promise and captained a team to the Stanley Cup. As the Olympics loomed, Sidney Crosby, 22 and so long a phenom, realized that he was chasing a dream not just for himself but also for his hometown and his nation. —*from* SI, FEBRUARY 8, 2010

THE SIGNS GOT TO HIM AS he rode through the crowd on the old fire truck, flashing that boy-band grin, one hand on the massive silver prize. They passed the town limit—COLE HARBOUR, HOME OF SIDNEY CROSBY—and then the signs kept coming: WELCOME HOME at the Petro-Canada station, HAPPY BIRTHDAY at Kyte's Pharmasave, CONGRATS! at Chris Brothers Meats. And the thought began to rise: *I didn't dream this alone. They wanted it for me too....*

Coming home like this had been the plan since, shortly after leading Pittsburgh to the 2009 championship, Crosby had reserved his day with the Stanley Cup: August 7, his 22nd birthday. Now people packed in along the roadsides, whooping and smiling and waving their own signs that they had brought here to Nova Scotia from Ontario, from Alberta, from across the nation. Here was the neighborhood where Sidney had Rollerbladed to his buddies' homes. Here was the pizza place that made the family dinner on Friday nights, the sports store that supplied the tape for his first sticks and the stone to sharpen his little blades. He was blocks from the house where his parents, Troy and Trina, struggled to pay the mortgage, to buy oil for a few months' heat—but made damn sure that Sidney had new skates each season.

He came back each summer, loving how his celebrity shrank among old friends. With space to roam, no traffic or crowds, Cole Harbour boasts a rare quiet. But not today. As the fire truck turned and began the last mile of the route Crosby suddenly saw what lay ahead: tens of thousands more people, a roiling, sunblasted sea of faces lined 10, 20 deep. He would later describe the scene in an almost incredulous tone: "There was no . . . *empty*."

Crosby's ascension has often served as a vehicle for matters beyond his ken. It wasn't enough that he was charged, at 18, with saving the postlockout NHL. When Paul Mason, one of Crosby's youth coaches, says "the NHL needed another Wayne Gretzky," he means more than just another great player who sells tickets. He means another in the line of Canadian transcendents, another hair-raising Howe or Orr to provide what Andrew Podnieks, the author of *A Canadian Saturday Night: Hockey and the Culture of a Country*, calls "marketing in a psychological or spiritual sense." Crosby reassures his nation that, when it comes to hockey, the Great White North is still No. 1.

Fans have pilgrimaged to Cole Harbour for years, hoping for a glimpse of Canada's Next One, leaving items at his parents' house to be signed, knocking on the door. Last summer a van from Vancouver pulled up and a man asked if this was, indeed, Sid's boyhood home. When Trina said yes, he screamed, "It's her!" and more than a dozen people spilled out of the van.

Such approachability is part of Crosby's appeal. His low-key demeanor dovetails with the Canadian self-image—self-effacing, deceptively tough. Today he is the face of Team Canada's bid for Olympic gold and his role as defender of the faith has never been clearer than in a commercial, released just after he was named The Canadian Press male athlete of the year in December. The spot opened with Crosby declaring, "Hockey? Hockey is *our* game."

After the ride through the packed town and a few moments on a stage holding the Cup aloft as the crowd roared, the most personal part of Crosby's day arrived. He and eight friends, the ones he played with from ages six to 15, shed their clothes and hustled into pads and Rollerblades. The other men had moved on from the hockey dream—gone to school, gotten jobs, watched their friend live it for them on TV; Crosby could recite each of their old phone numbers from memory.

This had always been part of the plan too, ever since he joined the NHL. If he won, they would play one more time, three-on-three, the way every kid played it on the street or pond: *O.K., this one's for the Stanley Cup.* But now they'd do it for real. Crosby, as he did as a kid, squatted in goal, wearing oversized pads. Everyone was nervous—who plays road hockey in front of hundreds of people?—but once the sweat broke, it was as if nothing had changed. Sidney made 11 saves, took a tumble when one buddy flew into the crease and, of course, his team won, 7–3.

And then this: Crosby insisted that each player, winner or loser, hoist the Cup and act as if he had earned it. And one by one they did, setting off on wheels across a hard court, but feeling as though they were on the sharpest skates, on perfect ice, in a packed arena. Crosby stood back, grinning. For the first time in hours, or maybe months or years, he wasn't the center of attention or the vessel for so many hopes; he looked at ease. "This is why you do it: to share it with people," Crosby said. He knew, better than anyone, that even this day was hardly about him at all.

CROSBY WAS left off Canada's 2006 Olympic team as an 18-year-old. In 2010, by then with a Hart Trophy on his résumé, he went to Vancouver and made history.

GREGORY SHAMUS

vancouver 2010
vancouver 2010

2010 | AN OVERTIME GOAL by Sidney Crosby sent his teammates overboards in celebration of Canada's gold medal win over the U.S. | *Photograph by* ROBERT BECK

22
22
EASTON

1980 | IN ACTION in Inglewood, Canadiens center Keith Acton's dive had the Kings' Glenn Goldup bowled up and on his way over. | *Photograph by* ANDY HAYT

2007 | IN HIS 17th NHL season and playing in a preseason game for Columbus, Sergei Fedorov (91) was still charging after the puck. | *Photograph by* GERRY BROOME

1924–25 | MONTREAL REACHED the finals. From left are Aurel Joliat, Georges Vézina, Odie Cleghorn, Sprague Claghorn and Curley Headley. | *Photograph by* IHA

> Artifacts

Wool Works

Today's NHL jerseys are synthetic, sleek and lightweight. Yesterday's? Not so much. The woolen sweaters kept players decidedly warm, while over the years the logos have provided food for thought—and food for moths

KONRAD JOHANNESSON
Winnipeg Falcons/Team Canada 1920 Olympics

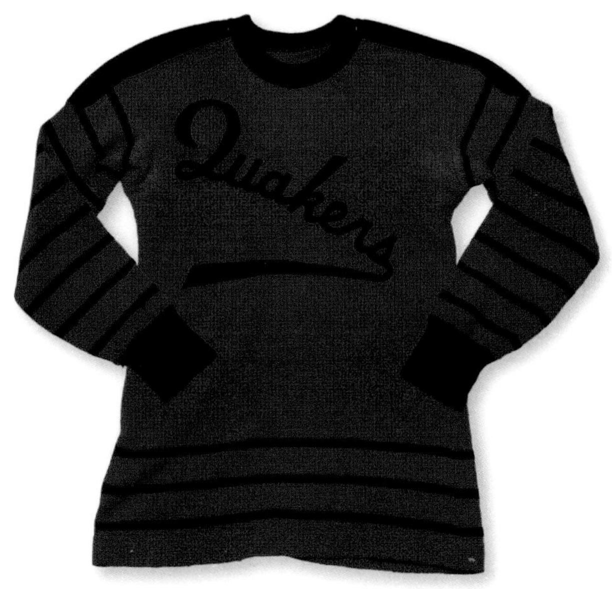

BILL HUTTON
Philadelphia Quakers 1930–31

HARRY (HAP) HOLMES
Seattle Metropolitans c. 1918

BENNY HAYES
Trail Smoke Eaters, 1939 World Champions

DAVID N. BERKWITZ; COURTESY OF HOCKEY HALL OF FAME

THE PANTHEON >> *Coaches*

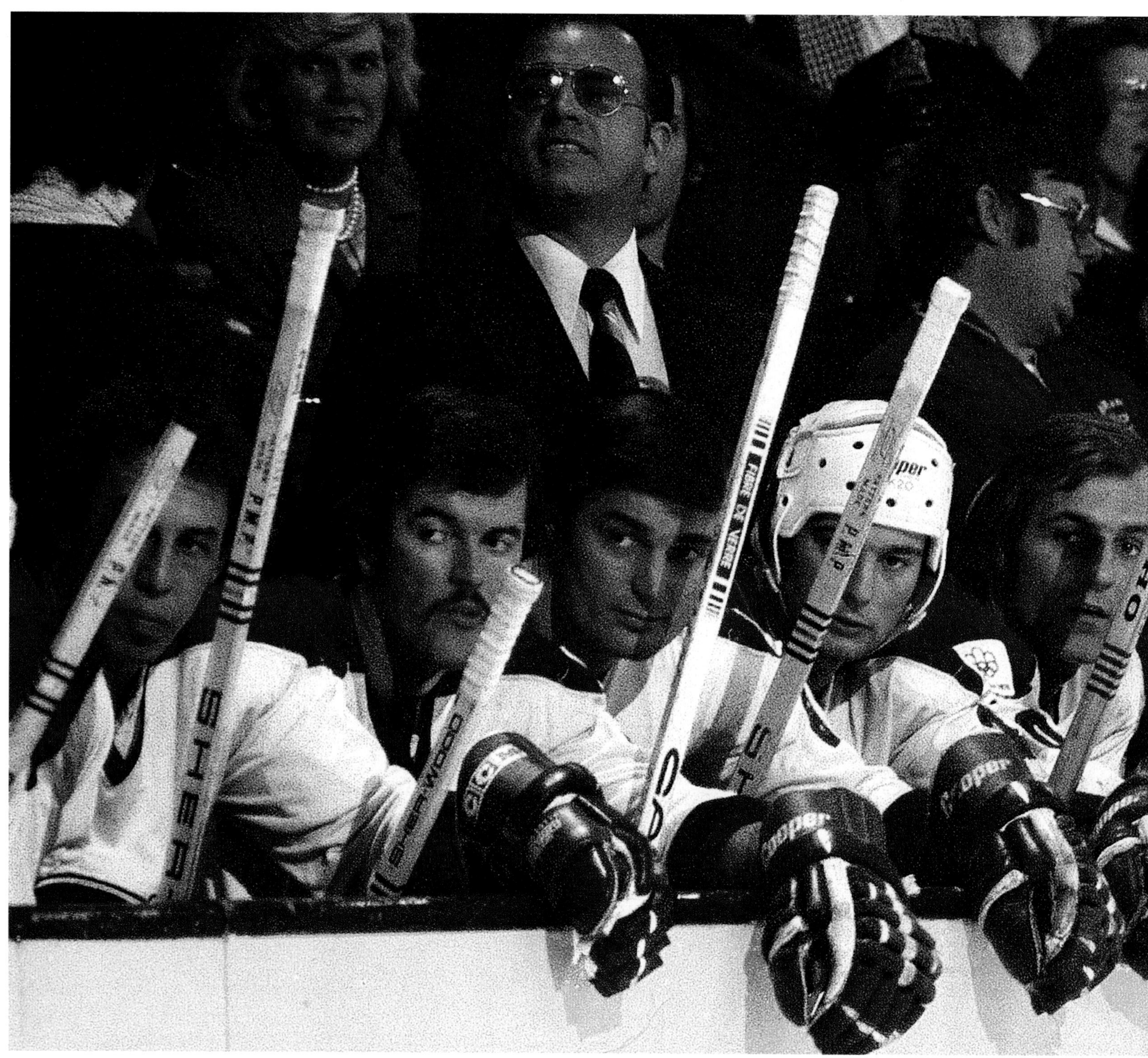

1976 | BOWMAN WON five of his record nine Stanley Cups with Montreal. He's the NHL leader in games coached (2,141) and won (1,244). | *Photograph by* MANNY MILLAN

SI's TOP 25

Jack Adams
Al Arbour
Mike Babcock
Father David Bauer
Toe Blake
< Scotty Bowman
Herb Brooks
Pat Burns
Hap Day
Pete Green
Punch Imlach
Dick Irvin Sr.
Tommy Ivan
Bob Johnson
Mike Keenan
Brian Kilrea
Ron Mason
Roger Neilson
Jack Parker
Lester Patrick
Glen Sather
Fred Shero
Anatoli Tasarov
Viktor Tikhonov
Jerry York

EXPORT
12
20

WORRYING IS THE WAY TO WIN

BY MARK KRAM

Toe Blake would coach the Canadiens to eight Stanley Cups—this excerpt ran between numbers six and seven—and he never stopped brooding along the way. —*from* SI, NOVEMBER 22, 1965

WATCH HIM AT A hockey game and then compassionately slip him a straight razor. It seems the only kind thing to do as Hector (Toe) Blake, coach of the Montreal Canadiens, spends an evening in his small, rectangular cell at rinkside, in the shadows of a larger, more perceptible hell inside himself. During the game Blake's teeth, like jackhammers, forever blast into a chunk of gum and at times, it appears, his lower lip. His head rolls like a cue ball with English on it, and his voice—constantly discharging epithets—is that of a foreman in a stamping mill. High-voltage moments send him bolting up and down in a jagged line but, when confronted with obvious defeat or victory or excruciating blunder, he somnambulantly stumbles about in tight little circles. Right now the thing most troubling Toe Blake, the Captain Bligh of the National Hockey League and everybody's candidate for a long vacation in a nice, quiet country place with high walls around it, is the fact that the experts have once again picked his team to finish in first place.

A Canadiens game is always, quite simply, the third day at Gettysburg for Blake. He is, true, avuncular at times, but more frequently he is despotic or desperate—a human fusillade of stinging ridicule and penetrating anger. "It's the way I am," says Blake. "It's the only way I know how to get there."

Since 1955, when he succeeded the Habs' highly obstreperous and successful coach, Dick Irvin, Blake has flogged both his opposition and his players. He has given the Canadiens 385 victories, 187 defeats and 128 ties in the regular-season schedule, seven league titles and six Stanley Cup championships, five of them consecutive. His most recent Cup victory—the first after a four-year drought—came last season, to the bewilderment of every expert in hockey and the embarrassment of all those who have persisted in portraying Blake as just a caretaker coach.

As a player, Hector (or Hec-toe, as his younger brother called him as a child), was a leftwinger and captain of the devastatingly successful Canadiens in the mid-1940s. He was a star but not a superstar, a scuffler who had to work hard for his success. "I could never let up," he says. "I had to drive myself."

He has proved no different as a coach. True, he is a technically solid hockey man, a patient master at handling young players and one who is consistently successful at getting competence from those who do not have it to give too often, but it is his attitude and his cutting tongue that drive the Canadiens. After a series of defeats, or even just one game notable for desultory play, Blake can usually be heard profanely disparaging the abilities of his players. "The dressing room just shakes," says one reporter.

"I'm not sure such a technique is right," says Blake. "I've tried the silent treatment on them, but it gets me more upset than it does them."

Blake is 53 now, and his 10 years of big-league coaching have marked him badly. He has frequent and persistent headaches, and he doesn't sleep well. He is a loner who is lonely. On the road, away from his family, there is nobody to drain the frustration and misery of defeat from his mind. Sometimes he can shake it by walking the streets, but usually he can be found in his big hotel suite late at night, alone and moving from the bed to the chair to the bed and back to the chair again. Once in a while he will turn on the late show, and just when his mind is being hooked by, say, a story of lost love in a Western town, gossamer figures on skates will glide through his thoughts in slow motion. *Damn it, Blake, why were you so tough with the players before the third period? Are you sure you had the right combination on the ice in that big moment of the second period?* He never remembers the good moves, nor does he ever remember the good things he has done for people.

Blake is not insensitive. He knows that his circle of friends is not as large as it once was. He knows that he has hurt some people profoundly—through his words and his actions. He has, for instance, had to bench or release old friends at various times during his career, and he has never been callous about it. Each incident has taken a piece out of Blake. "It is a very, very difficult thing to do," he says. He is also aware of the deep scar that has been inflicted by his job. "Once I was a very happy man," he says. "I am a bitter man now, a very bitter man."

THE CANADIENS were riddled with injuries and in the rare position of being underdogs during the 1965 playoffs, but Blake's strategies helped them take the Cup.

JOSEPH CONSENTINO

15

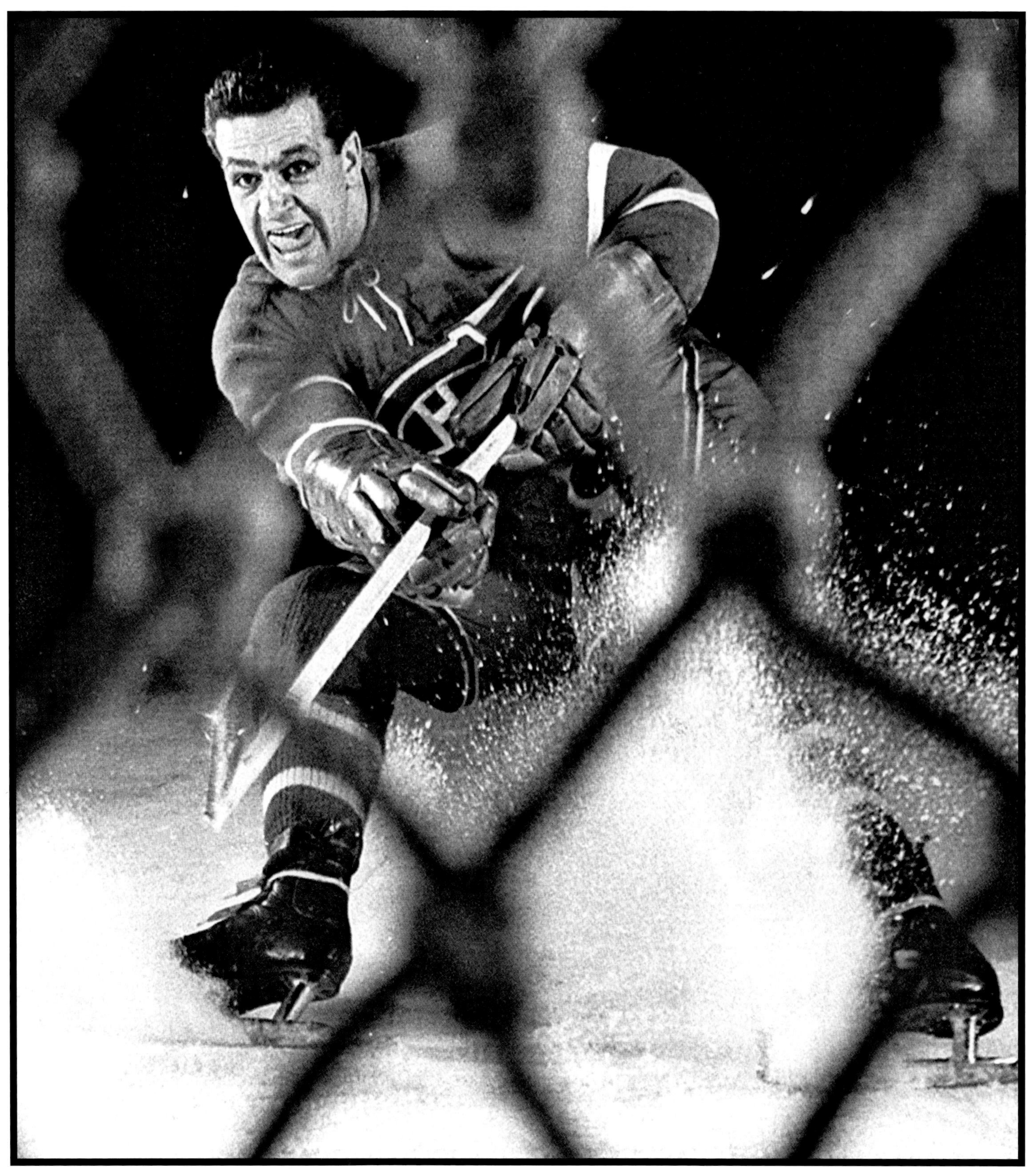

1955 | THE CANADIENS' Bernie Geoffrion was called Boom Boom for his thundering slap shot, then one of the game's true phenomena. | *Photograph by* YALE JOEL

1981 | THE PHENOM: Bobby Carpenter was in a Massachusetts prep school when he made SI's cover. He would be drafted third overall by Washington. | *Photograph by* MANNY MILLAN

1957 | BROTHER, CAN you spare a puck? Montreal's onrushing Henri Richard (top) looks to receive a pass from older sibling Maurice. | *Photograph by* HY PESKIN

COURTESY HOCKEY HALL OF FAME

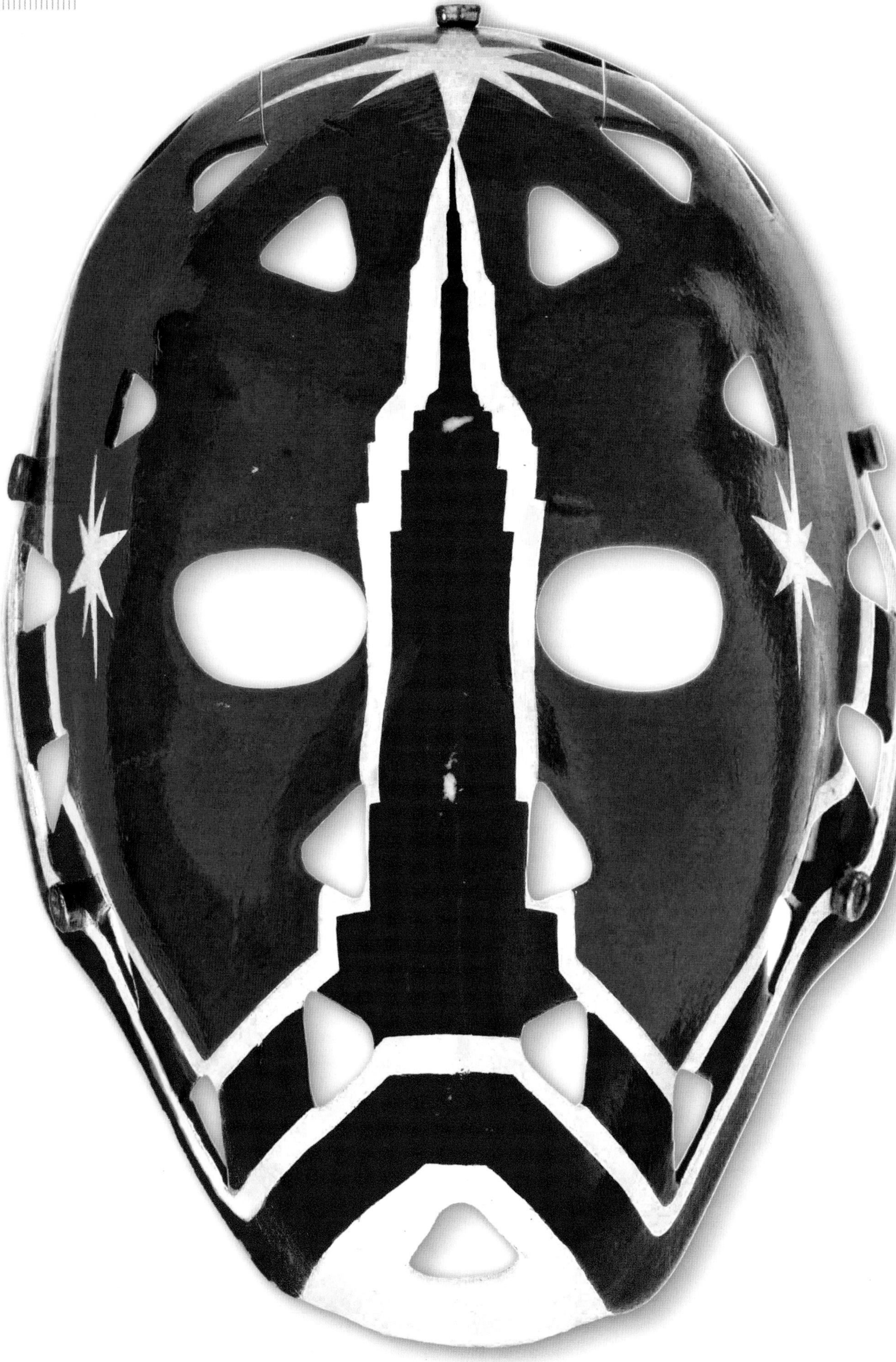

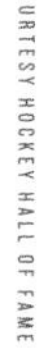

1980 | STEVE BAKER played 57 games with the Rangers, donning this mask and building his name by losing just once in his first 10 starts. | *Photograph by* MATTHEW MANOR

2002 | NEAR THE END of a 17-year career in which he won 484 games, Eddie (the Eagle) Belfour landed in Toronto. | *Photograph by* DAVE SANDFORD

bal network of innovation.
SIEMENS
LEAFS
SIEMENS SIEMENS SIEMENS SIEMENS SIEMENS
Glob
19

CHERRY BOMBS

BY LEIGH MONTVILLE

The essence of Don Cherry's blustery message—and his xenophobia and his vitriol—was his resistance to change. Why can't things be the way they were? Where is the honor? —*from* SI, MARCH 29, 1993

HE KNOWS THE END WILL come someday. Maybe someday soon. Maybe tonight. He is pushing, pushing, pushing the limits too far, saying too much. One final piece of outrage will bubble from Don Cherry's high-volume mouth, and that will be that. *Ka-boom!* He will self-destruct in full public view, the carnage strewn across the living rooms of an entire country, from the Maritimes to British Columbia. *Ka-boom!*

"I can't keep saying these things," he says. "How can I keep saying these things?"

Things like what?

"Like asking someone to break [Pittsburgh Penguin defenseman] Ulf Samuelsson's arm," he says. "How can I say that on television? I asked someone to break Ulf Samuelsson's arm between the wrist and the elbow."

Ka-boom!

He cannot help himself. The lights come on, 4½ minutes to fill on a Saturday night, a tidy little show called *Coach's Corner* between the first and second periods of *Hockey Night in Canada*, and he might as well be holding a lighted stick of dynamite while he gives his commentary. How can 4½ minutes, once a week, be so dangerous? He will say anything, do anything. He will tweak noses, pick fights. He will ask for the arm—if not the head—of a Penguins defenseman he doesn't like.

Four-and-a-half minutes. One week he suddenly unfurled an eight-foot-long Canadian flag and talked about the "wimps and creeps" who opposed Canada's participation in the gulf war. Another week he was wearing sunglasses and an earring in his left earlobe and talking with an exaggerated effeminate lisp. Wasn't the subject supposed to be the opposition of Los Angeles King star Wayne Gretzky and King owner Bruce McNall to hockey violence? Wasn't the subject supposed to be hockey? Couldn't he simply say what he thought? An earring. A lisp.

Cherry still can't believe he did that. He could not help himself. "I come off after wearing the earring, and I'm just shaking, eh?" he says. "I was so pumped up. Scared. I was just shaking."

Everything has become so much bigger than he ever expected. He says these things—says anything that comes into his head—and the entire country seems to stop and listen. He is 59 years old, moving hard on 60, and he has become Canada's Rush Limbaugh and Canada's Howard Cosell. All in one. He is George C. Scott and Willard Scott and Randolph Scott. He is John McLaughlin and Dick Vitale and Bobby (the Brain) Heenan and Roseann Roseannadanna and Cliff Clavin, mailman, and George Will and Henry David Thoreau and maybe a little bit of Mighty Mouse, here to save the day.

Polls have shown that he is the most recognizable figure in the country, more recognizable than any pop star, any politician, any hockey player even. He is so big that he cannot walk on any street in Canada without drawing a crowd. He is so big that he doesn't do banquets anymore, can't, because the demand is so great. He is so big that there have been petitions to put him on the ballot to replace the retiring Brian Mulroney as prime minister. Prime minister? How did this happen?

"Tomas Sandstrom," he said once on the air about the Kings' forward. "A lot of people think he is Little Lord Fauntleroy, but Tomas Sandstrom is a backstabbing, cheap-shot, mask-wearing Swede." Actually, he's a Finn, not a Swede.

Is that something a prime minister would say? The words just came out.

Educators decry his misuse of English, his fractured syntax, his mangled pronunciations, worrying that he will breed a generation that says "everythink" and "somethink" and won't have any idea how to make verbs agree with nouns. Hockey executives often paint him as a Neanderthal, out of touch, arguing for violence and against style, trying to defend a frontier that already has been opened wide to the arrival of international talent. Interest groups pick out one outrage after another, the shelves beginning to shake as soon as he speaks, politically correct ideas falling to the ground one after another as if they were pieces of cut glass or bone china. Oops, there goes another one.

None of this matters. The Canadian public simply can't get enough of him. He points. He shouts. He sneers. He laughs. His clothes come from the wardrobe of some road company of *Guys and Dolls*, flashy suits and fat-checked sport jackets, custom-tailored, elongated shirt collars starched to the consistency of vinyl siding, riding high above his Adam's apple. His head juts out like a hood ornament in search of a collision. Put on a small screen, he is a larger-than-life terror.

EVEN LOUDER than Cherry's bombastic words is the array of garish suits with which he has been overwhelming viewers of *Hockey Night in Canada* since 1980.

CLOCKWISE FROM TOP LEFT: BRUCE BENNETT/GETTY IMAGES; LOU CAPOZZOLA; BRUCE BENNETT/GETTY IMAGES; TOM SZCZERBOWSKI/US PRESSWIRE

HEISTEN
27

2002 | GOPHER IT! Grant Potulny (18) was mobbed by his Minnesota mates after his overtime goal against Maine in the NCAA title game. | *Photograph by* DAVID E. KLUTHO

CANADIEN

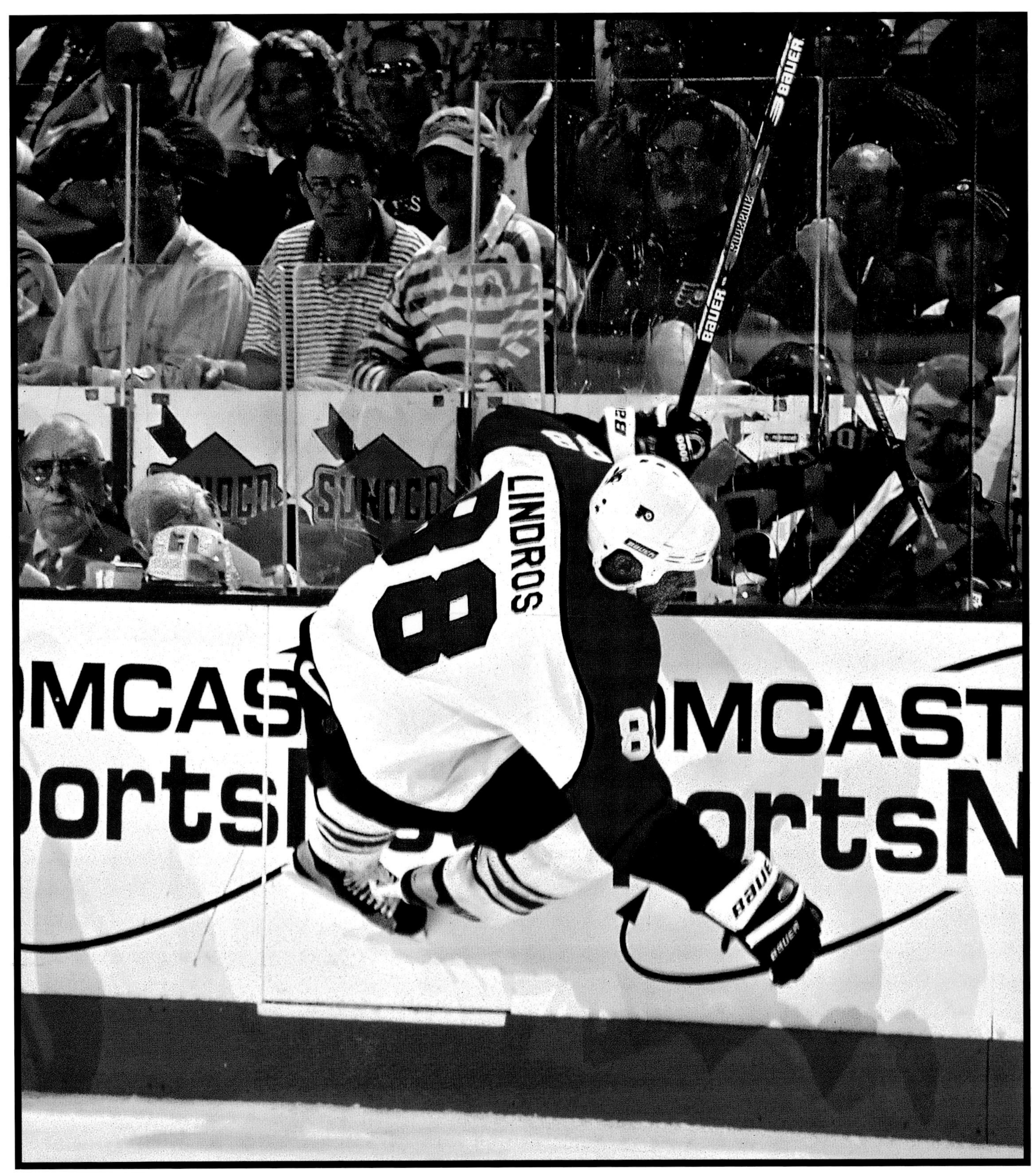

1998 | TOUTED AS the Next One as a kid, Eric Lindros would excel in the NHL, but pay a price for his aggressiveness, suffering a series of injuries. | *Photograph by* LOU CAPOZZOLA

1978 | THE BRUINS' Brad Park had Canadiens forward Jacques Lemaire in the air here, but Montreal landed up a winner in this Cup finals. | *Photograph by* MANNY MILLAN

New Game
2005–06 *to* present

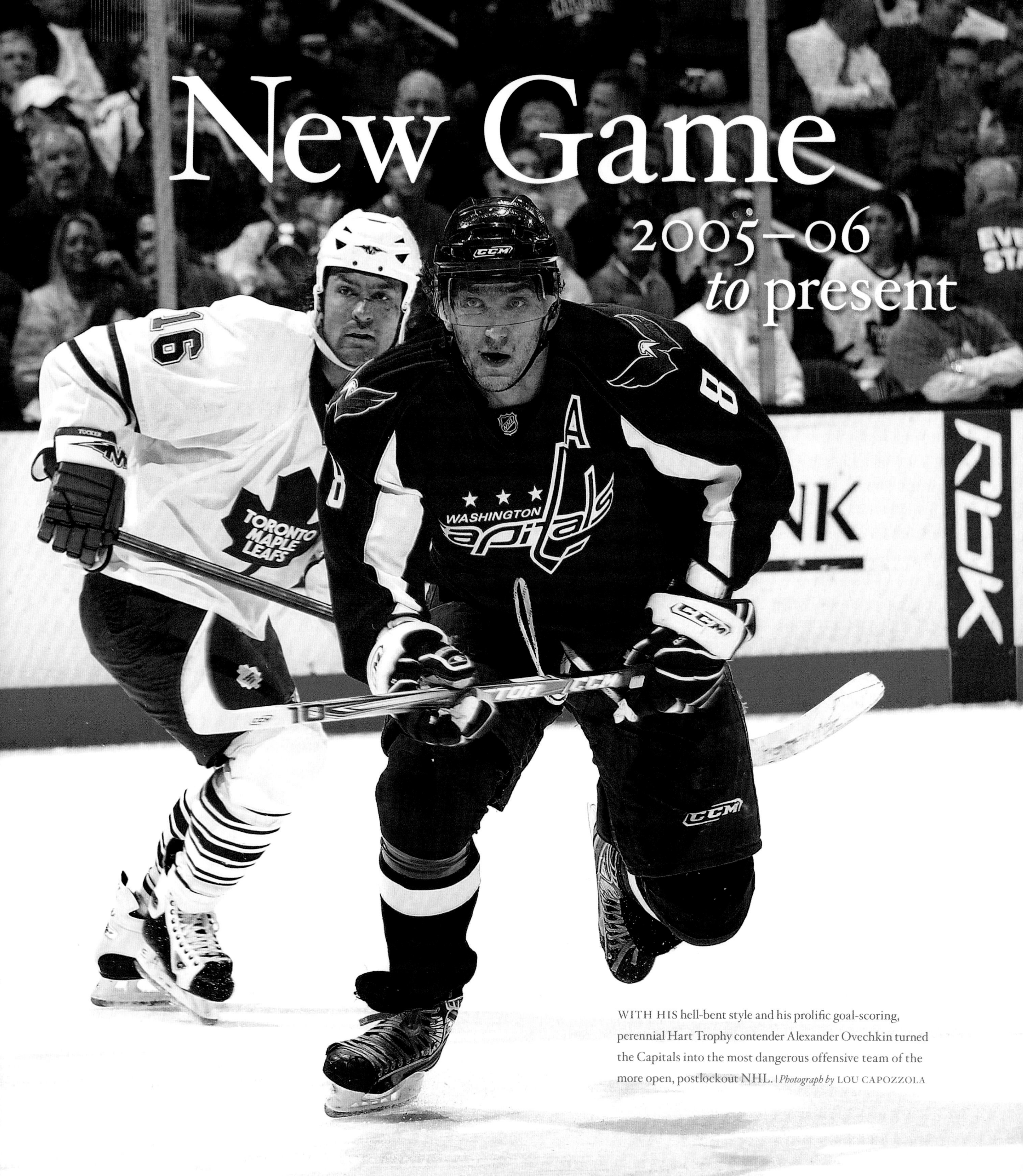

WITH HIS hell-bent style and his prolific goal-scoring, perennial Hart Trophy contender Alexander Ovechkin turned the Capitals into the most dangerous offensive team of the more open, postlockout NHL. | *Photograph by* LOU CAPOZZOLA

> ALL-STARS OF THE ERA <

FIRST TEAM	SECOND TEAM
LEFT WING ALEXANDER OVECHKIN CAPITALS	LEFT WING DANY HEATLEY SENATORS, SHARKS
CENTER SIDNEY CROSBY PENGUINS	CENTER JOE THORNTON BRUINS, SHARKS
RIGHT WING JAROME IGINLA FLAMES	RIGHT WING DANIEL ALFREDSSON SENATORS
DEFENSE NICKLAS LIDSTROM RED WINGS	DEFENSE ZDENO CHARA SENATORS, BRUINS
DEFENSE CHRIS PRONGER OILERS, DUCKS, FLYERS	DEFENSE SCOTT NIEDERMAYER DUCKS
GOALIE MARTIN BRODEUR DEVILS	GOALIE MIIKKA KIPRUSOFF FLAMES

COACH
MIKE BABCOCK
RED WINGS, TEAM CANADA

> NICKNAMES <

Jason [Spezz-Dispenser] Spezza ^
Sidney [Sid the Kid] Crosby
Derek [Boogey Man] Boogaard
Kyle [Grease] Calder
Brian [Soupy] Campbell
Todd [Fridge] Fedoruk
Johan [Mule] Franzen
Johan [Moose] Hedberg
Jonas [the Monster] Gustavsson
Cristobal [Hip Hip] Huet
Patrick [Big Daddy] Kane
Ian [Mumbles] Laperriere
[King] Henrik Lundqvist
John [Mad Dog] Madden
Evgeni [Geno] Malkin
Alexander [the Great] Ovechkin
Mike [Mickey Ribs] Ribeiro
Brent [Biscuit] Seabrook
Jordin [The Tootoo Train] Tootoo
Jonathan [Captain Serious] Toews
Marc-Éduoard [Pickles] Vlasic

STATISTICAL LEADERS

GOALS

ALEXANDER OVECHKIN	269
ILYA KOVALCHUK	230
DANY HEATLEY	219
JAROME IGINLA	191
SIDNEY CROSBY	183

ASSISTS

JOE THORNTON	385
HENRIK SEDIN	332
SIDNEY CROSBY	323
PAVEL DATSYUK	293
MARC SAVARD	292

POINTS (ALL SKATERS)

ALEXANDER OVECHKIN	529
JOE THORNTON	510
SIDNEY CROSBY	506
DANY HEATLEY	444
PAVEL DATSYUK	438

POINTS (DEFENSEMEN)

NICKLAS LIDSTROM	320
SCOTT NIEDERMAYER	264
CHRIS PRONGER	261
BRIAN RAFALSKI	260
SERGEI GONCHAR	259

WINS

MIIKKA KIPRUSOFF	201
MARTIN BRODEUR	199
ROBERTO LUONGO	190
RYAN MILLER	181
HENRIK LUNDQVIST	177

GOALS AGAINST AVERAGE*

MARTIN BRODEUR	2.30
HENRIK LUNDQVIST	2.33
NIKLAS BACKSTROM	2.37
EVGENI NABOKOV	2.43
CRISTOBAL HUET	2.47

*MINIMUM 200 GAMES PLAYED

>>WISH YOU WERE THERE

Team Canada 3, Team U.S.A. 2 (OT) >

FEBRUARY 28, 2010 • CANADA HOCKEY PLACE, VANCOUVER Playing for Olympic gold, the North American powers go to overtime when the U.S.A.'s top sniper Zach Parise ties the game with just 24.4 seconds remaining in regulation. But 7:40 into the extra session Sidney Crosby beats Ryan Miller with a golden goal, forever earning him a place in Canadian lore.

Boston University 4, Miami (Ohio) 3 (OT)

APRIL 11, 2009 • VERIZON CENTER, WASHINGTON, D.C. Trailing by two goals with one minute to go in the national title game, Boston University pulls off the improbable, erasing the deficit in 42 seconds to force overtime. Then 11:47 into sudden death the Terriers' Colby Cohen unleashes a big slap shot that deflects past Miami goalie Cody Reichard to cap the comeback.

Flyers 4, Bruins 3

MAY 14, 2010 • TD GARDEN, BOSTON After trailing three games to none in the second-round playoff series, Philadelphia rebounds to force Game 7, then finds itself down 3–0 late in the first period. But the visiting Flyers don't quit, tying the score in the second period and, after the Bruins get called for having too many men on the ice, getting the power-play winner from Simon Gagne with 7:08 left in regulation, becoming the third team in NHL history to overcome a three-game deficit in a playoff series.

Capitals 4, Penguins 3

MAY 4, 2009 • VERIZON CENTER, WASHINGTON, D.C. Hockey's biggest stars, Alexander Ovechkin and Sidney Crosby, each score their first postseason hat trick in Game 2 of the Eastern Conference semifinals.

Stars 2, Sharks 1 (4OT)

MAY 4, 2008 • AMERICAN AIRLINES CENTER, DALLAS Having taken a 3–0 series lead, underdog Dallas drops the next two games before this epic Game 6 battle. Stars captain Brenden Morrow, who had two goals disallowed in Game 5, beats Evgeni Nabokov 9:03 into the fourth OT to lift Dallas to the Western Conference finals.

Penguins 4, Red Wings 3 (3OT)

JUNE 2, 2008 • JOE LOUIS ARENA, DETROIT Between the second and third overtimes, with his team trailing three games to one, Petr Sykora tells his Penguins teammates that he will force a Game 6 by scoring the game-winner. At 9:57 of the third OT, Sykora makes good when, on a power play, he blasts an Evgeni Malkin pass past Chris Osgood.

Canadiens 6, Rangers 5 (SO)

FEBRUARY 19, 2008 • BELL CENTRE, MONTREAL Trailing 5–0 in the second period, Montreal rallies, feeding off of a deafening home crowd and stunning the Rangers by tying the score late in the third. The shootout win marks the first time the Habs—who got two goals each from Alex Kovalev and Michael Ryder—have overcome a five-goal deficit, and it matches the NHL record for biggest single-game comeback.

Canada Juniors 6, Russia Juniors 5 (SO)

JANUARY 3, 2009 • SBP CENTRE, OTTAWA In the World Junior Championship semis, Canada takes four leads, but rival Russia comes back to tie each time, then goes ahead 5–4 with 17:40 gone in the third period. But Jordan Eberle's second goal of the day ties the game for Canada with five ticks remaining. After a scoreless extra period, Eberle and John Tavares score in the shootout to clinch the win.

>MAYHEM MOMENT

JANUARY 17, 2010

Dave Keon Arena, Quebec

A video showing Rouyn-Noranda center Patrice Cormier's cheap-shot elbow to the face of Quebec defenseman Mikael Tam in a QMJHL game goes viral. Tam, who suffers a traumatic head injury, goes into convulsions on the ice. Cormier, a New Jersey Devils prospect, is suspended for the remainder of the regular season and the playoffs.

> "Frankly I found it distressing to see a young man like that suffering unnecessarily because someone decided that's how hockey is played."
>
> —*Quebec Premier Jean Charest*

> TEAMS OF THE ERA

^

DETROIT RED WINGS

Two Presidents' Trophies (2005–06, '07–08), four straight division titles, two trips to the Stanley Cup finals (one win, one loss) and a league-best 48 postseason victories are all indications of the Red Wings' recent dominance. In the first five seasons after the lockout, Detroit's Mike Babcock, who took over at the start of this era, had nine more regular-season wins (257) and 22 more standings points (566) than any other NHL coach.

PITTSBURGH PENGUINS

Starring Sidney Crosby and Evgeni Malkin—two of the three most compelling forwards in the game—and young goalie Marc André-Fleury, the Penguins shot from just 22 wins in 2005–06 to 45 or more victories in each of the next four seasons, finishing first or second in their division each time. Pittsburgh twice went to the Stanley Cup finals, losing to Detroit in six games in 2008, then rallying to beat the Wings in '09.

TEAM CANADA WOMEN

Undefeated in Olympic competition at the Salt Lake City, Torino and Vancouver games, the Canadian women are the unquestioned powerhouse of women's hockey. Eight members of the 2010 team that shut out the U.S. 2–0 in the final—among them Jennifer Botterill, Jayna Hefford, Becky Kellar and captain Hayley Wickenheiser—each have three gold medals and played major roles in a 15-game Olympic winning streak.

[DEBUT] [FINALE]

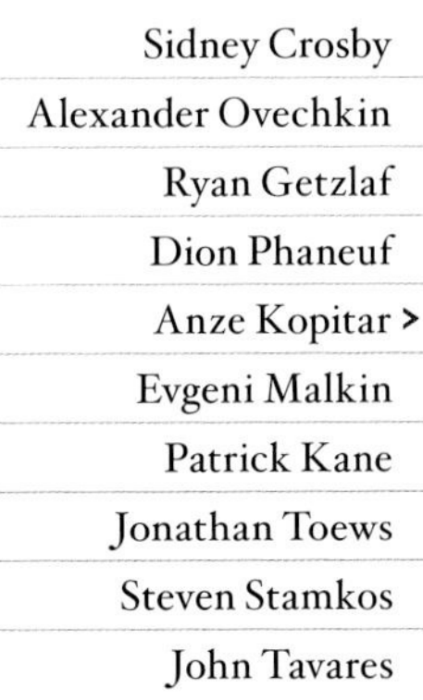

[DEBUT]		[FINALE]
Sidney Crosby	2005–06	Mario Lemieux
Alexander Ovechkin	2005–06	Brett Hull
Ryan Getzlaf	2005–06	Steve Yzerman
Dion Phaneuf	2005–06	Brian Leetch
Anze Kopitar >	2006–07	< Peter Bondra
Evgeni Malkin	2006–07	Eric Lindros
Patrick Kane	2007–08	Dominik Hasek
Jonathan Toews	2007–08	Jaromir Jagr
Steven Stamkos	2008–09	Joe Sakic
John Tavares	2009–10	Keith Tkachuk

> BY THE NUMBERS

301 | Days, the duration of the NHL player lockout, wiping out the entire 2004–05 season.

48 | NHL record for wins in a season, set in 2006–07 by Devils goalie Martin Brodeur. That same year he played an NHL-record 4,697 of a possible 5,024 minutes.

19 | Years, 244 days: age of Penguins center Sidney Crosby when in 2006–07 he became the youngest scoring champ of any North American pro sports league.

20 | Straight NCAA Tournament berths, beginning in 1991 for the Michigan Wolverines, a record. Michigan also holds the mark of nine national titles.

4 | Consecutive Lady Byng Trophies awarded to the Red Wings' Pavel Datsyuk (2005–06 to '08–09), the first player since the Rangers' Frank Boucher (1927–28 to '30–31) to win that many sportsmanship awards in a row.

37 | Career points for Finland's Teemu Selanne, the alltime leading scorer in Olympic hockey.

> PATRICK FACTOR

Recalling the 1938–39 Rangers when patriarch Lester coached sons Muzz and Lynn, Patricks unite on the 2005–06 ECHL Wheeling Nailers. Lynn's son Glenn coaches, Glenn's son Curtiss plays and Ryan, son of Craig Patrick, is an assistant. "There's been a legacy," Curtiss says. "I feel good to be part of it."

1967 | NO LONGER the oft-penalized "Little Devil" he was in his early years, dynamic Black Hawks center Stan Mikita won the Lady Byng and Hart trophies. | *Photograph by* NEIL LEIFER

1958 | HERE PREPARING to face the Black Hawks, Montreal's Jean Béliveau, known as le Gros Bill, played in 14 All-Star games and won the NHL's first Conn Smythe Trophy, in '65. | *Photograph by* JOHN G. ZIMMERMAN

2010 | AFTER HIS overtime goal in Game 6 stunned a Philadelphia crowd and won Chicago its first Stanley Cup in 49 years, Patrick Kane (far right) scooted jubilantly up ice, with teammates Andrew Ladd (16) Patrick Sharp (10) and Nick Boynton in close pursuit. | *Photograph by* BRUCE BENNETT

24
88
BAUER
WARRIOR
FINAL
BAUER
BAUER
BAUER

1952-1953
NHL Record
95 PTS
Art Ross

1953 | THE GLOVES were well-worn and the man was well on his way: Gordie Howe would win four more Hart Trophies after this record-breaking season. | *Photograph by* DAVID N. BERKWITZ

COURTESY OF HOCKEY HALL OF FAME

THE OLD GOALIES' DANCE

BY PETE AXTHELM

The Maple Leafs upset the Canadiens and won the Stanley Cup behind dissimilar goaltenders who would go on to the Hall of Fame, Johnny Bower and Terry Sawchuk. —*from* SI, MAY 15, 1967

THE TWO MEN SAT ON A SMALL bench in the corner of the locker room, separated from most of the players and well-wishers by the pile of pads and skates and tape that goaltenders use for equipment. In the center of the room some of the Toronto Maple Leafs were drinking champagne from the Stanley Cup, which few hockey men had thought they could win. Other Leafs were shoving fully clothed coach Punch Imlach toward the showers. But Terry Sawchuk and Johnny Bower, the goalies who had done the most to make the celebration possible, were by themselves, dragging deeply on cigarettes and grappling silently with the frayed nerves and many physical ailments that are an inescapable part of life for aging men who insist on enduring in a young man's game.

Sawchuk, 37, had played one of the best games of his career that night to beat the Montreal Canadiens 3–1, as the Maple Leafs clinched the Stanley Cup in the sixth game. Bower, who claims he is 42 but is probably older, had put in two big games the week before; now he had trouble walking because of a pulled groin muscle. But he had been in uniform on the end of the Leafs' bench all night, because Imlach said he deserved to be there. He looked happily around the room through bright eyes that have been narrowed into a perpetual squint by 22 years of watching pucks speeding at him. "I knew we would win it tonight," Bower said, "and I damn well wanted to be part of it."

Someone asked Sawchuk about his most dramatic save of the game, a desperate lunge behind his back to grab the puck just as it trickled onto the goal line. Terry shook his head. "No, I don't remember it. I don't remember any special saves once a game is over. How many shots did they take, anyway? Must have been a hell of a lot." The fast-skating Canadiens had taken 41, most of them from close range. Somehow Sawchuk had stopped all but one.

Sawchuk and Bower are the most prominent members of what the coach calls his Old Folks Home—a group of seven scarred warriors 36 or over, five of whom had helped win Imlach's first three Stanley Cups. Imlach, an intensely loyal man, had kept his veterans despite critics who said their abilities were gone. "Everybody said I'd never win another Cup with these old guys," said Imlach. "Well, maybe that makes this one the biggest kick of all. We sure shoved it down everybody's throats."

They could not have won without Sawchuk and Bower and it would be hard to imagine a pair of heroes less alike in their approach to the game. Sawchuk has been an established National Hockey League star for 17 years. Bower spent 12 of his first 13 seasons in the minors. "When I was playing in Cleveland at the age of 33," he admits, "I gave up all hope of being an NHL goalie." Sawchuk has thought of retirement for some time, and may quit now unless an expansion team offers him a contract he cannot refuse. Bower says he has "absolutely no thought of retiring. Too many guys quit this game too soon." Sawchuk believes in pacing himself carefully in practice. Bower is probably the hardest working member of hockey's hardest working team.

The two goalies complemented one another perfectly against Montreal. Bower was brilliant in a 3–0 victory in the second game; and in the pivotal third game he made 60 saves as Toronto finally won 3–2 in double overtime. "I love to play hockey," said Johnny with a smile, "but a game like that can hardly be called fun."

Bower's season ended in the warmup before the next game, when he kicked out at a puck and got the muscle pull. Sawchuk was rushed in—for his worst game of the playoffs. On four of the Canadiens' six goals he seemed almost immobile. In the fifth game Sawchuk was a different player. "We talked before the game," said Imlach. "I told him he had brought us this far, and he had the records to prove he was a great clutch player. He was entitled to one bad game. I knew he could win as long as he played aggressively in goal." Sawchuk did that, challenging the Canadiens forwards, moving out of the net, scrambling to the ice, and stopping almost everything in the last two games.

With the exception of the exciting, wide-open overtime game, the Toronto wins were masterpieces of rugged checking, defense and, of course, superb goaltending. "It's like a poker game," said Imlach. "You've got to drop out of a lot of hands to protect yourself. If you try to score on every play, you get killed." Cynics around the NHL have said that this cautious philosophy produces boring hockey. Imlach, who is never boring himself, laughed when the objection came up. Resting an elbow comfortably on the large silver Stanley Cup, he wondered, "Were the Toronto fans bored with us this spring?"

THE 1967 FINAL marked the fourth Stanley Cup that Bower won with Toronto. He would not win another—and neither has the franchise.

LEE BALTERMAN

22
TORONTO

1984 | MARIO LEMIEUX arrived in Pittsburgh at age 19 after a wildly successful juniors career and commanded immediate attention. | *Photograph by* LANE STEWART

1999 | PITTSBURGH ICON and five-time scoring champ Jaromir Jagr left the Penguins in '01 to sign a monumental $77 million deal with the Capitals. | *Photograph by* NICK CARDILLICCHIO

KOHO
KOHO
KOHO

1944 | THE PUCK stopped on the skate of Chicago defenseman Earl Seibert (17) in Game 3 of the Cup finals. The Canadiens, and defenseman Glen Harmon (8), were bloodied but undaunted, winning 3–2. | *Photograph by* BROWN BROTHERS

1993-94
CENTRAL
DIVISION
CHAMPIONS
PONTIAC
56
13
EASTON

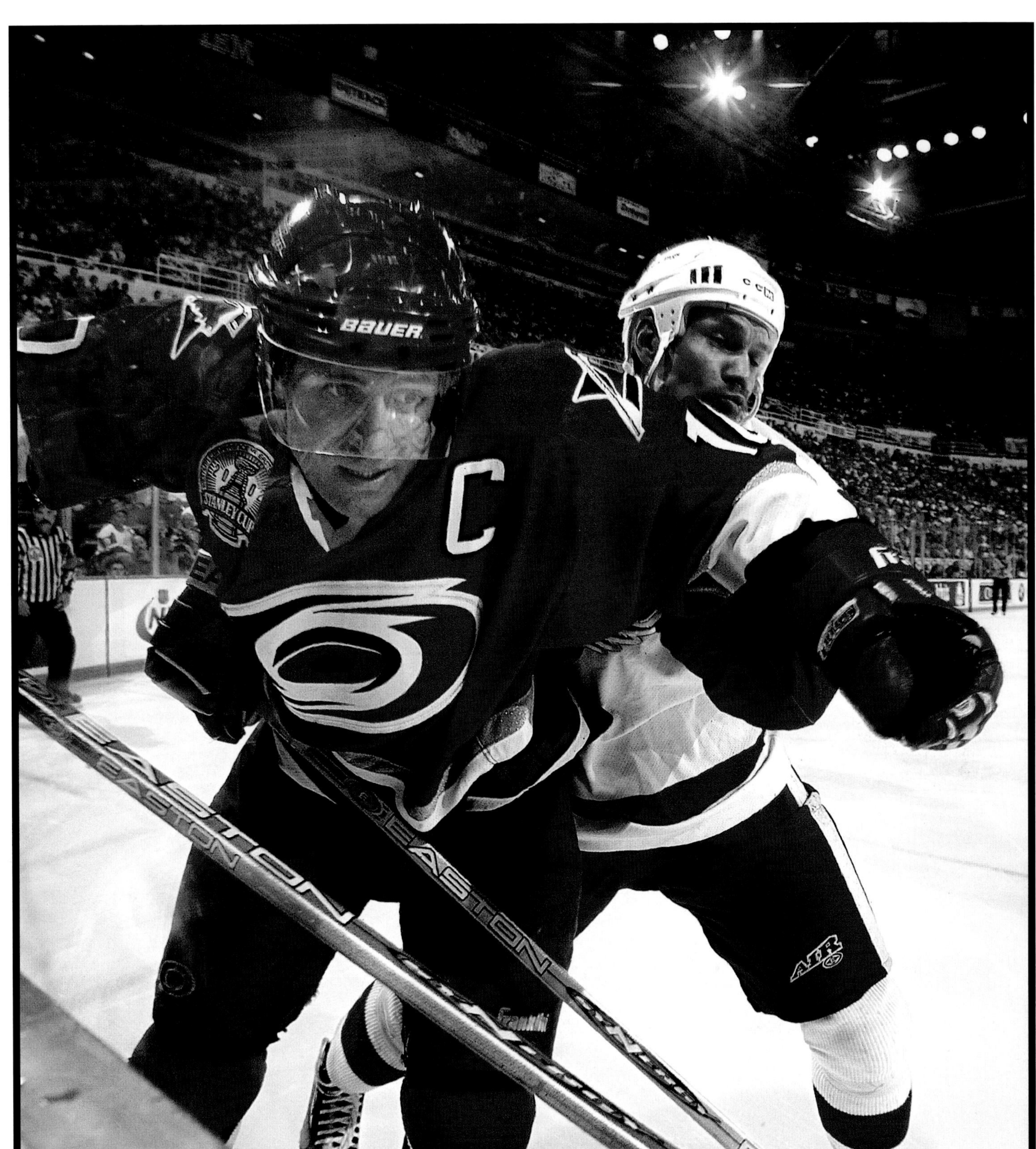

2002 | CAROLINA CAPTAIN Ron Francis was nearing his third Cup until Nicklas Lidstrom and the Wings pushed the Hurricanes aside in the finals. | *Photograph by* LOU CAPOZZOLA

2008 | DALLAS DEFENSEMAN Sergei Zubov (56) and Detroit's Pavel Datsyuk clashed in a chippy Conference finals that was won 4–2 by the Wings. | *Photograph by* DAVID E. KLUTHO

GOODBYE, GREAT ONE

BY E.M. SWIFT

After a 21-year professional career that transformed the game, Wayne Gretzky skated away. —*from* SI, APRIL 26, 1999

HE WAS CERTAIN. YOU COULD see it in his eyes, now clear and bright, though an hour earlier, as he took a final lap around the Madison Square Garden ice, they'd been brimming with tears. You could hear it in his voice as he described the phone calls he'd received that morning from Michael Jordan and Mario Lemieux telling him how much he'd enjoy his retirement. You could read it on his face as he described the final timeout that Rangers coach John Muckler called with 30 seconds left in a 1–1 game, while the sellout crowd chanted his name. "He called me over and told me, 'Wayne, I found out I had a grandson today. You've got to get me the game-winner.' When I was younger, I might have."

When he was younger, he would have. The Great One's magnetic north had always pointed toward the dramatic, and he'd made a career out of shining brightest when the most eyes were on him. Instead, it was the Penguins' Jaromir Jagr who scored the game-winner. Then Gretzky went to center ice, and before an assemblage of former foes, teammates and friends who'd come to New York for his send-off—Mario Lemieux, Mark Messier, Paul Coffey and Glen Sather among them—soaked in a throat-choking 15-minute ovation given by 18,200 fans who'd come to see hockey's greatest player leave the ice for the final time.

Gretzky again led the Rangers in scoring (nine goals and 53 assists in 70 games) this season, but his numbers were way down from his usual output. On a given night Gretzky was capable of thrilling even the most jaded observer with his uncanny passing, but he'd lost too much speed. "We were watching a tape at home the other night," he told SI a few hours before his final game. He was relaxed, autographing pictures and programs and some of the 40 sticks he would use against the Penguins that afternoon. His father, Walter, had come with him to the dressing room and was pouring himself some coffee. "My wife said, 'Boy, you were quick.' I always played up how slow I was, but if there was an opening, my first step to the net was as quick as anyone's, and there weren't many guys who beat me to loose pucks." At 38, though, Gretzky was seeing the loose pucks go to younger legs.

It's difficult to overstate Gretzky's impact on the game. He is both hockey's greatest scorer and its greatest ambassador, the man who almost single-handedly made the NHL viable in California with his headline-grabbing trade from the Oilers to the Kings in 1988. He leaves the game with a mind-numbing 61 NHL records, many of which will never be broken. During the six seasons from '81–82 through '86–87, Gretzky averaged 203 points per year. What was he doing, bowling? No other NHL player has ever scored 200 points in a season.

His record of 92 goals in an 80-game season, which he accomplished in '81–82, is "unreachable," in the view of Bruins general manager Harry Sinden. But Gretzky admits, with a rueful smile, that even with that record and even with his 894 career goals, the most in NHL history, "10 years from now they won't talk about my goal scoring; it'll just be my passing."

That was his genius. Gretzky's vision and imagination were such that he routinely created plays no one had seen. He played hockey like a chess master, several steps ahead of everyone else. Teammates learned to get open and be ready because Gretzky would find a way to get the puck on their sticks. If Gretzky had never scored a goal, he'd still be the NHL's alltime leading scorer on the strength of his 1,963 assists (the last one came during his finale), a staggering 861 more than Coffey, his closest pursuer.

He had two signature moves. Gretzky would set up behind the net—the Rangers painted 99 behind both goals on Sunday in his honor—from where he would feed breaking wingers or dart out in front for a wraparound. (Once, Muckler recalled, Gretzky used a third option: getting the puck flat onto his stick blade and, lacrosse-style, firing it into the goal off the back of Blues goalie Mike Liut in a 1981 game.) Gretzky's second innovation was to break over the blue line and spin toward the boards, eventually passing to a teammate who broke late into the zone. "He made the late man coming into the zone the most dangerous man," said Sinden. "Gretzky could hold the puck for so long, turning toward the boards and stickhandling in place, that even if you knew what he was going to do, you couldn't stop him."

Yet it's the man, not the record-breaker, that the NHL will most miss. He is the sport's only transcendent star but his deep love of the game is still farmboy-simple. The gift Gretzky's New York teammates gave him at his final practice said nothing of his records or accomplishments. It was a leather sofa in the shape of a baseball mitt, with a brass plaque at the base bearing the message THANK YOU FOR YOUR PASSION.

GRETZKY KEPT his plans to retire secret for months, but once he'd decided, he said, "I never wavered. This is a great game, but it's a hard game. It's time."

LOU CAPOZZOLA

POWERADE
SABRETT
IBM IBM
NHL
FOX
99

1998 | AFTER THE Czech Republic (in white) defeated Canada in the Olympic semifinals, the teams lined up for one of hockey's grandest traditions. | *Photograph by* DAVID E. KLUTHO

ZAMUNER
KUCERA

2003 | DOMINIK HASEK came out of retirement to join goalies Manny Legace and Curtis Joseph on the Red Wings' roster, creating a logjam in the net—and in the locker room. | *Photograph by* CARLOS OSORIO

GACE 34
JOSEPH 31
BAUER
BAUER
SUPREME
SUPREME
BAUER
SUPREME